THE CRACKED MIRROR

'This explosive and radical book is a dialogue between a philosopher and a social theorist based in India on the nature of experience, theory, ethics, and politics. In addition to its many other virtues, it is also a remarkable reflection on the logic of untouchability and thus of caste in Indian thought and experience, one which should force all social scientists concerned with inequality and humiliation in Indian society to rethink their most cherished dogmas.'

—**Arjun Appadurai**
Goddard Professor of Media, Culture and Communication,
New York University, USA

'The outcome of a dialogue between two of India's leading thinkers, one a philosopher, the other a political scientist, *The Cracked Mirror* marks an intellectual event of international importance. Not only is lived experience brought forcefully back into social theory, but it is the inassimilable experience of the Dalit, which for centuries has been distorted in the consciousness of the dominant. This is real "theory from the South", and it demands to be read everywhere.'

—**Sheldon Pollock**
Ransford Professor of Sanskrit and Indian Studies,
Columbia University in the City of New York, USA

'This book deserves to be read with care and interest, and marks a genuine advance in current debates. There is much food for thought in their exchanges for all of us. This is only to say that more such dialogues (or multilogues) are the need of the hour, to bring further experiences to light and in order to develop more theories for our collective liberation.'

—**Mary E. John**
Senior Fellow at the Centre for Women's Development Studies,
New Delhi, India

THE CRACKED MIRROR

An Indian Debate on Experience and Theory

GOPAL GURU

■

SUNDAR SARUKKAI

OXFORD
UNIVERSITY PRESS

OXFORD
UNIVERSITY PRESS

Oxford University Press is a department of the University of Oxford.
It furthers the University's objective of excellence in research, scholarship,
and education by publishing worldwide. Oxford is a registered trademark of
Oxford University Press in the UK and in certain other countries.

Published in India by
Oxford University Press
22 Workspace, 2nd Floor, 1/22 Asaf Ali Road, New Delhi 110002, India

© Oxford University Press 2012

The moral rights of the authors have been asserted.

First Edition published in 2012
Oxford India Paperbacks 2017
23rd impression 2024

ISBN 13: 978-0-19-947459-2
ISBN 10: 0-19-947459-1

Typeset in 11/13 Adobe Garamond Pro
by Excellent Laser Typesetters, Pitampura, Delhi 110 034
Printed in India by Replika Press Pvt. Ltd.

Contents

Acknowledgements

We would like to extend our gratitude to the many interlocutors who played a crucial part in making this debate possible. Our special thanks to A. Raghuramaraju and Udaya Kumar for their critical engagement in the debate and comments on the text, Nikhil Govind for his responses to the manuscript, Dhanu Nayak for discussions, Rammanohar Reddy and *Economic and Political Weekly* for permission to republish four articles as chapters in this book, many unnamed students in different institutions around the country who provoked, questioned, and engaged with us, and all those academics who have given us the benefit of reading our work and listening to us even if they were not entirely in sympathy with what we have had to say. Our sincere thanks to the editorial team at Oxford University Press for their enthusiasm and support for this project.

In addition, each of us would individually like to thank the following. Guru acknowledges the support of Barbara Harris-White, Director, South Asian Studies Programme at Oxford University for inviting him as a Fellow to the Programme and also for critical comments on the chapter, 'Experience, Space, and Justice'; Nandini Gooptu for inviting him to present the draft version of the same chapter; his colleague Gurpreet Mahajan and his student Satish Jha. He acknowledges the late Krishna Raj for his initiative in publishing the article on egalitarianism in social sciences, which eventually led to this debate.

Sarukkai is grateful for the intellectual support and camaraderieship of his colleagues at the Manipal Centre for Philosophy and Humanities—George, Meera, and Nikhil—as well as the students of the MA programme for their questions and responses to the many aspects of this debate. For their support at Manipal University, a special word of thanks to Ranjan Pai, Mohandas Pai, and K. Ramnarayan, the Vice Chancellor. He also thanks Samir and Rangan for many discussions on social transformation. Seshadri and Sampath helped in the translation of the Tamil text in the chapter on untouchability, and also taught him ways of understanding the texts and their traditions—his lasting gratitude to them for this and much, much more. He remembers his father, S.K. Rangarajan, who was instrumental in catalyzing these attempts at integrating philosophy with social and intellectual practices, and expresses his gratitude to Ramaa and Jayanth for many years of sharing memorable experiences.

Finally, both of us offer our humble thanks to our respective spouses, Hema and Dhanu, both of whom would embellish even cracked mirrors.

Abbreviations

BDD	Bombay Development Department
EPW	*Economic and Political Weekly*
ICSSR	Indian Council of Social Scientific Research
JNU	Jawaharlal Nehru University
NGO	non-governmental organization
OBC	Other Backward Classes
OUP	Oxford University Press
TTB	top of twice-born
UGC	University Grants Commission

Introduction

Gopal Guru and Sundar Sarukkai

The idea of 'experience', particularly in the Indian context, is becoming respectable as an object of study in academic discourse. A major impulse for this revival of interest in the category of experience is the continued frustration with Indian social theory. The emergence of the politics of identity is a grim reminder of this deficiency in theorizing social reality. The politics of identity seems to have entered the disciplines of the social sciences in a visible and aggressive manner. Claims of identity are often grounded in specific experiences. The specificity of experiences seems to demarcate different notions of self and community. There is nothing new in this observation, but what is perhaps more topical is the attempt to validate diverse experiences, and this, by default, involves a critique of any attempt to categorize diverse experiences into a few universal categories. The suspicion of universal categories particularly holds for those categories that are in, or catalysed by, the cognitive domain of dominant communities and cultures.

There is a need to move resolutely from the politics of identity to ambitions for original ideas. The debate in the present volume revolves around the contestation of certain well-entrenched beliefs about theory and its relation to experience, in particular, presuppositions based on variations of a Platonic theory of ideas. It revolves around the contestation of such disembodied notions of ideas, for they imply that experience is subordinate to ideas. In contemporary terms, this subordination can also be read as one between experience and theory, where experience is posterior to theory in the sense that theory orders experience. In contrast, there is the argument for the primacy of experience, from which theory not only follows but also cannot exist without this foundation. Primarily, this is the larger space of debate in this book and we believe that contemporary social theory cannot but engage with these issues creatively and comprehensively.

The very idea of social theory has had a long and troubled relationship with the notion of experience. Inspired by the theoretical structures of natural science (which, in turn, was modelled on the unique structures of mathematics), social science kept aside experience as a useful theoretical term. The reason is simple: for natural science, experience is problematic since it explicitly involves the human subject and, more importantly, is completely private. Any claim to universality (and thus duplicability/replicability) is seemingly lost in the domain of experience. On the other hand, it is evident from the writings of some political philosophers that experience plays an important epistemological role in the production of thought. Experience is prior to thinking and knowing. But it is susceptible to radical improvement by means of theory and philosophy. Ambedkar follows this methodology while developing his thought. Experience becomes important for him because the existing society, according to him, is mostly driven by texts like *Manusmriti*, which has formidable cognitive influence on conservative social consciousness. This makes it difficult for Dalits or women to rely on such texts. Ambedkar uses the Mahabharata only as a means of confirming existing experience. In a society confronting moral chaos it is experience that is the major content of self-consciousness. Ambedkar writes, 'I did not know what was untouchability till I was asked to sit separately in my school. I did not know till then it was written in the *Manusmriti*' (Ambedkar burned it at Mahad, in Ratnagiri district, in 1927).[1] Ambedkar's critique of classics like the *Bhagvat Gita* is to be seen in terms of the category of experience. It is through this category that he attempts a radical critique of the *Gita*. Even Ramabai Pandit uses this category of experience to attack the *Manusmriti*.[2] Finally, experience as the source of reflective consciousness denies a text the advantage of being authorial. It is in this sense that existing experience guides a person

[1] Khairmode (1990b: 254–5).
[2] Saraswati (1976: 47).

to make a careful selection of a text or (intellectually) inherit that text, which can establish a link between historical and contemporary experience, as for example the experience of untouchability that was transmitted from one generation to another through the complex mediation of caste and patriarchy.

Given this, why this continued distrust of experience in the construct of the theoretical? Partly, it is a product of a particular intellectual history in which theory was separated from experience; as mentioned earlier, the origins of natural science had much to do with it. Theory in the natural sciences can perhaps make do without explicitly factoring in the experience of the individual (although there exists a growing body of literature in the philosophy of science that questions this possibility). But this does not happen easily; the history of science can well be read as a systematic negation of the experiential. Galileo's dictum that launched modern science was fundamentally about the removal of secondary qualities in scientific descriptions. Secondary qualities are suspect only because they are experiential and depend on the nature of human experience. Science also succeeds in this enterprise because it focuses on the description of the properties of the world (and not on the experience of those properties).

But this again is not an easy task. As philosophers have long argued, descriptions of the properties of the world are, primarily and fundamentally, descriptions of our experiences of the world. The phenomenological traditions, both in Indian (where almost all traditions are fundamentally phenomenological) and Western philosophy, embrace this basic insight and, instead of artificially breaking up the subject and object, they look for ways to extract the objective from the omnipresence of the subjective.

The appearance of experience in the social sciences, as an important category of the act of theorizing, is indebted to critical theories of subjectivity drawn primarily from what is usually referred to as Continental philosophy. The concomitant critique of universality allowed the possibility of seriously engaging with issues such as local knowledge, ethnocultures, and so on. At the same time, and perhaps partly inspired by this revolution, groups and communities began to assert the primacy of their experiences. Moreover, they began to resist attempts by 'outsiders' to describe and re-categorize *their* experiences and in so doing concepts such as the 'outsider' and the 'other' began to be thematized more seriously.

But these reactive mores tend to dissipate—as has happened with postmodernism, for example—primarily because of the lack of attempts to theorize the idea of experience by drawing on different conceptual frameworks. In other words, even when individual or group experiences came to be valorized, the theories of experience were largely Eurocentric! Theories that spoke for the primacy of experience did not draw on the conceptual framework available in traditions such as the Indian, Chinese, African, and so on. Ironically, this generated universal theories of experience that were based on the critique of universality itself. Perhaps this paradox lies at the very heart of theorizing. This inherent paradox has serious consequences for social theories in/of non-Western societies, who have inherited (at many times without 'due process' and due thought) theories from the Continental and Anglo-American traditions. The problem of understanding 'their' experiences through 'their' framework is indeed a problem of great urgency for these societies.

This book is one small attempt to consider ways of thinking about experience, in particular the experiences constituting the complex entity called 'India'. It brings together four published articles and also four new chapters. Obviously, we do not in any way claim to have engaged with the multitude of Indian experiences but focus on a few in order to illustrate one particular mode of thinking about such experiences. While predominantly dealing with—and at the same time not fully dealing with—the Dalit experience, we nevertheless look to expanding the possibilities of describing other experiences through attempts similar to ours.

As authors, we come with completely different experiences. One is a political scientist and the other is a philosopher (without any implication that these are mutually disjoint categories!). Perhaps one can see how these territorial preoccupations influence the debate in this book. There is a historical narrative to this book. Gopal Guru, after having lost patience with the Indian social science community, wrote a piece in the *Economic and Political Weekly* (*EPW*) about the appropriation of the Dalit discourse by non-Dalits (Chapter 1). Guru's piece catalysed very few responses, which were generally critical, and in large part was ignored by the social scientists. The few negative reactions as well as the silence about Guru's challenge to the practice of social science in India perhaps not only reflected the tension between the community of theorists and the fieldworkers but also betrayed the unease about using experience as a legitimate category in theoretical social science. Most importantly, it illustrated the obduracy of theorists (which seems to be a universal phenomenon) towards recognizing the place of ethics in the act of theorizing.

Sundar Sarukkai wrote a delayed response, also published in *EPW*, which attempted to take Guru seriously even as it delimited his claims (Chapter 2). Sarukkai's paper focused on the conditions needed for theorizing and also attempted to discover what in experience could function as the special ground of theory. In so doing, Sarukkai highlighted the question of ethics inherent in Guru's argument and brought it to the forefront of the act of theorizing.

These two papers led to many informal and formal debates, particularly with students in places like the Jawaharlal Nehru University (JNU) and the University of Hyderabad. It also brought us together in exploring issues raised in these two papers. These two papers were increasingly being defined as a debate and that led us to consider the possibility of engaging in another debate related to the earlier papers.

That opportunity arose when Guru invited Sarukkai for a seminar on Ambedkar at JNU. Sarukkai's contribution to that seminar was a tentative attempt at conceptualizing untouchability. After presenting that work there was a hiatus of many months. But fortuitously another international conference on phenomenology gave Sarukkai an opportunity to fully develop these ideas and that led to a larger paper titled 'Phenomenology of Untouchability' (Chapter 7 is a more elaborate version of this published paper).

Guru wrote a response to Sarukkai titled the 'Archaeology of Untouchability' (Chapter 8) and the two of us decided that we would like these two papers to be published together so that the debate between the two of us could become a public debate or at least could be presented as such. The editor of *EPW*, Rammanohar Reddy, agreed to this proposal and the two papers were published together in *EPW*.[3]

---

[3] See Guru (2002) and (2009); Sarukkai (2007) and (2009a).

The untouchability debate provoked interesting responses.[4] But it also led to many questions, which we felt could be answered only by discussing these issues in greater detail in the form of a book. So with the four papers from *EPW* as the base, the two of us wrote two more chapters each: one each on experience and on the ethics of theory.

The title of this book followed from our attempts to make sense of the relationship between experience and theory. In searching for a meaningful relationship between the two, we kept stumbling upon the metaphor of a mirror where experience and theory seemed to reflect each other. However, we invoke the image of a cracked mirror to suggest a more complex and distorted reflection between experience and theory. Literally, the cracked mirror is what is available to a large segment of the poor population in India. The world as reflected in that mirror really symbolizes, to both of us, this subterranean reality that underlies any discussion on experience and theory. Our ideas in this book perhaps best inhabit the crack in the mirror.

We decided to present the eight chapters as a debate in the sense that we respond loosely to each other but also leave enough space for others to add their positions. We also decided to retain the authorship of the respective chapters so as to clearly delineate our agreements and disagreements without letting these differences get subsumed under joint authorship. In so doing, we also wanted to highlight the importance of debates in intellectual discussions. Raghuramraju's work on debates in ancient and modern India[5] provided an added impetus to retaining this format and the support of the editorial team at Oxford University Press (OUP) gave us the confidence to retain this structure.

We explicitly invoke the idea of debate in order to revitalize a forgotten aspect of debate in earlier intellectual discussions in India and bring it into contemporary academic practice. Rather than a general response to specific theories, a debate between two individuals allows the creation of a space not just for these two individuals but for others to inhabit. It also catalyses the possibility of agreements and disagreements not being reduced to personal likes and dislikes—a trend that

[4] Cybil (2009) and Natarajan (2009).
[5] Raghuramaraju (2006).

unfortunately seems to characterize much of theorizing (and not just in social science) in India today.

Although there is a sense of responding to each other throughout the book, there is also an added dimension of anticipating and responding to potential questions that could be raised by the readers of this book. Even as we do this, we do not presume that we have addressed or tried to address all these issues. We only hope that we have given a framework for other responses, which are as yet unarticulated. In particular, we have tried to react to the constant challenge of discovering ways of interpreting Indian experiences. We have also tried to seriously engage with some Indian intellectual traditions to generate new ideas and vocabulary for describing contemporary experiences.

The debate began with Guru's *EPW* article on the non-egalitarian practice of social science in India (Chapter 1). The next chapter is the response by Sarukkai to this article. Chapter 3 is a philosophical attempt to describe the nature of experience. By drawing on both Indian and Western philosophical traditions selectively, this chapter attempts to give the reader a sense of the theoretical problems related to the very idea of experience. Chapter 4 describes Guru's invocation of the ideas of space in the context of experience. In this chapter, an attempt is made to sequence the concepts that add significance to the idea of experience and that offer the epistemological and hermeneutic background for the possibility and intelligibility of the concepts of space and justice. Thus, theory proceeds through experience and acquires flesh through concepts such as space and justice. Chapters 5 and 6 explicitly engage with the nature of theorizing and in particular the ethical stance that is so necessary to the act of theorizing in the social sciences. These chapters also offer a critique of some of our own earlier arguments about the autonomy of experience and question the possibility of experience ever being outside a theoretical framework. But most importantly, these chapters foreground an ethical stance that we feel is necessary to the very act of thinking and theorizing about social reality. We conclude with two chapters that were published as a debate between us on untouchability. Chapter 7 is primarily an attempt to understand the experience of untouchability through phenomenology and draws on both Indian and Western concepts to expand the ways by which we could

conceptualize untouchability. Chapter 8 develops on these alter-
nate attempts to make sense of untouchability but takes a different
approach, the archaeological instead of the phenomenological.

While we very much hope that this book will interest social scientists, we also hope that it will lead to creative dialogues between
disciplines such as philosophy, literature, arts, and the social sciences.
Our primary target though are the students in India who, we find,
are faced with a deluge of theories from the 'West' and who, at the
same time, are untrained in and unexposed to Indian and other
non-Western intellectual traditions. This colonization of the mind
is a fundamental impediment to the growth of original and creative
reflections on the nature of diverse Indian experiences. This in no
way is a call to completely depend on ancient, medieval, and modern
Indian intellectual resources (although the West has done exactly this
in drawing *only* upon ancient Greek and later European and Anglo-
American thinkers!) but is a call to integrate different ways of knowing
and thinking by drawing on intellectual resources from all parts of
the world. It only reflects our unease that there is a huge asymmetry
between the use of conceptual resources of the 'theoretical West' as
against those from the 'empirical East' (paraphrasing Guru's invocation of the 'theoretical Brahmins' and the 'empirical Shudras') as well
as a great asymmetry between representations of the non-West by
Westerners and the representations of the West by non-Westerners.
In this sense, theory in the social sciences has shown little inclination
towards a democratic exchange of world views, ideas, and concepts.
Our hope is that this work perhaps affords glimpses of how we can
reduce at least one of these asymmetries.

1

Egalitarianism and the Social Sciences in India*

Gopal Guru

The recent debate involving some of the more sensitive scholars in the pages of the *Economic and Political Weekly* (EPW) has drawn attention to the problems that surround the future of social science disciplines in India. These interventions cover various dimensions of the malady of social science. For example, Ramachandra Guha underscores the absent liberals in the social sciences, while Partha Chatterjee underlines the colonization of social science by certain metropolitan centres in the country. These claims, particularly Guha's, have been contested on nuanced grounds by scholars like Peter de Souza. The present chapter argues that the introduction of the principle of egalitarianism into the debate seeks to extend and not undermine Guha's, de Souza's, and Chatterjee's criticisms of social science practice in India.[1] The principle of egalitarianism, as we shall spell out in greater detail in the following sections, becomes relevant in the context where the social sciences are divided into empirically inferiorized and the critically privileged domains of knowledge. As the last fifty to sixty years of academic experience with Indian social science shows, social science practice in India has harboured a cultural hierarchy, dividing it into the vast, inferior mass of academics who pursue empirical social science and the privileged few who are

* This chapter was previously published in 2002 as 'How are the Social Sciences in India', *Economic and Political Weekly*, XXXVII (51): 5003–9.
[1] See Chatterjee (2002), de Souza (2002), and Guha (2001).

considered the theoretical pundits with reflective capacity that makes them intellectually superior to the former. To use a more familiar analogy, Indian social science represents a pernicious divide between theoretical Brahmins and empirical Shudras. This pernicious dichotomy indicates the lack of egalitarian conditions in social science practice in the country.

This chapter is divided into four sections. The first deals with the justification of the egalitarian principle for critiquing the practice of social science.[2] This would of course include a critique of the cultural hierarchies that operate through certain academic and institutional structures. In the second section an attempt is made to discuss the conditions that seem to adversely affect the growth of reflective capacity within the intellectually deprived groups such as Dalits, tribals, and even OBCs (Other Backward Classes). This section addresses the question of why certain groups lack this capacity as the primary condition for doing social science at a more abstract theoretical level. This would include analysis of factors that have a bearing on the possibility of reflective capacity. The third section concerns *moral stamina* as the necessary condition for doing theory. In the final section, an attempt is made to critique the theoretical claims that have been made on behalf of Dalits by non-Dalits and to carry out a moral critique of the intellectual representation of Dalit issues in social science in India.

THE EGALITARIAN PRINCIPLE AND SOCIAL SCIENCE PRACTICE

It is argued here that the egalitarian principle provides both moral opportunity as well as the capacity to interrogate the exclusionary (in terms of the purity–pollution divide, an *agrahara*, the exclusive dwelling space of top of the twice-born) nature of social science practice in the country. Moreover, it also provides normative direction to alternative modes of reorganizing the boundaries of social science so as to make them more inclusive. The reorganization of social science on egalitarian lines seeks to question the 'gatekeeping' by some. The egalitarian principle thus is both interrogatory and suggestive. This can be justified by providing the following reasons.

[2] Berlin (1978: 87 and 102).

First, the egalitarian principle has a capacity to bring out within the practitioner of social sciences a sense of moral responsibility that would force the latter to offer a justification as to why she is privileging a particular social science language, say, of only theory over the empirical description of a particular phenomenon under investigation. To put it differently: egalitarianism would interrogate all kinds of intellectual mores for their arbitrariness. For example, the egalitarian principle in social science would not accept the following explanations: 'one has an innate ability to do only theory', 'doing theory is a part of one's natural disposition', and 'one is privileged to do only theory because one has been born from the thinking head of pure bodies'. Second, and a corollary to the first, the egalitarian import therefore basically interrogates the hierarchical division that suggests that some are born with a theoretical spoon in their mouth and the vast majority with the empirical pot around their neck. Here the analogy of the pot is suggestive of the social evil that was expressed through an earthen pot tied around the neck of untouchables during the Peshwa rule in nineteenth-century Maharashtra. The untouchables were forced by the Brahminical state to tie this pot around their neck so that they could spit in the pot and thus save the space around them from getting ritually polluted. Others, the upper castes, were free to spit anywhere but not the Dalits. To emphasize the absurdity of the issue, we could say that the Peshwa rule did not promote democracy in spitting, as is the case in contemporary India.

Third, the egalitarian principle would also interrogate the epistemological imperialism that empowers non-Dalits or tribals to launch intellectual expeditions to conquer newer epistemological territories that belong to the Dalit or Adivasi intellectual universe. The egalitarian principle would puncture this modernist (over)confidence by questioning on moral grounds the competitive element that renders every field of knowledge a free zone of investigation that can be taken over by anyone who follows the ground rules, procedures, and protocols that are devised by the 'gatekeepers' of the social sciences. Thus, the egalitarian principle undermines the competitive model of doing the social sciences. It would put moral pressure on the modernist to keep off some fields of knowledge that might get better intellectual treatment from others. The interrogatory dimension also has a bearing on the suggestive thrust of the egalitarian principle. The interrogatory character of the egalitarian principle fundamentally opposes all forms and contexts of formal exclusion from the field of intellectual inquiry.

The egalitarian import into understanding social science practice in India is suggestive for the following reasons. First, it would not approve of arguments like 'one cannot demand equal treatment in all fields of intellectual pursuit'. Similarly, it would not approve of the intellectual position that some fields of inquiry must be left free for the specialists. Secondly, the egalitarian principle would not approve of rigid ground rules, procedures, and protocols that are restrictive in nature. Further, the egalitarian principle, at least at the theoretical level, offers a promise to those cultural groups whose entry into the intellectual field has been historically prohibited by social forces in India. For example, one of its epistemological variants can render the field of knowledge (both theoretical and practical, as the episte-mology of social action) communicable across cultural borders with persons of any cultural background in principle capable of utilizing it.[3] Thirdly, this kind of egalitarianism presupposes a possibility of a common stock of concepts and categories that are equally available for use and even misuse by a person from any caste or social origin. It only suggests that the epistemological field in itself does not establish a copyright for certain cultural groups to control categories. On the contrary, it would question the politics of naming catego-ries or assigning boundaries to intellectual practice in an arbitrary manner. It is in this sense that the egalitarian principle promises to undermine the dominant epistemological practices that are not only exclusionary but also authoritarian in their intention and tend to become a force that seeks to discipline, denigrate, and even deny epistemic status to certain concepts and categories that do not fall in line with the intellectual discourse that feeds on cultural hierarchy as a hegemonic necessity. Theory as an authoritative practice has destructive implication particularly for the young scholars who in their desire to follow the authoritative academic personality sacrifice their insights that can flourish outside the authoritative intellectual practice. In other words, without the egalitarian principle, hegemon-ic social science practice might make a lot of negative difference to

[3] Raina (2000).

cultural groups such as Dalits and Adivasis. As an intellectual force this kind of hegemonic practice would lead to caricaturing of the Dalits or Bahujans as epistemologically dumb, push them into empirical ghettoes, or confine their intellectual or theoretical ambitions to the dominant methodological modes to a significant degree. Thus the lack of a genuine egalitarian principle within mainstream social science practice, as we shall argue later, would crush the confidence of the marginalized (Dalits, Adivasis), lower their self-esteem, and humiliate them through epistemological patronage or charity.

In this context it is necessary to ask the question whether we have followed the egalitarian principle in the practice of the social sciences. The answer to this question cannot be given in the affirmative. On the contrary, it is possible to give a very mixed answer. Scholars have failed to address this question squarely. Instead they have lamented the falling standards of social science practice, particularly its theoretical components.[4] Thus it is suggested that there is a poverty of political theory in India. While these are valid observations, they do not comment on the authoritative and intimidating character of social science practice in the country. What is ironical is that the lamentation has been about the shrinking social base of political theory in India, not so much about the content and form of theory. The authoritarian character did not attract scholarly attention even in the recent report on social science research in India.[5] This chapter argues that social science practice in India is still exclusive and undemocratic in character. It is self-serving and self-satisfying as well. It lacks a genuine egalitarian character.

Social science discourse in India is being closely disciplined by self-appointed juries who sit in the apex court and decide what is the correct practice according to the canons. These juries decide what is theory and what is trash. It is a different matter that these canons lack authenticity as they are borrowed from the West rather unconditionally. The 'apex court' in social science with its full bench in Delhi keeps ruling out subaltern objections as absurd and idiosyn-

---

[4] Many political theorists share this lament. More particularly, Bhiku Parekh (2010: 19–30) has written about the poverty of political theory in India.

[5] Chatterjee (2002: 3604–12).

cratic at worst and emotional, descriptive-empirical, and polemical at best. Among other things, 'bridgehead' methodology is deployed by the juries to silence dissenting voices that are questioning this cultural hierarchy and are threatening to offer alternative ideas of social science.[6] However, as we shall see in the following sections of this chapter, Dalits or the Bahujans have been finding it less motivating to invest in an alternative imagination of social sciences in India.

SOCIAL CONTEXT OF INTELLECTUAL HIERARCHIES

Any discourse, including the social sciences, emerges within a specific material and social context. In other words, it is the material context with appropriate conditions that shapes reflective abilities among individuals or groups. What was the material context that would have prompted Dalits to go for experimentation, innovation, and imagination? Skilled occupations do facilitate a certain degree of innovation among their members. Generation of knowledge takes place basically in the labour process.[7] It is the labour process that creates the concrete possibilities for such epistemological abilities. But reflective abilities develop only in certain kinds of labour processes. For example, if the labour processes are imaginative, innovative, and interesting, then they provide sufficient scope for the agent to reflect continuously on the tools of production. The progressively transforming labour process unfolds umpteen opportunities for reflective capacities. The intellectual history of the West is proof enough in this regard. In India, social groups, particularly the artisan castes who were forced, if not privileged, to handle labour processes with innovation could produce innovative knowledge systems. But certain groups like the Dalits, who did not form part of the organic labour process, ultimately failed to develop an intellectual capacity to reflect. By and large they were always kept out of such a social context. Generation after generation, they were pushed into occupations that were completely devoid of any possibility of innovation and imagination and hence were not impregnated with any possibility of knowledge. For

---

[6] For example, the forum called Dalit Intellectuals' Collective based in Mumbai.

[7] Patil (1982: 17).

example, they were pushed regularly into occupations like scavenging, sanitation, and other types of manual labour that had inherent limitations in preventing them from doing anything extraordinary in terms of creating knowledge. Until the arrival of modernity in India, particularly with independence, Dalits were not included in the differentiated spheres of production that offer the context for imagination. In other words, ghettoization into inferiorized manual spheres, reflecting the closed character of society, resulted in loss of the confidence that is so important in developing the theoretical potential in the social sciences.[8]

In the Indian context these occupations were alienating and humiliating, and stalled any possibility of imagination or innovation within the Dalit communities. Thus, before independence, the Dalits lacked both the context and the conditions. Differentiated spheres of production both intellectual and material and destigmatised occupations are necessary for acquiring intellectual calibre and confidence. After independence, labour processes did offer differentiated spheres for the Dalits; but they did not create sufficient conditions that made reflectivity possible. We shall discuss this point in greater detail later. Suffice it to say that lack of conditions stalled the growth of any reflective faculty among Dalits, who may have had reflective capacities but could not develop them. They were denied the conditions that are necessary for the development of reflective faculties. One of the crucial conditions of reflectivity is the availability of freedom. Freedom from the immediate context, is absolutely necessary for making sense of the immediate at an abstract general level. It is necessary to make connections through the vast body of details that are embedded into the immediate. Freedom is also necessary to seek detachment from the immediate for illumination at the general level. If one does not enjoy that freedom and is completely trapped in the ceaseless struggle for survival, one is hopelessly handicapped in developing any reflectivity. Ultimately it is those with economic security who can pursue philosophy and theory in the formal sense of the terms. The rest are forced to do only the empirical side of social science. Ambedkar himself had realized the need for such freedom and took time off to detach himself from the immediate *chawl*

---

[8] Gellnar (1982: 182). The English translation is by the author.

(working-class tenement) life in Bombay and went to different places of higher learning abroad. But he was not as fortunate as others to enjoy steady support from the intellectual circles that existed during his time. His reflectivity flourished almost like Ekalavya's. What is necessary is feedback from liberal interlocutors, support from institutions with strong traditions of solid theoretical research, and financial support that might help the scholar to pursue the academic agenda at a more abstract level and on more meaningful and dignified terms.

Scholarship programmes are not enough to provide material security for Dalits for two reasons. First, they are meagre and second, they do not guarantee the jobs that are so crucial for any reflectivity. Along with these conditions, the resources of the community along with historically accumulated intellectual resources assure a congenial cultural context, making one's choice of theoretical research look natural. Members of the twice-born communities are fortunate to enjoy these conditions both in India and abroad. The Dalits lack these community resources.

The Hierarchical Past Survives in the Cultural Present

There are historical reasons that gave a structural advantage to the top of the twice-born (TTB), which is the section of the upper layer of the social hierarchy in India, in consolidating its privileged position in doing theory. Historically accumulated cultural inequalities seem to have reinforced Dalit epistemological closure. This in effect left the realm of reflectivity entirely free for the TTB. Such closure has its sanction in Manu's thinking. The Shudras, according to Manu are born from the leg and hence are deficient in terms of the capacity to think. Manu's code denied Dalits and women access to formal education, which is necessary to achieve the capacity to speak in an abstract universal language. This division, with religious sanction behind it, was conveniently naturalized within folk consciousness, as is evident in this Marathi ditty:

Brahmanchy ghari lihina [at the Brahmin's you write and learn]
Kunbay ghari dana [at the tiller's you thrash]
Mahara ghari gana [at the Dalit's you sing)[9]

[9] This saying is very common in Maharashtra's cultural life.

The privileged location of the TTB was further legitimized through the writing of both Indian and foreign scholars. Prominent among them is P.V. Kane, who argued that Brahmins were the founders of Indian philosophy.[10] In the same vein, Louis Dumont also mentions (with reservations) that Brahmins as the renouncers were the creators of value and of different branches of knowledge.[11] It is generally believed by some scholars that Brahmins have always pursued theoretical or pure reason with the help of intricate arguments, while Buddha was always following practical reason in order to tackle practical problems such as maintaining peace in society. However, people like Ambedkar and Sharad Patil may not accept this claim and would argue that the Buddhist philosophical tradition is the thinking tradition based on the dialogical mode, which was much more democratic than the Brahminical mode.[12]

Members of the TTB have consolidated cumulative advantage over Dalits or Bahujans for the following reasons. First, the TTB were fortunate enough to receive modern education from the imperialists. Many of them did not mind migrating to Western countries even though that went against the spirit of their religion. They were also the recipients of different kinds of fellowships that were showered upon them by both several princely states and the colonial state. Even after independence, they received the attention and appreciation of those in power. For example, a member of the TTB served as adviser to the Maratha chief minister in Maharashtra. Many prominent Brahmins led intellectual–cultural bodies in the state. They have been the major beneficiaries of intellectual opportunities that are available in India and aboard. They do not mind migrating abroad, leaving the Dalits or Bahujans to take over the empire of empirical research. Cambridge, Oxford, Harvard, and several other universities abroad and privileged institutions and premier universities at home are frequented by the TTB. The doors of certain premier institutions within India continued to remain closed to Dalits for almost five decades. It is only in the recent times there have been some attempts to accommodate at some level Dalits and tribal scholars in such institutions.

[10] Patil (1982: 17).
[11] Dumont (1980: 275).
[12] Ambedkar (1957).

It is only in recent years that Dalits have been accommodated in these institutions, of course at the lower levels of the fellowship programmes. It is also interesting to note that even places like Oxford, if not Cambridge, and Harvard have become quite hospitable to Dalits and their issues, thanks to the fellowship programmes offered by such universities.

There is no doubt that these institutions, including the Indian ones, have promoted quality research. But these institutions' obsession with modernity as a governing condition seem to have seriously undermined the egalitarian principle that, as seen earlier, requires equal access to intellectual resources. Many scholars who have managed to become part of a globally operating academic network latch on to every new opportunity, thus pushing those who lack this connection to relatively less attractive institutions within India. Even in India, scholars other than Dalits use Dalit themes to jump from one fellowship to another without much moral problem, while some other scholars hold fellowships simultaneously at different places in India and abroad, seriously violating the Rawlsian justice principle that would not allow such monopoly leading to the exclusion of a number of persons qualified for these positions. In any case, Dalits are the latecomers to such opportunities. They were excluded from the benefits as they could not pass the modernist test. Now that they are ready to compete for entry, the rules of entry have been changed to the disadvantage of these underprivileged groups at the institutions that continue to remain available to privileged scholars who, as mentioned above, can jump from one scholarship to another and thus are the beneficiaries of a soft landing at several premier research institutions in India.

Dalits and tribals are thus denied the intellectual conditions that are necessary for developing more reflective capacities. It is frustrating, if not tragic, for Dalits to languish in raw empiricism. In the absence of such opportunities, the only alternative that is available to Dalits, Adivasis, and OBCs is to approach central bodies such as the University Grants Commission (UGC) and the Indian Council of Social Science Research (ICSSR) for help. It would be interesting to know how many tribals and Dalits have been the beneficiaries of various national and international fellowship programmes that are offered by these bodies. In the absence of reliable evidence, one can hazard a guess and say that Dalits and tribals are, by and large, kept out of the fellowship programmes. One of the primary reasons that can explain this exclusion from the opportunity structure is that there is active discouragement at both ends of the opportunity structure. Dalits find the UGC and ICSSR functioning too bureaucratic and hence intimidating and actively discouraging. We have several examples that show that Dalit students were forced to give up more attractive UGC fellowships in favour of less attractive ICSSR ones.[13]

On the other hand, there is a constant flow of opportunities to the TTB. The Shudras have been, as remarked earlier, left with the earthen pot full of empirical details that are thoroughly despised by the TTB as inferior. The pot overflows in seminars and in magazines and government offices as and when it is required to overflow. Apart from the monopolization of institutions to maintain the historical lead in epistemological status, the TTB deploys different strategies such as canonizing the discourse with the help of well-defined ground rules, procedures, and protocols, and compartmentalization of institutions around chosen themes. For example, the high priest in theory seeks to canonize the social science discourse around ground rules that are often inhibiting, protocols that are discouraging, language that is definitely frightening, and procedures that cause anxiety among those who want to move away from the empirical to the theoretical. This kind of TTB professionalism strikes fear among the Dalits and Bahujans, who then do not dare to enter the theoretical 'agrahara'. The failure to elevate the discourse to higher levels of complexity and the formulation and approximation of experience results in displeasure displayed by these gatekeepers of social science towards the Dalits, tribals, and OBCs.

The creation of language becomes another effective weapon to restrict the entry of Dalits into academic circles that are based on a particular syntax, mostly Anglo-American. Some of the more nasty guards of these circles would point out the grammatical mistakes of the Dalits publicly, not just for crushing the intellectual confidence of the Dalits through humiliation but also for hiding behind the language

[13] This is the story of a Dalit scholar who is working towards a PhD in social work in Chennai. The JNU, New Delhi also has various Dalit students who have joined various different centres there and receive ICSSR fellowships.

game. This restricted exchange ultimately leads to the creation of mutual admiration societies (Delhi is full of such societies). Such societies certainly achieve a certain kind of height but hardly any depth in the social sciences. Due to their shared habitus,[14] Dalits lack the imagination to invent new conceptual instruments. Thus they keep producing more of the same. We will deal with this issue a little later. Such societies cause epistemological isolation of the Dalits. The strict observance of a language code, protocols, body language, and ground rules effectively converts seminar halls into a hostile structure that very often inflicts humiliation on the Dalits, who then feel too nervous or intimidated to enter such structures. Ultimately, Dalits are denied access to knowledge and its articulation. They are also denied the critical faculty to interrogate the dominant mode of thinking. For example, the Dalit may have a genuinely insightful point that might challenge the big boss in social science, but the moment the Dalit questions the premise of the big boss, immediate loud laughter full of crushing derision is collectively produced in such gatherings. Does not this kind of institutionalized exclusion show the dent in social science confidence? Let us look at another example, one that involves the humiliating exclusion of Dalits from the established discourse in social science. If some Dalits were speaking about Gramsci, suddenly the champions of Gramsci would raise objections: *'Aj kal koi bhi aira gaira nathu khaira Gramschi ke bare me bol raha hai'*[15] or 'Poor Gramsci must be turning in his grave'.[16]

In fact, Gramsci would rest in peace in his grave, seeing his thought being resurrected by the right kind of subalterns, who are ridiculed as *aira gaira* (which basically means any Tom, Dick, and Harry) by these 'defenders' of Gramsci. The so-called defenders of Gramsci are actually offending Gramsci and holding social science hostage to their intellectual fanaticism. However, the high priests of theory do not mind Dalits doing empirical studies. Some of them base their theoretical premises on data collected by Dalits. Social science practice therefore lacks moral standing. Theory does not attract

[14] This is a cue from Bourdieu in Butler (1990: 119).

[15] Loosely translated as 'Nowadays, anybody can speak about Gramsci'.

[16] This is from a collection of poems by P.I. Sonkamble (1986: 29) from Aurangabad, Maharashtra.

the Dalit also because the latter lacks internal moral reasoning based on the notion of sacrifice and endurance. Doing theory is a moral responsibility based on sacrifice that the Dalits have to make in terms of pursuing spiritual rather than temporal power. It requires that one be not moved by immediate success or solution or glamour or charm. Let us see how this affects the doing capacity of reflectivity.

Moral Conditions of Reflective Capacities

Doing theory demands enduring moral stamina for successfully resisting the temptation of temporal gains that have the capacity to demotivate a person from pursuing intellectual projects. Doing serious theory also demands that one should overcome the sense of anxiety that involves an element of compulsion to perform. Performance, whether on the stage or in seminar rooms, is aimed at getting immediate recognition from the audience. In such performances what become important are body language, speech, sound, and speed of words, and not so much the careful arrangement of the content. Doing theory requires discipline, patience, and endurance that go into making a theoretical statement that is made carefully and not superficially or polemically. Doing theory does not therefore bring you immediate recognition. Ambedkar's sociological, economic, and jurisprudential work took a long time and Rawls invested nearly twenty years in his theory of justice. Against this, the temporal fetches immediate here-and-now recognition.

Most Dalits are vulnerable to the attraction of the temporal power that does not flow from theoretical practice but from what are considered to be the easy if not more glamorous spheres of mobility. These might include formal politics and networking with institutions that demand that intellectuals always be ready with data. When ambitions for the temporal grow out of proportion to theoretical consciousness, then theoretical concerns get completely driven out of the cognitive map of the Dalits. Practical reason takes precedence over theoretical reason. Along with the state, Dalit politicians from both the non-governmental organizations (NGO) sector and formal politics promote such practical reason because in the case of the former, the empirical details come in handy to impress donor agencies, while in the case of the latter, the data helps in constructing the self-serving rhetoric that serves very well the everyday forms of Dalit petty politics on the one hand and the liberal state on the other. With such moves, the official intellectuals among the Dalits are ever willing to convert the figures of atrocities into such rhetoric, which are later parroted by Dalits in national and international forums. One can even mix in some emotion to make the details more interesting!

In such an intellectual atmosphere, promoting theory requires transcendence of emotions to reach rationality, and anybody offering theory looks like a stranger to this brand of Dalits, who have a stake in maintaining the collective theoretical inability. The logic of the temporal dominates the academic agenda of the Dalits. Thus, many of them go in for soft options rather than tough courses such as philosophy and theory that do not promise temporal power. It is this professionalization of Dalit interest that, on one hand, makes them more individualistic in their attitude and, on the other, is responsible for their casualness, if not callousness, towards theory.

Dalits try to compensate for theoretical deficiency by substituting it with brilliant poetry. It is this sense of compensation that has led to the creation of brilliant poetry in Maharashtra from this class. In this regard, it is really interesting to note what a Dalit poet has to say about intellectual relations reversing the traditional positions of the Dalits and the TTB. The poet says,

When we were tearing you were tearing us
Now we tear you while you tear.[17]

This particular ditty suggests that while the Dalits were skinning dead cattle, the TTB were tearing off the personality of the former through humiliation and intellectual exclusion. Now the TTB skins hides, maybe in sophisticated tanneries, and the Dalits are deploying knowledge to tear down the TTB through social auditing and intellectual intervention at various levels.

But poetry cannot be a substitute for theory. Most poetry, including Dalit poetry, is based on aesthetics and metaphors and this no doubt makes things interesting. It is true that Dalits have developed a good sense of aesthetics but it by definition belongs to the particular,

[17] This is a transalation by the author of an oral poem by P.I. Sonkamble from Aurangabad.

though it is based on rich experience and therefore has the potential to become the guiding standard for the universal. Besides, it also generates inwardness and tends to keep some things hidden from the public imagination. But poetry has no conceptual capacity to universalize the particular and particularize the universal. It does not have that dialectical power. By contrast, theory demands clarity of concept, principles, and the open examination of one's own action to see whether it is justified. Poetry helps the Dalit in making connections through metaphors, but not through concepts. It is theory that is supposed to do that. It makes connections through concepts and also helps in illuminating the meaning that is embedded in complex reality. (However, Gadamar asks: '[I]s it right to reserve the concept of truth for conceptual knowledge? Must we not also admit that the work of art possesses truth?'[18] These are serious questions).

It is not entirely true that Dalits turn towards either poetry or empirical research out of compulsion. On closer observation it is found that they also make a very conscious choice to undertake empirical research for the following reasons: First, they would argue that their lived experience is rich enough and can stand on its own authentic terms and that it does not require any theoretical representation. Experience for them is a sufficient condition for organizing their thought and action and for ignition of everyday experience into resistance. Second, Dalits argue that since they have privileged access to their reality, they can capture it with a full view without any theoretical representation. This claim is obviously based on ontological blindness. The assumption in such a claim is that non-Dalits have an innate inability to comprehend Dalit reality because of their different social location. Thus, though Dalits do not generate any theory, their research can always contain some valuable theoretical insights and their experience alone can illuminate aspects of human relations. Third, in defence of empiricism, some of the Dalits still argue that doing theory is undesirable because it makes a person intellectually arrogant, egoistic, and socially alienated if not irrelevant. In this regard, it is interesting to note that the critique of abstract thinking goes back to the fourteenth century in Maharashtra. The forerunner of the non-Brahmin tradition Sant Tukaram criticizes this intellectual

[18] Gadamer (1987: 39).

tradition for its egoistic implication in the following *abhanga* (a form of folk or devotional poetry):

It is all to the good! O God! That you made me Kunbi
Otherwise I would have been done to death
through Brahminical cant and hypocrisy.
As a Brahmin, I would have floated full
of arrogance and ego;
and would have been led to the lowest of
the lowest naraka (hell).[19]

This particular reaction of Tukaram is too self-explanatory to require any further elaboration. These are some of the reasons that are advanced by the Dalits to defend their empiricism. The question that still remains to be answered is: Should the Dalits, tribals, and the OBCs be forever lost in their unique experiences? Should they not look at theory as a moral responsibility to accord respect to their experience that otherwise is caricatured by both the snobbish theorist and politicians from TTB? Should they not move from the immediate to the abstract and restore subjectivity? Should they not stop making guest appearances in somebody else's formulations and restore to themselves the agency to reflect organically on their own experience? Thus doing theory becomes a social necessity for the Dalits.

DALITS NEED THEORY AS A SOCIAL NECESSITY

It is argued here that moving away from the empirical mode to the theoretical one has become a social necessity for Dalits, adivasis, and OBCs. It has become a social necessity for the following reasons. First, theory is a social necessity for them to confront the reverse orientalism that treats Dalits, tribals, and OBCs as the inferior empirical self and the TTB as the superior theoretical self. The descriptive mode is often deployed by the TTB in order to wrap the insult and derision that is inflicted on the Dalits. Thus, description of the body language of the Dalits and the OBCs becomes an erotic need for the cultural and political satisfaction of the TTB. It is due to this reason that the TTB did not find it necessary to offer theoretical treatment to

[19] More (1999: 37).

the theatrical language of the OBC chief minister from Bihar or the Dalit chief minister from Uttar Pradesh. The theory of theatrical language offers an unique opportunity for Dalit or Bahujan scholars to escape derisive description of their cultural symbols. It is in this sense that doing theory becomes a social necessity in order to fight inverted orientalism. This should become a social necessity in order to become the subject of their own thinking rather than becoming the object of somebody else's thinking. To put it more crudely, the asymmetrical relationship that characterizes inverse orientalism seeks to caricature Dalits, tribals, and OBCs as amusing objects. Dalits have been portrayed as amusing objects in several studies that were initiated by the UGC and ICSSR on Dalits and tribals (and now women) through separate study centres. These studies of Dalit and tribal communities seek to 'museumize' the latter as amusing objects.

Anthropology and, to some extent, sociology have taken the lead in caricaturing Dalits and Adivasis. Huge funds are provided by the ICSSR and UGC for promoting this enterprise. This kind of social science practice raises the issue of whether social science in India is not reproducing the same tormenting forms of orientalism against which it had fought in the first instance. In what way are the practitioners of social sciences morally superior to the orientalists? In view of the complete lack of theoretical intervention from Dalit or Bahujan scholars, some non-Dalit messiahs have offered to represent Dalits or Bahujans theoretically. Their claim to fight this reverse orientalism on behalf of Dalits looks attractive. It is argued by the TTB that they need to intervene in the Dalit situation at the theoretical level only to restore voice and visibility to Dalits, and ultimately advance the Dalit epistemological cause. But this also ends up producing reverse orientalism in a very subtle way. The claim to offer epistemological empowerment to Dalits involves a charity element which by definition is condescending. This epistemological charity has several implications for Dalits. First, speaking for the Dalits (or anybody) constitutes a *jajmani* relationship, structurally involving a patron and a client. In the present case, the *muknayak*[20] becomes the patron and the 'dumb' becomes the client to define the patron. The patron, in a very ironical sense, tends to reproduce the Brahminical mechanism of first controlling

[20] Leaders of the 'dumb' masses.

knowledge resources and then pouring them into the empty cupped palms of Dalits. It happens in the same humiliating way—the TTB still pours water into the hands of the thirsty Dalits. This relationship makes the muknayak intellectually indispensable and the dumb almost crawl before such messiahs for rhetorical appreciation and designated empowerment rather than real theoretical elevation. We come across umpteen cases of such designated empowerment when Dalits publicly bask in the intellectual glory of their muknayaks. This structured relationship creates legitimacy for the patrons' existence in both the Dalit soul and Dalit society. As a result the patron does not find it necessary to exit from the epistemological fields that are specific to the Dalit and Bahujan situation.

This jajmani relationship also has another implication for the Dalits. This representation tends to undervalue or underplay the discursive capacity of such groups who in favourable hermeneutic conditions can develop an epistemic stamina. But the muknayaks make a very smart move, prompting the dumb to throw up more interesting details so that the former can use these details for either grand formulation in a liberal mode or its postmodernist deconstruction. This by implication restricts the Dalits to the empirical and pushes them into the frozen essentialist trap. This postmodernist construction of Dalits remains blind to the hegemonic politics that would feel happy to celebrate such a construction, as it replaces the need to make connections between several local experiences that belong to the same logical class of collective suffering and exploitation.

Finally, this epistemological enthusiasm of the non-Dalits also suffers from another and rather serious malady. This intellectual representation remains epistemologically posterior. That is to say, the discovery of the Dalit epistemological standpoint fails to explain who has arrived—whether the object (Dalits) or the subject (muknayaks). This question becomes absolutely important because such claims have been sustained on the basis of throwing up completely new conceptual landscapes from the Dalit experience. This inability to either recover or throw up an alternative concept happens because these scholars choose to theorize Dalit experience while standing outside the Dalit experience. This representation thus remains epistemologically posterior. In view of this posterior epistemology, its standpoint remains a mere assertion that feeds on the critique of the mainstream

Marxist or feminist framework. This externality hardly enables the Dalits to secure theoretical advance for their revolutionary understanding and politics. To put it more crudely, such epistemological enthusiasms may turn Dalit epistemology into an exegetical horizon of difference that may radically undermine any possibility of the fusion of epistemologies that are egalitarian in nature. It is in this sense that the patronizing or posterior epistemology fails to belong to the realm of social necessity. It comes up as a choice to transcend the personal intellectual frustration of those middle-class former radicals for whom the old frameworks have ceased to be charming options.

It is true that the old liberal or Marxist discourses tried to tighten the conceptual boundaries of social science in India, almost pushing the social science discipline into a state of suffocation. But these discourses did compete with one another, like the caste versus class discourse for deciding protocols, procedure, and ground rules for the social sciences. In the process, these discourses took over the theoretical task of discovering concepts and categories for Dalits, Adivasis, OBCs, and women. For example, the Marxist discourse introduced concepts such as class, exploitation, proletariat, labour, and alienation for everybody, including Dalits. In the liberal discourse, caste, nationalism, citizenship, rights, and multiculturalism are the potent categories for everybody. This by implication suggests the Dalit failure of historical imagination to do theory.

Although such rendering does pose a huge theoretical challenge to provide alternative sets of categories, this is a challenge that is worth taking up. Dalit theory, in order to become a social necessity, has to be vertically critical of the limitations of Marxist and liberal methods and be horizontally sensitive towards those Dalit or Bahujan critical impulses that may be still present in the methods mentioned above. Thus it would be unfair to dispense with everything from Marxism or liberalism for their epistemological deficiencies. In fact, doing theory is also an inner necessity for the Dalits.

DALITS NEED THEORY AS INNER NECESSITY

There seem to be different factors that become the preconditions for the realization of this inner necessity. These are the moral conditions. For Dalits to realize doing theory as an inner moral necessity, they must make a conscious moral choice to use their sense of freedom for understanding and reflecting on the Dalit experience. They should treat this freedom to walk out from the Dalit experience as the initial condition for achieving theoretical heights in their reflections. They may go to Oxford and Cambridge for achieving height for their experience but they should also make a moral choice to walk back into the Dalit experience in order to accord depth to their reflections. This becomes an essential condition for doing theory. Thus, the modernist theorist who is driven by the individualized intellectual triumphalism of conquering newer epistemological territories becomes a morally undesirable option for the Dalits. This kind of epistemological imperialism is one-sided as it shows commitment to scholarship and not to the cause. For Dalits, theory comes as a double commitment both to scholarship and also to the social cause. As a part of this moral commitment the Dalits should avoid walking into pure empiricism or 'experientialism', which come as alternatives in the competitive forms of tokenism in the realms of both academics and politics. For Dalits, theory should not begin and end with Oxford or Cambridge or some institution within India that is devoted to promoting theoretical work. Their theory should not be caught in the self-serving professionalism and stupefaction adopted by the TTB in the country. Dalits should test the tenacity of their theory not with the certification of juries of social sciences, howsoever attractive that may be, but on the basis of how much influence these theoretical formulations enjoy in the popular mentality.

It is a Gramscian project that demands impeccable commitment on the part of the theorist to translate technical content into an ordinary idiom and common speech so that it becomes accessible to the common people and does not remain confined to seminar rooms only. In fact it should be practised from the Red Fort in Delhi. That would, by the way, re-signify the fort by dispelling the deceitful rhetoric of interested parties ritually on every 15 August. Dalits are expected to take the initiative in giving moral lead to doing theory in the country. This orientation would thus remove the cultural hierarchies that tend to divide social science practice into theoretical Brahmins and empirical Shudras. Ultimately social science in India would fulfil the fondest hopes by expanding the social base of its conceptual landscape.

2

Experience and Theory
From Habermas to Gopal Guru*

Sundar Sarukkai

In the previous chapter, Gopal Guru has made some important observations about the nature of social sciences in India. The most important one, in my view, is the one about the right to theorize—in Guru's terms, a moral stamina that is needed before theorizing is possible. This is an issue that is not limited to Guru's concern about the 'theoretical exploitation' of Dalits. Rather, this is an issue that has occurred in almost all areas of discourse, especially in recent times. Perhaps reflecting the consumer age, individuals and communities now want copyright and patent over theories about themselves or their communities. The most common way of legitimizing this demand for copyright or for a 'moral' right to theorize is by taking recourse to the notion of lived experience, as indeed Guru does. But what is lived experience? What are the elements that constitute lived experience? And most important for this copyright view of theory making, what is the relation between lived experience and theories about this experience?

WHO HAS THE RIGHT TO THEORIZE?

In recent times, the notions of authority and authenticity have become dominant to the concerns of theorizing. Guru's argument that the

* This chapter was previously published in 2007 as 'Dalit Experience and Theory', *Economic and Political Weekly*, XLII (40): 4043–8.

lived experience of Dalits constitutes the only valid and authentic experience, and moreover that theorizing this experience should be limited only to the Dalits, is yet another voice in this trend.

The question that is at the foundation of many of these views is basically this: Who really has the right to theorize in the social sciences? This is a problem that has affected many of us, both in academics and outside. Consider the theorization of Indian culture, its many aspects such as religion, society, psyche, films, music, and so on. While there are some eminent theorists based in India, there are more who are outside India. The theories about the Indian experience—as experienced by those who live in India now—are largely derived from 'outsiders' who, at the most, may visit India during breaks in their teaching schedules or during vacations. Because of their position, both as competent thinkers and as being part of cultures that are connected with publishing, much of what is written about India and accepted by the world arises from such 'outsiders', whether they be of Indian origin or not. Unfortunately, the idea of 'participant observation' legitimizes fieldwork by outsiders who can sample the Indian experience for a few weeks in order to theorize about its many components. This can, at times, be frustrating. As much as it is frustrating for Guru when he sees non-Dalits taking over the Dalit experience in order to theorize about it. But being frustrated is not enough. What is important is to find arguments that can help us establish the validity or otherwise of this position.

An important subtext in Guru's article is the anger, sometimes justifiable, about non-Dalits theorizing Dalit experience. This anger is common to many, if not all, communities who exhibit a strong dislike to being objects of study of those who do not 'belong' to that community. We routinely hear this when non-Indians make observations about Indian society, culture, or its people. We routinely hear this from scientists when non-scientists write about science, especially on the problematic issues of science. Is this anger towards the outsider justifiable? Or can an 'outsider' be in a position to make meaningful comments about a community s/he does not belong to? And who really is the outsider?

Almost every activity has generated this problem. Artists have questioned critics of art along the same line: if you are not an artist yourself, what gives you the competence—and the right—to talk about a piece of art? Scientists and technocrats have often responded to writings about science or technology in a similar fashion. In fact, it has become fashionable for scientists now to be vocal in their attack on philosophers or sociologists of science. The Nobel Prize winner Weinberg claims that philosophy of science is a gloss on science; and a few years back Sokal and Bricmont launched a frontal attack on postmodernists for 'abusing' scientific terms.[1] Technocrats often believe that philosophers and sociologists of technology are actually 'anti-technological'. But the point is that while it is useful for philosophers of science to understand science, it is also evident that in many cases philosophy of science draws upon philosophy more than science. It uses philosophy to reflect on the practice and discourse of science. As philosophy, it is indeed an outsider to day-to-day scientific practice. Yet, its observations on science are very profound and often illuminate the nature of science far better than the practice of science does. A more pervasive example is the insights into the nature of language gained by philosophers of language and linguists, even though such insights are rarely visible even in a person's competent use of language.

Similar concerns are true of religious communities, where at various times community members react to any writing about religion or their community by saying that unless one believes (or shares a lived experience of that particular religious belief), one has no right to criticize that experience. Consider another illustrative example: Indian language writers, especially after Indian English writing became newsworthy, have taken the position that Indian writers who write in English cannot claim to speak for Indian society since a large number of Indians are not English speakers. Here the claim is that narratives written in English are inauthentic. Here since lived experience is equated to 'lived language'.

However, there are also many human activities in which a theorist cannot—in principle—have lived experience. Should political theory be written only by politicians? History, for instance, cannot live up to this demand, for according to this position, unless a person has had lived experience of an historical event, any written history about that event is inauthentic. Similarly, we cannot theorize about religious

---

[1] See Sokal and Bricmont (1998) and Weinberg (1993).

fundamentalism unless we are part of fundamentalist organizations. When we talk about empathy with a suffering person we are able to project something of the other's experience into ourselves although we do not in any sense have a lived experience of the suffering of the other. When we claim that untouchability is a crime, we do not have to have been an untouchable. When we ask for equality of citizens, including women, we do not have to be a woman or Dalit to say that. That is, there are experiences that allow us to theorize based on other principles, for example, principles of human freedom and liberty.

But there is a crucial difference in all these claims for authenticity and Guru's arguments. In many of these cases the recourse to authenticity and lived experience comes primarily when something unfavourable is written about the community or about an experience. When an outsider writes what the community perceives as good, the outsider is not only accepted but often also valorized. For example, scientists have rarely reacted to outsiders writing about the greatness of science, especially when these writers have helped in creating a legendary status for science and scientists. It is largely when science comes under criticism that scientists attack non-scientists writing on science as not having any 'authentic' experience or understanding of science. So also is the case with writing on Indian culture, religion, and society. When outsiders write about contemporary or ancient India in a flattering manner, the outsider status is conveniently forgotten or is sometimes invoked to show how even outsiders can recognize the greatness of these societies. But the moment there is some form of criticism, the outsider status is invoked to debunk the criticism. Most often, the problem of the outsider status is situated in the absence of a lived experience.

At the outset, it may seem that Guru is doing the same thing when he claims that non-Dalits should not theorize about Dalits. That is not really the case. Guru does not take the position that it is impossible for theorists to write about a community they do not belong to. As he rightly notes, that would involve his inability to theorize about non-Dalits. For Guru, theory has a particular role to play and that role has to be based on experience and universal reason. As he suggests, the route is from the initial to the essential. But what is important is that this is a position that he takes prior to any value attached to what non-Dalits write about Dalit experience. That is, he is not interested in whether the writing of the non-Dalits is complimentary or derogatory about Dalits but only that non-Dalits have no moral right to theorize about Dalits. This is a much stronger view than that discussed earlier and needs a critical analysis to see if it is tenable. The basic difference from the other view is that the former reacts to epistemological claims about something, basically choosing to call somebody an outsider based on a judgement on what the outsider writes, whereas Guru's position is ethical and normative, and has no place for the theoretical outsider. (Another way to understand Guru's claim is to situate the act of theorizing as a political activity, and given the current politics of the asymmetry of representation alluded to in the Introduction, it is necessary to raise such fundamental questions about this process). To understand the complexity in these claims, we need to look more carefully at the notion of lived experience.

EXPERIENCE AND LIVED EXPERIENCE: THE DIALECTIC OF CHOICE AND NECESSITY

'Lived experience' is a catchy term popular primarily among phenomenologists. In the debate about experience and theory, the notion of lived experience also plays an important role, as it indeed does in Guru's arguments. But what exactly is the nature of lived experience? What makes lived experience unique only to the community or individual who lives it?

Experience consists of many elements—the subject who experiences as well as the structure and content of the experience itself. The impetus to experience may be internal or external to the subject. Having the experience of burning my hand, for example, involves an external event that causes a particular experience in me. But one may also have entirely internal experiences such as feeling hunger, joy, or angst.

What does the word 'lived' add to 'experience'? Experience is often confused with the cause of the experience. This allows us to objectify the notion of experience and transport it everywhere to generate similar experiences, leading us to believe that there is a materiality to the whole complex of experience. This materiality, seen as the cause, is taken to be independent of the experiencer. Consider this illustrative example. There are now restaurants whose theme is rural ambience. This experience, which is now accessible to a customer of such a restaurant, is presumed to be similar to the experience of a rural person. The kind of food, the earthiness of the surroundings, lack of what is seen as urban sophistication, and so on, are supposed to recreate the experience of eating in rural places. Let us say I go to such a place and eat ragi balls, a staple rural food in Karnataka. What is it that I am experiencing? What is it that I am supposed to experience? And what is the relation between this experience and the 'authentic' experience of a rural person who eats ragi balls?

The first point to note is that a naïve view of experience is based on the belief that an experience can be replicated—not the experience of the subject but the materiality that constitutes the experience, that which is thought to be 'disassociated' from the total experience. Thus, in principle, we usually believe that we can simulate all and any experience. The possibility of simulating all and any experience is based on the belief that there is no *necessary* connection between the experiencer and the experience. For example, I don't have to travel to the moon but I can, if I train to be an astronaut, get the experience of walking on the moon in anti-gravity chambers. Almost any experience can be duplicated in some sense. Any experience that is commodifiable can be replicated. What this view of experience does is to remove the subject as an essential component of experience. All experience is thus similar to the experience of fun fairs and anybody who pays can participate in the experience. Thus, what is experienced is to seen to be independent of the subject who experiences. Such a view of experience influences our common beliefs about the nature of experience. But can experience really be materialized, commodified, and transferred without taking the subject of experience into account?

Now we can understand the importance of the idea of lived experience. The most useful way to thematize lived experience is to recognize that there is no element of choice or freedom associated with it. In general, we find ourselves placed in a situation and we have to live with what we are given. When a rich man partakes of the experience of the food of the poor, he has a choice and he is asserting that choice. This also implies that he has a choice of *not* participating in that experience. It is the subject's will that decides on whether a particular experience is experienced or not. Experience of this kind, often referred to as vicarious experience, always comes with three important characteristics: one, the *freedom* to be a part of an experience; two, the freedom to *leave* any time if the experience is not satisfactory; and, three, to *modify* the experience, if necessary, to suit one's needs.

Lived experience exhibits, in general, none of these three characteristics. Lived experience is not just about living any experience in the sense that we participate in an experience. If lived experience has to play an ethical and epistemological role, if it has to be the adjudicator of some notion of authenticity, then lived experience should be used only for those experiences that are seen as *necessary*, experiences over which the subject has no choice of whether to experience or not. (The very notion of necessity is itself a complex philosophical problem and one which different cultures seem to have thematized differently).[2] Even if the experience is unpleasant, there is no choice that allows the subject to leave or even modify it. The experiencer comes to the experience not as a subject who has some control over that experience but as one who *will* have to live with that experience. (This necessary experience may have some notion of choice in its genesis—that is, I may choose to put myself in a situation over which I have no control). All this makes lived experience qualitatively different from mere experience. Consider this example. I am bouncing around in a room without any gravity, simulating the experience of walking on the moon, and suddenly the oxygen runs out. As long as I have control over the experience, there is really no serious problem because I can get out of the simulated experience. I can go close to the experience of dying and that is an experience that can be savoured because I know that at the end of it, I can get out of the situation. Contrast this with the (lived) experience of the person who is on the moon and who doesn't have an escape valve. The panic engendered in this person, the will to survive, the understanding that is generated in being in such a situation are indeed quite different from simulated experiences where there is always a choice to get out or modify the experience to suit our needs. In the example of the urban restaurant

---

[2] See Sarukkai (2011).

with a rural theme, suppose I go to eat ragi balls and I find that I don't like the taste. If so, I eat something else or go to some other restaurant. If the Ferris wheel is making me sick, I just get off it. But lived experience offers no such easy choice: if living your experience makes you feel sick, then too bad!

What this means is that the structure of lived experience is one that acknowledges the essential unbreakable relation between the subject who experiences and the context and content of experience. This unbreakable relation is the relation of necessity and creates the absence of choice. Thus, while experience can be duplicated and simulated, lived experience cannot be opened out for experience by *any* subject.

To take Guru's arguments seriously, we have to understand lived experience in this manner. For his arguments to hold, lived experience should be seen as the experience of *being* a subject and not an experience *by* a subject or about a subject. That is, the first prerequisite for an experience to be considered as lived experience is that there is an experience of what it means to *be* the subject who experiences. This automatically places an element of no choice—there is indeed no choice in whether I want to be the subject of experience, although I may have choice about particular aspects of what I experience. You cannot have a Dalit experience unless you are a Dalit yourself or at least experience what it means to be a Dalit subject with *no choice to be otherwise*. Thus, participant observation would also not constitute lived experience as long as the observer, who may otherwise live in and like the community, has a choice to leave when the going gets tough or when the observer decides to leave. Suppose we say that to be a Dalit subject is to be oppressed with no choice of escaping this oppression. Then the lived experience of Dalits is not about sharing their lifestyles, living with them, and being like them, but *being them* in the sense that you *cannot* be anything else. Or, in other words, to be a Dalit is not to share all that they have but to share what they cannot have. Lived experience is not about what there is but is about what there is not. *Lived experience is not about freedom of experience but about the lack of freedom in an experience.*

It is this sense of lived experience that allows us to understand why lived experience is in fact factored into an essential ethical principle that expects the experiencer to become the subject of experience. But

Guru goes a step further. He wants lived experience to justify an ethical principle to do theory. That means that it is not enough to use lived experience as a validation but it is asked to do more, to become the ground for social theory. Can it live up to what Guru demands of it?

Guru's notion of lived experience as essentially related to theory is only one part of the theoretical element of an experience. This is the experience of *being* a subject and not experience *about* the subject. Being a subject is one part of the experience—an essential part, no doubt—but it does not encompass the complete experience. If one follows Guru's prescriptions, then we will have to acknowledge the possibility of expanding what we define as theory and knowledge. If lived experience is to be the final validation for theory, then we will have to look at autobiographies as epistemologically legitimate in a fundamental sense. Interestingly, this is a view that has been expounded some years ago by M.N. Srinivas.[3] He believed that autobiography could be a legitimate tool to understand societies. His argument was based on the idea of learning to trust subjective experience and subjective description as being true to the subject who has experienced or who speaks that experience. We can extend this argument further, as I have indeed done, to claim that fiction based on lived experiences could actually be seen as a legitimate mode of theorizing.[4] But this mode of autobiography or fiction runs counter to the modernist view that depends on the empirical–theoretical dichotomy to generate objective knowledge. If Guru wants to hold on to this structure of empirical and theoretical, then he should reconsider his emphasis on lived experience. Or if he wants to place lived experience at the centre, then he should modify his view of theories, especially his understanding of the empirical. One of the ways of doing this is to demand that ethics be integral to the act of theorizing. If this is allowed, then lived experience becomes the ground for such ethical intertwinement with theory.

[3] M.N. Srinivas (1996). Also, we have to note the importance of autobiographies in Dalit literature.

[4] Sarukkai (1997).

THEORY AND EXPERIENCE: OWNERSHIP OR AUTHORSHIP?

One way to distinguish the nature of experience and theoretical reflection about that experience is through the notion of authority. Is an individual an author of her experience? What is the nature of authorship between an individual and the theory she constructs?

Authorship is an important criterion in distinguishing experience and theory. A person who experiences is not an author of that experience like a person who theorizes about that experience. We are not authors of our experience in the sense that we do not create that experience within us. It is part of our nature to have such experiences and there is no extra agency needed to initiate such a feeling within us. The experiences that we have can be broadly classified into two types: one arising from being in situations not of our making and the other arising from situations we consciously put ourselves in. For example, the experience of being a Dalit belongs to the former type and experiencing the feeling of being drunk is often a consequence of a conscious act. In the first case, we are definitely not authors in any sense. We are neither authors of the events in which we find ourselves nor authors of the experience that is caused by such events. But it could be argued that we are authors of our experience in the second type: we simulate the experience of being drunk because individuals choose to drink and in doing so are aware that they could have that experience of feeling drunk.

If we are not authors of our experiences, then how are we related to our own experiences? We are related to our experiences as owners: we own our experiences but do not author them. It is perhaps similar to the way we own books that we do not author. Ownership confers a set of rights over what we own and authorship confers a different set of rights over what we author. In the historical trajectory of these ideas, we can see a sense of private and public playing out in these terms. (Authors have copyrights and owners have certain other rights). For the purposes of the discussion related to the rights of theorizing our experiences, I suggest that it is the dichotomy of ownership and authorship that is most illuminating.

Once we make this move, Guru's claim can be rephrased in the following manner: an owner has a stake as an author. The extreme case of claiming that only those who experience can theorize implies that only an owner can be an author. Is this a tenable position?

To understand this, we need to look at the notion of the owner in greater detail. What does an owner actually own? The owner of a book owns something of that book—in this case, only the material constituting a particular book. The owner has no rights over that book. She cannot print it and distribute it, for example. She cannot, in principle, change a few lines here and there and publish it as her own. Actually, there is very little an owner can do with a book other than buy it and perhaps read it! The owner owns that *particular* book, meaning thereby that there are *specific* acts that are allowed under that ownership—for example, getting rid of it if she doesn't like that book. Experience is like this: we own our experience, meaning thereby that there is only little we have control of in that experience. Most often we do not have control over what causes that experience; we do not have any say in how the experience should be; we have nothing at all to add consciously to that experience—that is, we cannot either delete unpleasant elements or add pleasant elements to a given experience.

Here is why experience enters into a problematical relation with theory. To theorize is to have a say, it is to be able to say. To theorize about a particular experience is to have a say about that experience. And who can really have a say in having a say about an experience? Guru's position would mean that it is the owner who has the final say in saying anything about that experience. However, we can only partially accept this view because there are many elements of that experience that the owner is not really an owner of. We own our experience only in a particular meaning of that term and we may have control over only some elements of that experience.

In principle, we can theorize about another person's experience because there is a space within that experience that is not related to the experiencer. For example, consider the element of oppression which a Dalit experiences. The Dalit who experiences oppression legitimately owns that experience of oppression. However, the experience of oppression also involves an oppressor, either as an individual or a system, and the Dalit has no control or ownership over this oppressor. So, how much of the experience of oppression can be owned by a Dalit who experiences oppression in a particular act? Moreover, does a person who experiences oppression own that particular experience or larger categories that describe that experience? Is there a difference between a person who experiences oppression once as against somebody who experiences it repeatedly? Who has a greater ownership claim to the *idea* of oppression?

These questions are relevant because theory does this job of moving away from the particular. One's experience may not be enough to validate one's right to have a say about the conceptual world that describes that experience. On the other hand, not having any experience but theorizing about it also seems intrinsically problematical. It is this tension about theorizing that is manifested in two radically different approaches by two thinkers. At one end, we have Gopal Guru and his argument that only the people who own an experience can theorize about it. At the other end, we have Habermas, whose theoretical impulse, I would argue, arises in response to an experience but does not expect the theoretician to have anything to do with the experience. Interestingly, one can see a parallel in the different modes by which the Greeks—and the modern West—and the Indians formulated logic. Logic is fundamental to theory but logic itself was described in different ways by these traditions. In the Indian case, the logicians insisted that inference had to be grounded in the empirical whereas the Greeks, particularly following Aristotle, formulated the logical in opposition to the empirical. One can read this difference as an insistence that theory had to be grounded in experience—the Indian view—against the view that theory is in some fundamental sense independent of the empirical—which is the position in Greek and modern logic, and mathematics.[5]

There are different ways of understanding these oppositions. One way is through the binary of emotion and reason. Experience is often placed under the idea of emotion and related terms whereas theory is something that presumably arises under the action of reason. To hold Habermas's position is to give in to this absolute dichotomy between emotion and reason. There are many pointers to why such a dichotomy seems to make apparent sense. Experience is first-person; reason overcomes individual capacity and also limitations. Experience is local and context-specific. Reason attempts to establish the universal

[5] See Matilal (1998) and Sarukkai (2005).

present in local specificities. But these two terms also share similarities. Both of them seem to be outside wilful and conscious behaviour of individuals. We have experiences just as we have reason. We make mistakes about deploying both our reason and our experience but the fact is that we have an innate capacity for both.

Guru's position, in contrast to Habermas, is to erase this distinction and construct an essential relation between them. Asking for theory to be essentially related to experience is asking for reason to be essentially yoked to feeling, emotions and such terms. This yoking is not at the level of legitimacy: that is, Guru is not claiming that it is epistemologically illegitimate to *not* relate reason to emotion. He would like to claim that experience and reason are in some sense ontologically related: that is, they are related as facts of the matter. That is the reason why he finds an ethical component in this relation—it is ethically wrong to theorize about experience when one has not experienced the same oneself.

The Habermasian approach is actually one that tells us what the role of theory is. In phrasing his approach in this manner, we can see a clear distinction between what he does and Guru's demands on theory. As will be discussed in the next section, Habermas's approach should be seen against the background of his support for modernity in general. It should also be placed against a historical trajectory and in particular to his response to German fascism.

THEORY AS DISTRIBUTING GUILT: HABERMAS AND THE PUBLIC SPHERE

The German role in the Second World War (and related horrific consequences such as the Holocaust) has inspired important theories. To give two well-known examples, particularly of relevance to this chapter, consider the responses to this event by two thinkers, Habermas and Levinas.

One of the influential ideas examined by Habermas is that of the public sphere. The idea of public sphere has been so much appropriated that many 'Indian experiences' are facilely described in terms of the public sphere. Whether these ideas can be universalized as easily as some do is another question altogether, one that has already been addressed by Guru in the previous chapter. The point that interests me is this: How is it that we come to believe, often effortlessly, that categories defining another society, another experiential space can be easily appropriated to describe a different set of experiences? One way is through the use of concepts, which seemingly transcend particular societies and cultures.

This idea of universality is indeed strongly present in Habermas's theorization of the public sphere and principles of communicative praxis. Habermas's support for the larger project of modernity is in consonance with specific ideas related to his theorization of the public sphere. He is also responding to his and his country's historical journey and engagement with fascism. Shocked at the depravity of the Nazi period, Habermas wants to find a theoretical way to engage with what had happened. (Engaging theoretically has the associated danger that it could become a means of absolving oneself from the sin of somehow even being related to these atrocities). Rational communication, for him, is potentially one way to stop such acts from happening again.

Pensky notes that the historical trajectory of the German land— including the pre-War era, dominance in Middle Europe, the Nazi years, partition, and reunification—define the relation of the universal and particular in Habermas.[6] Given this historical experience, the only way out for Germany was to be a democratic society with liberal principles and it is these principles that Habermas wants to universalize.

Universalism for Habermas is a collectively shared mentality, 'a sense of solidarity inhabiting a public space that is distinct from political or economic institutions'.[7] Pensky understands mentality as referring to a 'mode of conduct with its accompanying capacities for self-deliberation, for self-examination and self-criticism'.[8] Although distinguished from the particular forms of life, it has to be rooted in some such culture. For Habermas, the real force of universalism is in the moral domain, manifested, for example, as plurality and the

[6] Pensky (1995).

[7] *Ibid.*, p. 69.

[8] *Ibid.*, p. 71.

response to a different other. Habermas's writing on the nature of the German state, its relation with the past, and its problems after reunification all point to his attempts to construct a philosophy that is essentially beholden to the German experience.

However, remember that Habermas's concerns are nothing new: they are part of the articulations of a collective German guilt. Karl Jaspers already wrote this in 1945: 'Germany cannot come to [regain consciousness] unless we Germans find the way to communicate with each other... we want to learn to talk to each other... we do not just want to assert but to reflect connectedly, listen to reasons, remain prepared for a new insight.'[9]

Strong and Sposito argue this case of an indebtedness of theories to their social origins much more strongly. They begin by noting that 'the theory of communicative action makes the case that rationality is a relevant moral *social* concept'.[10] Speaking to each other places us in a moral position. The authors point out that Habermas believes that the resources needed for the 'ethicopolitical democratic' project are available in the Anglo-American and European traditions. Habermas tries to rehabilitate Western thought not as Western thought alone but as something universal. The specific 'Western' thought that he privileges is that associated with the Enlightenment. Universalization displaces Enlightenment thought from its specific European origin and becomes a model for other cultures and societies displaced both spatially and temporally from Europe.

But why is it important to preserve and continue the Enlightenment? Strong and Sposito suggest that it is largely because of the politics of Europe, which included the specific German experience with fascism. The authors note that although the early Habermas does not view even a thinker like Nietzsche as dangerous, in later works he attacks Nietzsche, Derrida, and Heidegger as being 'politically dangerous'.[11] An important reason for such a shift is the growth of neo-Nazism in Germany. His attack on the postmoderns is fuelled by his reaction to the Nazi rule. The Nazi experience 'makes it not

[9] Pensky (1995: 90).
[10] Strong and Sposito (1995: 263).
[11] *Ibid.*, p. 264.

only possible but necessary to think in universalist terms'.[12] Thus, for Habermas, the fact of Nazism means that we 'must think in universalistic ethicopolitical terms as long as we remember the fact of Nazism'.[13] Habermas writes in terms of the 'we' and 'our'; but who is this 'we'? Strong and Sposito suggest that in the use of the 'we', Habermas is suggesting that 'because of their historical experiences Germans now carry the world historical burden of the universal'.[14]

What is the relation between theorizing and the creation of such universalities from the specific German experience? Under what conditions can those in a different society accept such universal categories that arise from specific experiences? What exactly is Habermas doing in creating theories as responses to certain social events?

I suggest that what he is doing is using theory as an agent to distribute guilt. Theory does this very effectively in many ways: depersonalizing traumatic events, creating new categories to place these events in, creating explanatory structures as part of its structure, abstracting concepts and ideas that then simulate universality, and so on. Habermas could have responded to the Nazi experience in many different ways; but as far as he uses theory to respond to it, he is deploying theory for a particular purpose, that of distributing his guilt among others. His guilt is phrased in terms such as abhorrence of the Nazi experience, fear that neo-Nazism is rising, and so on; but in effect, theory—in the way he construes it—functions as a distributor of guilt. Just as much as the Germans 'now carry the world historical burden of the universal', it is theory that carries the guilt of the inhuman acts of a culture. When others 'participate' in such a theory, they dilute individual sense of guilt for those somehow associated with a guilt-inducing action: universalization is the ultimate dilution of guilt. Guru's trenchant criticism, in the earlier chapter, of the attempt by non-Dalits to theorize the oppression of the Dalits can also be seen as an example where theory is used by the dominant and forward castes to distribute their guilt.

There is a precondition for theory to do this job: namely, its capacity to establish a distance between itself and experience. Habermas's

[12] *Ibid.*, p. 266.
[13] *Ibid.*
[14] *Ibid.*, p. 267.

support to modernity and his thematization of the public sphere with its concomitant ideas of rational communicative praxis are not theoretical moves that arise from lived experience as formulated by Guru.[15] In fact, the crucial point here is that experience cannot dictate authorship. Habermas's theory is for *us*—namely, those who have not participated in that experience. It is we, who are outside this experience in all sorts of ways, who can build upon this theorization. It is we, as complete outsiders to this experience, who will carry on and pass on this universal guilt—that is, it is we as outsiders who will theorize about this experience that is receding further and farther away from us.

For Habermas, then, theory is legitimated by its distance from experience. If he accepts Guru's position, then he would have to say that only those who have suffered under the Nazi rule should theorize about it. So both Guru and Habermas stand for two opposite views in their approach to the relation between theory and experience.

However, Habermas's approach can be usefully contrasted with the Levinasian attempt to theorize about the Holocaust. Levinas's theory arises from lived experience: a lived experience of Nazism that he and his family had to endure. His construction of an ethical theory is directly mediated not just by an experience but by a lived experience in which the idea of necessity (as described earlier) is strongly encoded. Guru's approach to theorizing about the Dalits is a Levinasian approach in contrast to a Habermasian one. For both Levinas and Guru, guilt is not to be distributed and shared among non-experiencers through the guise of theory. Theory is to be felt, is to embody suffering and pain, is to relate the epistemological with the emotional—that is, is to bring together reason and emotion. That is really the challenge that Guru forces on the practice of social science in India.

[15] See Raghuramaraju (2010) for a criticism of our positions regarding modernity and Habermas.

3

Understanding Experience

Sundar Sarukkai

We have referred to experience in different contexts in the earlier chapters. In this chapter, I want to explore the foundational ideas related to experience, drawing on some Indian and Western philosophical discussions on this theme.

Experience is a synonym for many things that are essentially human: life, sentience, consciousness, awareness, feeling, knowing. Experience is the foundation of human existence and it is not possible to make sense of this existence without understanding the nature of experience. The problems in theorizing experience lie precisely in the fact that it is so matter-of-fact and immediate. There is no need to work towards having an experience. We just have experiences, whether we like it or not. We have experiences of pain, pleasure, hunger, illness, joy, sorrow, sight, touch, and smell. We also have experiences of recollecting, remembering, forgetting, and dreaming (including daydreaming). Our actions are also experiential, such as the experience of speaking, writing, running, jumping, swimming, and so on. There are also a range of psychological experiences that define our response to the world such as anger, humiliation, power, and insecurity.

What are the common characteristics in all these diverse experiences, ranging from the experience of seeing to the experience of anger or the experience of dreaming? One common characteristic is the notion of 'feeling'. All the experiences that we have are 'felt'; and it is indeed significant that the description of feeling draws upon the sensation of touch. We are in touch with our experiences and experiences touch us in a most primitive way. This invocation of touch is significant, for it illustrates an essential nature of experience: that it is most immediate, just like touch is 'immediate'. The metaphor of sight involves a distance between the seer and the object of sight. But touch has no perceptible distance between the 'toucher' and the touched. Experience is more like touch than sight because there is really no distance between the experiencer and the experience. (The last two chapters of this book will explore the experience of touch in greater detail). It is this immediacy, this obviousness of experience that makes it unique as well as problematic.

Experience is fundamentally a feeling. What then is it to feel? Feeling is associated most often with a psychological state. We feel emotions like joy and anger. We feel upset or feel hungry. One immediate contrast is with thinking. When we think, we do not say we 'feel thinking'. While there is definitely an experience of thinking (what it is to feel when we are in the act of thinking), the feeling of thinking seems to be different in the sense that we do not—in common parlance—talk about feeling our thoughts, but only of thinking our thoughts. Feeling is intrinsically associated with the experiencer, in that to be an experiencer is to have the capacity to feel. This is often expressed equivalently by saying that feeling is first-person in that only the individual who has the feeling can really access it. Nobody else can have the experiential access to my feeling, although they may have linguistic and non-verbal access to my feeling. Thus, somebody can infer on seeing my face that I have a headache or can know my state on hearing it from me; but they can never experience the headache that I experience. It is this aspect of experience that has often been seen to be problematic as far as the relation between experience and knowledge is concerned. It is this aspect that so often grounds the problematic element of subjectivity, since the world of experience seems to be completely private, one in which nobody else can share. This means that accepting somebody's account of their experience as being true needs a great deal of *trust*.

We should also recognize that there are other human capacities that are not restricted to feeling. For example, consider the capacity for language. When we speak, do we have the 'feeling' of language? How is language really 'felt'? Even the question of meaning does not easily transfer to the vocabulary of feeling—we do not say that we *felt* a particular meaning of a sentence. Instead, we discover meanings or construct them. Such acts of discovery and construction are reflective of prior experiences.

Part of the problem lies in the isolation of the category of experience. If experience is fundamentally about feeling, then it gets associated with notions such as the first-person experience, subjectivity, and so on. Therefore, it also gets placed in opposition to ideas such as objectivity and reason. The suspicion towards experience in Western epistemology (particularly the analytical tradition) is due to this interpretation of the nature of experience. Specifically, processes of thinking are distinguished from experience, thereby leading to the enduring binary of reason and emotion, where reason is associated with thought and emotion with feeling.

There is another way of acknowledging the pervasiveness and the immediacy of experience without placing it within ideas such as the subjective and objective, as well as not placing it in opposition to objective knowledge and truth. This is by invoking the notion of cognitive states. As experiential beings, we are forever in one cognitive state or the other. Cognitive states are transitory: they begin, proceed, and end. One cognitive state is replaced by another. Cognitive states are immediate and pervasive, like experience; but the subjective, first-person aspect of experience is only one kind of cognitive state. Reason and reflection are also cognitive states. While one is reasoning, one can describe the cognitive process involved in it. Thus, a description of experience through cognitive states seems to be a more general description of the human experience. In such a description, the problematic notion of feeling is only part of the cognition related to experience.

Shifting the description to cognitive states thus has important consequences to the larger question of the relation between experience and theory. While we will not be able to discuss this in greater detail here, it must be noted that Indian philosophical traditions are primarily about cognitions. As we will see later, the descriptions of experience as subjective feeling does not occupy a dominant role in these traditions. First-person experience is only a particular kind of cognitive state, and experience in general is more encompassing.

Cognitive descriptions of experience, as in the Indian traditions, are embodied descriptions. To have an experience, we need a body.

We are not pure consciousness in the world. We have a body through which we experience the world. The five sensory organs generate sensations in us and thus these organs are the windows through which we experience. But the five organs are not enough in themselves. Rather, a better way of describing this would be to say that the physical organs by themselves do not guarantee experience. They are only the mediators of experience. What binds these inputs from the organs as 'one' experience is consciousness. An equivalent way of saying this is to note that the organs by themselves do not 'feel'. The aspect of feeling—it is believed—needs something more than the physical organs. The body is the complex that consists not only of the physical organs but also consciousness. Such a view is common to Indian philosophical traditions. (Modern Western thought adds another ingredient to this complex by viewing mind as another kind of entity, one which is not physical. It is interesting to note that for Indian philosophies, in general, the mind is seen as constituted by 'matter' and is seen as the sixth organ, albeit one that is an internal organ. The function of the mind is to synthesize the sensory inputs from the other five senses).

Emotions are fundamentally experiences. Since these emotions are understood to be psychological states and purely subjective, their epistemological status is always in question. So to the extent that experience overlaps with emotion, there is no possibility of having a well-established relationship between experience and knowledge—at least for many accounts of knowledge in contemporary and mainstream Western traditions. Even empiricism, which would base knowledge on sensory experience, does not base knowledge on emotions but only on sensations of the world received through the body. One can articulate the basic problem in this manner: While we see an object, we receive information about various aspects of the object such as its colour and shape, but we do not receive any 'emotions' from it. A flower might give a particular person joy, while in another it may evoke sadness; but these emotions are not seen to be part of the descriptive characteristics of that flower. Hence, emotions do not generate empirical knowledge; at the most, they can only generate knowledge about the nature of the subject. For example, if I experience sadness on seeing a flower, this experience has some information about me that would explain why I feel this emotion. This emotion says nothing about that particular flower.

One cannot underestimate the importance of this belief. The foundation of modern science rests on this distinction between emotion and knowledge. Galileo's dictum that science should be concerned only with primary qualities and not the secondary ones (those like emotion and taste, that are primarily human responses to things) means that scientific knowledge begins by keeping emotion away. The rhetoric of knowledge that followed has extrapolated this removal of secondary qualities to the rejection of any notion of experience and the subjective. Such a move also allowed modern knowledge systems to disengage with the question of ethics in relation to knowledge. (I will discuss this point in greater detail in Chapter 6, on the ethics of theorizing).

However, emotions are an integral part of our experiences in this world, particularly so in the social world. As social scientists, we do feel emotions towards the subject matter of our work in ways that natural scientists do not. While the practice of social science keeps out this emotional aspect of experience, both in method and in writing, there is nevertheless a looming presence of emotion within social theory. This complex relationship between experience, emotion, and knowledge is another challenge to theorizing experiences.

EXPERIENCE AND KNOWLEDGE

In the context of both natural and social sciences, the relation between experience and knowledge is a difficult yet recurrent theme. The basic contour of this debate is as follows: It seems to be the case that without any experience, there can be no knowledge. By experience, I mean the world as experienced through our senses. Our senses are the windows to the world and our senses appear to each one of us as an experience of the sensations. For example, the colour of a tree is available to me through my visual sense and the colour is experienced by me in a particular way. Yet, even though we may think we are all seeing the same colour, there is no guarantee that the way I experience that colour is the same as others do. At least this is the dominant argument from some philosophical traditions. In many epistemological traditions, the suspicion towards experience is encoded in different ways, such as placing emotion against reason and the intellect, and the mistrust of a first-person report as opposed to a collective one. (This suspicion also leads to sceptical and dismissive views towards art). Fundamentally, the problem is that there is no guarantee for truth or falsity of experience, and hence experience—in itself—cannot be justified.

Part of this problem has to do with the way one defines knowledge. In the Western tradition, largely influenced by early Greek views on epistemology, there is a clear distinction between 'theoretical' knowledge and 'practical' knowledge. Echoes of this are found in the theory–empirical distinction. Following Plato, knowledge is characterized by its capacity to be justified and to guarantee certainty. This leads to a long tradition in Western thought that distinguishes between the ideal form of knowledge (as in formal logic and mathematics) as against empirical forms of knowledge (as in the sciences). Until the beginning of modern science, knowledge was primarily associated with certainty untainted by empirical knowledge, and it was the influence of the chemist Boyle and the physicist Newton that legitimized scientific, empirical knowledge.[1]

One cannot underestimate the importance of this Greek view of knowledge. Ideas of necessity and absolute certainty inform this view of knowledge. Truth in logic and mathematics embodies these virtues. These forms of knowledge are independent of input from the world and are quite indifferent to the way our world *actually* is. Thus, the idea of the possible becomes an important marker as against the idea of the actual. One can then rephrase the meaning of necessity by claiming that the necessary is what is true in all possible worlds, a view that is dominant in contemporary philosophy. And what is true in all possible worlds cannot obviously depend on the way *our* world is, and hence empirical knowledge, knowledge of the world we inhabit, cannot in any sense be the ideal form of knowledge.

The conflict between these forms of knowledge leads to a long debate between rationalism and empiricism in Western thought. On the one hand is the rationalist belief that knowledge should be grounded in mental capabilities and on the other is the empiricist

[1] Osler (1970).

who would insist that knowledge be grounded in sensory experience. A strong version of rationalism would claim that ultimately all knowledge can be derived from the mental capacities alone and a strong version of empiricism will insist that all knowledge can be reduced to the sensory inputs alone.

Interestingly, such a distinction between rationalism and empiricism does not occur in the Indian philosophical traditions.[2] For example, formulations that define necessity in terms of being true in all possible worlds would not be acceptable to these philosophers for the simple reason that there is a strong streak of empiricism in all Indian philosophical traditions. Their view of knowledge is not based on an ideal notion of logical and mathematical knowledge. In contrast, both Indian logic and mathematics are themselves 'empirical'.[3] Experience is thus the ultimate grounding of all Indian formulations of knowledge. But in saying this, we should note that their understanding of experience is broader than that used in the rationalism–empiricism debate.

The rationalist critique of the experiential basis of knowledge influences modern epistemology, including the epistemologies associated with the natural and social sciences. In particular, it privileges knowledge making that tries to erase the presence of experience. Even in the empirical sciences, the role of theory has often been seen as something that transcends experience. Theoretical structures, like the structures of logic, mathematics, or syntax, are superstructures that order the empirical experience. Hence, the essential idea of knowledge is something beyond or behind or before experience. Therefore, invocation of experience in scientific descriptions is a taboo.

Natural science has been very successful in eradicating not just personal experience but also the individual herself. The rhetorical strategy of scientific writing that does not allow the author to use 'I' in a scientific paper is a constant reminder of this attempt to keep the individual out of the knowledge claims of a community.[4] Scientific theory is a continued attempt to replace the experience of the individual with properties that belong to the world. This approach

[2] Matilal (1985, 1999) and Mohanty (2002).
[3] Sarukkai (2005).
[4] Gross (1990).

has influenced social sciences but it has been successful in varying degrees. I will discuss the relation of theory and experience later on in the book; here I will restrict myself to the comment that this attempt to keep experience out of valid knowledge impacts social science much more than it does natural science.

Kant's response to the problem of experience is also helpful in addressing the relation between experience and knowledge. The most important insight that we can take from Kant in this context is that our experiences are intrinsically related to our cognitive capacities. While the external world may catalyse our experiences, the final structure of our experience is built from innate cognitive structures of 'understanding'. Thus, certain a priori concepts order the sensory input we receive, and that ordered input is what constitutes our experience. In this sense, our experience is already conceptually filled and these concepts do not derive from the external source of experience but from our internal cognitive structure. In this description, there is no explicit invocation of the individual subject since the a priori concepts are not subjective but rather are universal structures of human understanding.

Although in a sense Kant could be seen as belonging to a phenomenologist tradition, it is Husserl's phenomenology that develops a complex reading of experience and its relation to knowledge. For Husserl, and in general, for the phenomenological tradition, experience is all that there is. Everything that we say about the world has to be discovered in our experiences. But this does not mean that what we discover in these experiences is purely 'subjective'. In fact, a most important insight from Husserlian phenomenology is that the *very idea of the objective is a particular subjective experience of the world*! That we believe there are objective and subjective worlds is a unique characteristic of our experience. To assume that somehow we have access to the idea of objectivity outside our experiences is a completely mistaken notion.

We should remember that for Husserl, phenomenology was the highest of the sciences. It is the 'science of sciences', a pure eidetic science. What we discover in our experience are essences, and these essences are indubitable. Moreover, there is a method, the much-maligned phenomenological method, that helps us discover these essences. These essences are the highest form of knowledge and they have to be extracted out of experiences. Thus, the phenomenological approach to experience relates experience and knowledge in an intrinsic manner.

Indian philosophical traditions are fundamentally phenomenological traditions. Their major concerns are about experience, consciousness, the self, and related notions. Their description is fundamentally cognitive in character. Even logic is described cognitively. Immersed in experience, as it were, it is difficult to isolate experience itself as a special category, as it happens in some modern Western traditions. These particular views on experience in the Western tradition are a response to a specific history of the debates between empiricism and rationalism. Kant, as is famously known, attempts to mediate these two views. In the Indian traditions, such a neat distinction between the empirical and the rational does not develop. The rational and the empirical are intertwined just as latter-day phenomenology understands the intertwining between experience and knowledge. This intertwining is illustrated in the words used for experience in Indian languages.

The most common word for 'experience' in Indian philosophy would be *anubhava*, although many writers ranging from Matilal to Ramanujam point out that there is no exact semantic match between 'anubhava' and 'experience'.[5] Anubhava is closely related to the notion of the self, and so in Indian thought, it is impossible to talk of experience without invoking the self. In Western traditions, where such a distinction is made, we can note a parallel between experience and knowledge in the following manner. In modern traditions, particularly in the period corresponding to the establishment of modern science, the knower is differentiated from the known; consequently, the experiencer is not invoked in accounts of experience. The very nature of experience is such that there is always an experiencer. But our descriptions of that experience may or may not invoke this experiencer explicitly.

It is interesting to note that the commonly used terms for experience in Indian languages exhibit the intrinsic relatedness of experience and knowledge. In Tamil, one commonly used word for experience is

[5] For example, see Matilal (1986: 23).

pattarivu and in Bengali, it is *abhigyota*.[6] Both these words for experience have explicit connotations of knowledge in them. Even in common parlance, it is difficult to find words for experience that do not have terms for knowledge, skill, or wisdom (like *arivu*) stitched into them. So also is the case with anubhava. There is a similar analogy in German. The two words for experience in German are *Erfahrung* and *Erlebnis*. The latter is a specifically coined term that denotes 'lived experience', but both these words have a sense of the 'lived' within their semantic space. Lived experience suggests an immediacy that is not present in the other idea of experience, which is already refined through reflection, conceptual structures, and so on. The basic point I am making here is that the words for experience in different languages exhibit hidden presuppositions about experience. 'Experience' in English does not have a sense of the 'lived' in it. As is well known, this word is derived from the Latin *experientia*, which, among other things, supports the meaning of proof and experiment. One can, along this trajectory, see the explicit connection of knowledge with experience; but over time this connection has been drastically modified. In the Indian uses of the term, because of the explicit presence of synonyms for knowledge in the words for experience, this relation is always evoked when one talks about experience.

The intrinsic relation between experience and knowledge is reinforced through the explicit relation between the knower and the known. This relation had to be broken for modern knowledge (science) to be possible, since if this relation were to hold, then the morality of the knower could be seen to influence the moral status of the known and thus leads to difficult questions such as the following: If Dr Mengele, the infamous Nazi doctor, discovered some medical truths following his experiments on the Jews, should that become part of our knowledge system? Should knowledge be intrinsically associated with the morality of the knower and with the ethics of the means of acquiring that knowledge? Modern science becomes possible only after the splitting of the knower–known relation (see Chapter 6 for a longer discussion). Similarly, just as the knower–known distinction was created, so also was the experiencer–experience relation broken to allow us to talk of experience without the shadow presence of the

---

[6] Thanks to Rakhi Ghoshal for alerting me to the Bengali use.

experiencer. As a consequence, we talk of experiences as if they are independent entities and as if they are available to us without the experiencer. Guru's argument (Chapter 1) about the practice of social science in India today can be seen alongside this historical debate on the importance of the knowing subject as well as the experiencing subject in any evaluation of knowledge and experience.

However, there is another philosophical debate that has brought back the relevance (or the uniqueness) of experience. This is an argument that claims that there is a special knowing that is present in first-person experience that can be had only by the person who has that experience. This is an argument that is often referred to as the knowledge argument regarding qualia. Basically this is a claim that even though someone might have all the physical knowledge about a particular event, that person will still not have the knowledge of what it means to have experienced that event. In a sense, this is the argument that experiences cannot be reduced to some physical correlates.

Some well-known examples are these: Even if all information about a molecule, like ammonia, is known, one still cannot know how it would smell just from this information.[7] Jackson offers a variation of this argument by arguing that knowing everything (all physical descriptions) of a colour is still not complete knowledge about that colour since the experience of that colour cannot be known just by knowing the physical information about colours and the human sensory apparatus.[8] The basic point here is that experience has an associated body of knowledge that is available only to the experiencer. Nagel, in another influential rendering of a similar argument, points out that it is impossible to know what it is like to be a bat even though we may know everything about the bat's sonar apparatus.[9] The point about all these examples is that having a subjective experience is epistemically special. There is some knowledge in an experience that cannot be had by those who do not have that experience. This is yet another way of approaching Guru's challenge posed in the earlier chapter.

[7] Broad (1925).
[8] Jackson (1982).
[9] Nagel (1974).

I AND MINE

There is a fundamental relation between self and experience. Through the category of the self, ideas such as identity are conceptualized. Important notions of identity, belongingness, emotions, both personal and 'cultural', self-knowledge, recognition of the other, and the like are all intimately related to the idea of experience. So our understanding of experience and thus the self will influence the way we conceptualize these terms. It should not be a surprise to discover that the nature of the self, like experience, has been conceptualized in different ways in different philosophical traditions.

Although the concept of the self is different from that of experience, there is an intrinsic relationship between the two. One way to understand this would be to consider whether one can have experience without a self and whether one can have a self without any notion of experience. The most common ways of talking about these concepts tend to regard experience as needing a self that *has* the experience and that selves cannot be known except through their experiences.

However common the belief in self, there are many philosophical problems in the idea of self. Let us consider a view in which the self is equated with 'I'. We can begin with a simple question as to whether we have an experience of 'I'. When I say 'myself', I am referring to the 'I' that characterizes me. Now, do we have an experience of 'I'? Or of 'I-ness'? Or indeed of 'myself'? Or is the self granted to us only through thought and conceptualization that, for example, could occur after the experience? If so, then not only is the self independent of experience but it is incapable of being experienced.

Even if the self cannot be 'directly' experienced as the self, yet the self is present in every experience. Every experience I have is 'my' experience. The pain I feel is 'my' pain, not yours, not somebody else's. Every experience is qualified by the prefix 'my' and since it is universally qualified as such, we do not need to invoke it in describing every experience. Instead, what we often do is to displace this adjective 'my' to the position of a subject 'I'. Thus, from saying that I feel 'my pain in the stomach', we convert it into 'I feel pain in the stomach'. But there is something lost when we—by a sleight of hand—replace the 'my' with 'I'. We lose 'myself' and discover a self.[10]

This shift from 'my' to 'I' is extremely significant. What it does is to make the 'I' a universal. Every 'I' is a universal 'self'. The idea of a universal 'subject' is thus born. The universal subject is related to the universal 'I' and not to the particular 'my'. Linguistically, the shift from 'my' to 'I' removes the idea of ownership present in the phrase 'my pain' (this pain is mine) and replaces it with pain as a property or a characteristic of a self. This is a wonderful and subtle example of nominalization, where an adjective (my/mine) is substituted with a noun (I). In so doing, it creates an object called the self, which has properties like pain, pleasure, and so on. The 'I' now has feelings; but we do not say 'I have this mine pain'. Instead, we are only left with 'I have this pain', which is just like saying 'A has this pain'. The substitutability of 'I' means that we could as well say, 'All have this pain'. The pain, the feeling, is no longer localized to the person who has that pain.

Another interesting illustration of this is seen in the difficulty of using 'I' and 'my' in a simple sentence. Although we can have a sentence such as 'I am carrying my purse', it seems impossible to say something similar about my feelings. For example, 'I am having a pain' seems more correct than 'I am having my pain'. This illustrates how the 'I' is invoked in order to absorb the first-person experience.

'I' is ontological and 'mine' is epistemological. Thus, 'I' becomes associated with the ontology of self while 'mine' is related to the epistemology of the subject. We do not say 'This is I', whereas we do say, 'This is mine'. Any invocation of 'mine' needs a guarantee and/or proof whereas the existence of 'I' makes the self an object that is present, self-present.

The nominalization that replaces the 'my' with 'I' converts feelings into properties of the self. The feeling of oppression is replaced with the property of being oppressed. That is, one's feeling of oppression gets replaced by a notion that a self is oppressed. Such processes related to nominalization have important consequences in the way

[10] For an interesting analysis of self, I, my, mine, etc., see K.C. Bhattacharya (2008).

we understand the relationship between experience and theory. (An intriguing analogy of this process is with scientific discourse, which is marked by the process of nominalization. Here, verbs are replaced by nouns and this has profound consequences for understanding the nature of science).

Therefore we should be careful in distinguishing different terms related to the self. One such is the 'subject'. Others include 'person', 'individual', and so on. In the next section, I will briefly discuss the trajectory of the idea of the self in Western and Indian thought.

Self and the Subject

When we talk of experience, are we talking of the self? Or of the subject? Or something else perhaps? Is the notion of experience different from those of self and subject? Or is experience that which is only *had* by the self?

The themes of self and the related notion of subject are too vast to be dealt with in a small section. Given the context of this book, I will restrict myself to two points: (1) the relation between rationality and the self, which is a defining relation for the 'Western' understanding of the self, and (2) some reflections on the nature of self as understood in Indian philosophical traditions. Both these aspects are integral to the creation of social theory in India.

As Steinvorth points out, the ideas of the self in Western thought are 'closely interwoven' with rationality.[11] There are two conceptions of the self that are available in Western thought. One is the Lockean conception, which is associated with 'utilitarian rationality', and the other is the Cartesian one. Until the seventeenth century, in the West, the idea of the self was dominantly influenced by Aristotle and the Stoics. In the eighteenth century, Locke's conception begins to dominate. As Steinvorth notes, 'the self has a central position in Western thought because the way it is conceived commits us to a conception of rationality and action, science and religion, and, most momentously, to a distinction of rational and individualist societies from less rational and more collectivist societies'.[12] Rationality was

---

[11] Steinvorth (2009: 4).
[12] *Ibid.*, pp. 5–6.

used as a marker to distinguish cultures and, among other things, it served to validate the subjugation of cultures, as well exemplified in later colonial discourses.[13]

Plato distinguished different faculties of the mind. The 'higher' faculty makes possible calculation and the 'lower' faculty is associated with desire. Similarly, Aristotle makes a distinction between active and passive reason. But what complicates the matter is the introduction of the will, which is the power to decide what to do even though reason might dictate only one possible path—that is the capacity to 'both to do and not to do a possible action'.[14] This idea of the will that has the freedom to choose, even when reason suggests otherwise, influences the later distinction created between self and subject.

It is not that there was a homogenous idea of the self in the history of mainstream Western thought. Although the Cartesian self has played an influential role, there were other formulations such as the Lockean self, which was identified with consciousness, the Humean position that denies the existence of a self (somewhat like the Buddhists), and the Kantian idea of the self as a transcendental idea.[15] Steinvorth makes an important point: the attempt to understand premodern societies in Hegel and Marx, and the psychologists' attempt to describe the transition from the self of a child to that of an adult have something in common—both of them were concerned with two kinds of selves and the shift from the 'collective and authoritarian' self of premodern societies to the 'individualist and fallible' self of modern societies. A child's self moves towards individual responsibility and fallibility, away from being under the authority of the parents. Weber and Freud are unified in their essential view of a self as moving from being under an authoritarian form to becoming an individualized one. Steinvorth argues that the 'West has produced a concept of two-faced self in which a collectivist and authoritarian self precedes an individualist and fallible one'.[16] The latter self is a sign not only of modernity but also of the Western self, and such a

---

[13] See Ada (1989).
[14] Steinvorth (2009: 6).
[15] *Ibid.*, p. 7.
[16] *Ibid.*

self is in opposition to premodern societies or traditional societies. (A similar dichotomy of two kinds of selves is seen in Heidegger's distinction between authentic self and inauthentic self: the latter guides ordinary action.)

The perceived superiority of the West is fundamentally related to the way the self is conceptualized in its many intellectual traditions. Such a view of the changing self influences Eurocentric and colonial discourses. It has also influenced modern social theory in India. But in this context, there is an important aporia that needs to be addressed. If we understand Weber and Freud's description of the two selves as indicative of hierarchies (premodern/modern and child/adult), then can we use them to describe the nature of selves in the Indian social context? Are the hierarchies of Indian society based on such distinctions between a self demonstrating individual responsibility and another self that accepts authority? Is such a formulation relevant to clarifying the selves of different caste groups? While I will not deal with these questions directly, perhaps the discussion in this book will help tangentially answer these questions.

The sense of rationality associated with the self is emphasized through the capacity for judgement. This is philosophically a profound shift, since judgement becomes a special capacity of human experience. The Cartesian self manifests this shift following Descartes's distinction between experiences (which includes desires, beliefs, and doubts) and judgement (*deciding* on the content of these beliefs and desires). This move 'splits' the 'self' into two, one part experiencing and the other judging the content of that experience. For Descartes, judgement is what finally defines the human: 'The deliberate judgment is what I cannot distance myself from; hence, it is myself'.[17] Thus, the notion of the self is primarily associated with that 'power' to judge and therefore functions as an agent of judgement. Moreover, for Descartes, as Steinvorth points out, the self is indubitable (as the method of doubt presumes to show) whereas the world is dubitable. I would extrapolate from this to argue that experience gets sidelined in this view since judgement is *in* the self but experience is *of* the world and if the world is dubitable, then so is experience.

---

[17] *Ibid.*, p. 8.

For the empiricists, knowledge about the world is founded on sense experience. But as has long been argued, the sense impressions have to be reconstructed and it has often been assumed that it is the self which does this task. But this means that the world that is so constructed is also extremely private. Such a view of the self also makes it passive, and as against this, as Steinvorth points out, the self for Heidegger and Wittgenstein is characterized by its capacity to 'act on the world' and not just to construct a world.

In the dominant Western tradition, as briefly alluded to before, there is a sense of the 'growth' of the self—we acquire a self as we grow from a child to an adult and presumably as we move from the premodern to the modern. What does it mean to say that we acquire a self? Primarily, it is the capacity of the self to judge and to act. As much as we judge worldly experiences, we also judge ourselves. Moreover, it would be difficult not to take seriously the possibility that an individual has many 'selves'. It should not be a surprise that the idea of shame—one that has interested many important thinkers—indicates the presence of these selves, since shame 'starts when I become conscious of my self as something observed by other selves in my body'.[18] Shame is fundamentally a consequence of the self's power to judge itself. The growth of a self is not limited to judging oneself, however. To grow into a 'full' self, many conditions are required, such as the use of 'propositional language', awareness of dependence on others, and capacity for 'initiating actions'.[19]

Understood in this manner, the self's relation to experience is ambiguous, particularly because of the domineering concept of judgement. In Indian philosophy, we repeatedly encounter the prevalent view that experience is always and necessarily tied in with an experiencer. The experiencer is the one who is aware of the experience. If the Cartesian self is the capability for 'deliberate judgement', then this self by itself cannot experience emotions such as suffering. That is, we have an experience and the self judges it to be a particular type of experience, such as humiliating, shameful, and so on. For some, then, there is therefore a need to distinguish between self and subject. Steinvorth suggests that what 'happens to us constitutes' only our

[18] *Ibid.*, p. 22.
[19] *Ibid.*, p. 23.

subject and not our self. He further adds that the 'self is what we are left with when we distance ourselves from anything that only happens to us'.[20] So, when we suffer because of a particular experience, the suffering is part of the subject and not of the self. One can extend this, as Steinvorth indeed does, to even claim that thoughts belong to the subject and the self judges them. In this view, then, the category of an individual is the 'sum' of the self and the subject. Thus, it is the individual who 'acts and feels', who feels and judges, and so on.

Does experience belong to the self or to the subject? If we follow the above arguments, then it seems that it must belong to the subject; the self merely judges the experience. In terms of understanding what kind of an experience one has, such as the experience of shame or humiliation, it is the self that does the job of categorizing experience under these concepts. So how these experiences are categorized under what concepts depends on the self.

I would argue that these formulations of the self and the subject, which has had a great influence on the relation between experience and knowledge/theory in the dominant Western intellectual tradition, need to be repositioned in the context of any debate on experience and theory in the Indian context. On the one hand, there is nothing Indian or European about the self and the subject as categories; but on the other hand, one should recognize that these categories are not independent of cultural presuppositions and world views. (We should, of course, keep in mind the fact that empiricists and some contemporary philosophers would not want to make such a distinction between the self and the subject; but nevertheless, these distinctions and what follows from them have had a seminal influence on the way social science has responded to the problem of experience and its relation to theory.)

What role does the notion of self play in Indian philosophical theories? There are many competing philosophical theories in Indian philosophy. It should not be a surprise to note that there are many different formulations of the self in these philosophies. One major tradition, which has had a great influence in talking about the self, is the Vedānta tradition. The Nyāya and the Buddhist schools differed with the Vedāntins, with the Buddhists most famously being

[20] *Ibid.*, p. 9.

known for the denial of the self. But in general there seems to have been some common elements in the many different schools of Indian thought (not including the views that deny the existence of self). First of all, the idea of the self is captured best by the notion of the 'I'. The nature of the self is also closely related to the theory of body, mind, and consciousness these theories hold. For many Indian traditions, the mind is not different from the body in kind, like it is for Descartes and modern thought. Mind (*manas*) is also matter like the body.[21] Moreover, in Indian thought, the self is always embodied.[22]

The descriptions of a self in these philosophical schools are similar to that discussed above. Advaita, Nyāya, and Mīmāṃsā are all concerned with the nature of experience, but tend to describe it in terms of consciousness. The first question that confronts these philosophers is this: Who perceives experience? Suppose I have a particular experience. When I say that I have that experience, does it necessarily imply that there is another self that is perceiving this experience? In the language of the Indian philosophers, what they were asking is whether consciousness needs another higher-order 'seer' to 'see' the experience. In the discussion above, we considered the possibility that the self judges experience. Nyāya and Mīmāṃsā hold a view that is closer to this description (but not in terms of judgement). For them, the self is the object of consciousness and it is available through the 'I' experience. But for the Advaitins, consciousness is 'self-luminent' and is thus able to see its own functioning.

The description of experiences in Advaita is influenced by its typology of three basic states, defined as the waking, dreaming, and dreamless sleeping states. All these three constitute what we would call ordinary experience. In all these three cases of ordinary experience, there has to be a common 'subject' who experiences them, for if this is not the case, then we should have at least three selves corresponding to the three states. Moreover, a pure subject (an experiencing subject who is not experiencing anything), also called 'the self', can never be experienced.[23] For Advaita, this pure subject is the 'true self' and the aim of liberation is to have knowledge of this self. To know

[21] Chakrabarti (1999).

[22] Ram-Prasad (2001: 381).

[23] Sharma (1993: 26).

the self, there must be an experience of the self, and this is really the problem. So Advaita accepts the idea of the self-luminosity of the self.[24] In all the three states, something is witnessing them all and that is the pure subject. Our experience is never of the pure subject but only of the subject who experiences. So our normal 'I' is not the pure I but only the imagined-I, which is also called the ego.[25] In general, for Indian philosophers, the ultimate knowledge is the knowledge of the self—that is, 'perception of its *true* nature'—whether the self is enduring or not.

While Indian theories of the self often end up with discussions on liberation, there is nevertheless an important point in these ideas of the self. Like the self–subject distinction discussed earlier, a similar distinction of the 'pure subject'–subject is present in the Indian views. Both the 'pure subject' and the 'self' are witnesses to the experience that is had by the subject. So, we might say that the 'pure subject' is the author of the experience, the one who 'perceives' all the experience happening to the subject and thus has an awareness of these experiences. In a similar manner, we could call the self the owner of the experiences that the pure subject becomes aware of.

For the Advaitins, this difficulty in describing experience is part of the problem of language. As Sharma points out, one cannot use the words 'knowledge' and 'experience' with reference to the 'pure subject'.[26] That this is nevertheless done only shows the 'poverty of language', which is that language 'itself involves a division into subject and object'.[27] This is the reason, as Sharma suggests, for the emphasis on silence. (Note here an interesting difference on the origin of the subject–object distinction. For some phenomenologists, it arises as the essential nature of experience itself, whereas for the Advaitins, it arises from the structure of language. Both are important insights that have some relevance to the experience–theory debate.)

In contrast, when the Buddhists reject the existence of the self, they are also rejecting an agent who is witnessing all the experiences. The Buddhist debate on the matter of self and experience actually

---

[24] *Ibid.*, p. 28.
[25] *Ibid.*, p. 32.
[26] *Ibid.*, p. 73.
[27] *Ibid.*

gives a clue to the structure of the self/subject. If there is no self stand-ing outside the experience, witnessing the experience (Advaitin) or judging it (Cartesian), then there must be something in the expe-rience that is self-aware. In this context, 'anubhava' stands for an immediate experience. Reflecting on this experience (which would include judging it) leads to a higher-order experience.

Thus, the real distinction for Indian theories of experience and self is between immediate experience and conceptual experience, that is, between conceptual and non-conceptual experience. I would argue that the question of judgement, which is so central to modern Western philosophy, arises in Indian thought through the consideration of conceptual and non-conceptual experience, a topic which is a major debate between the Naiyāyikas and the Buddhists. Experience that is immediate and direct is not mediated by concepts. I will interpret this experience as the experience of the subject. When this experience is seen through conceptual categories, then it has already been 'judged' and 'determined'. This constitutes the activity of the self as against the subject. For the Indian traditions, even if they do not follow the self–subject distinction in terms of judgement, they are following a similar path in their debates on conceptual and non-conceptual experience. These distinctions are not mere philosophical nitpick-ing but have a serious consequence for the question of the relation between experience and knowledge. It is of fundamental importance to issues of what kind of relation one has to one's own experience, what one can reasonably know about this experience, and so on.

Implications for Social Science Theory

What do these philosophical approaches to the self have to do with social theory? First of all, almost all essential ideas of the human, such as freedom, will, action, morality, and reason, have been associated with the self. The category of experience, as described earlier, is also related to the metaphysics of the self. In a way, the self is the com-mon site where theory and experience meet. However, there is a lot that is unclear in such descriptions. Primarily, there seems to be an implicit acceptance of an entity called 'the self' although there have been influential attempts to discredit this belief in the existence of such an entity.

In contemporary discussions, the notion of the self continues to be prominent. Almost any attempt to talk about ideas of freedom, identity, community, and so on, invokes the notion of the self. Moreover, in contemporary times, the self has become more complex, more divisive, and more unstable. Mansfield notes that contemporary global society, unlike earlier times in Western cultures, is one that places enormous premium on feeling.[28] Moreover, alienation in society, the rise of various crimes associated with a dysfunctional self, and the instability in the growth of a self, particularly in the teenage years, seem to have brought the idea of the self into prominence, although without much clarity on what is being referred to when one talks about the self. As already discussed above, the notion of the self goes along with that of the subject. Mansfield points out the subject is 'always linked to something outside of it'[29] and it is this character of being linked to other subjects and to the world that is an essential mark of the subject.

The notion of the Subject therefore negates the idea of the self as an isolated entity.[30] Mansfield notes four types of subjects: the subject of grammar, politico-legal subject, the philosophical subject, and the subject as human person. While the vocabulary of self and subject displaces the explicit presence of experience, there is an underlying link between experience and these two notions. When Mansfield notes that 'subjectivity is primarily an experience',[31] he is only echoing a common understanding of different subjectivities. There is an important consequence of seeing subjectivity itself as an experience. This follows from most contemporary accounts of the subject as something radically different from the Enlightenment subject. The latter guarantees an autonomous, individual self, but a legion of writers—from Freud to Foucault—break away from this model and instead describe the subject as a constructed entity. If the subject is constructed, then there are no 'natural' experiences that are possible. There are no innate experiences available to the human

[28] Mansfield (2000).
[29] *Ibid.*, p. 3.
[30] *Ibid.*, pp. 3–4.
[31] *Ibid.*, p. 6.

subject. All experiences, including sexuality, get constructed around themes such as power and culture.

Foucault's attempt to place the self within a discursive and power structure has been influential in social theory. We should remember that Foucault's move towards subjectivity and the self occurs through the engagement with the body. His attempt to make the body the site of power, at least in his work on the clinic and on discipline, was extremely influential; but it raises the question of what he actually means by a 'body'. The sociological body, that which is the site where power relations are instantiated, is not the simple physical body. As Fox notes, the body for Foucault cannot be the biological body, since this body is also 'discursively constructed'. In particular, the most trenchant criticism against this notion of the Foucaldian body is that it is passive and 'cannot be a catalyst for resistance'.[32]

Fox points out that Foucault's work on sexuality also meant a shift from the body to the self, in essence replacing a passive body with a reflexive self, which eventually leads to the ideas of technology of the self. The point here is this: in contemporary theories, the notions of self and subject have subsumed experience as the primary category; but there is enough that we can recover from these theories of self and subjectivity with respect to the problem of experience. As we will see in the later chapters, the political and cultural framing of experience is similar to such framings of subjectivity.

However, two issues that are central to this book remain out of the ambit of these contemporary theories. One is the explicit relation between experience and the *act* of theorizing, and the other is the relation between these views of self and subject with the formulations of self and experience in Indian philosophical and literary traditions. In the latter part of the book, we will explicitly engage with the ethics of the act of theorizing itself and, over the course of the next few chapters, we will try and illustrate how the Western conceptualizations of self and experience may not be enough to capture the complexity of social experiences in other cultures.

In the chapter that follows, Guru has already set the stage for such a re-conceptualization when he invokes the notion of space in the context of experience. He argues that the 'production of experience

---

[32] Fox (1998: 424).

hinges on the reproduction of spaces' (Chapter 4) and goes on to add that without experience, the spaces cannot fulfil their epistemological promise. I would argue that the shift to the notion of spaces allows Guru to describe contemporary social experiences in terms of categories that are also sensitive to the Indian historical discourse. In particular, the notion of place is central to ideas of religion and sacredness. This is most powerfully captured in the notion of sacred space that is common to both established religions as well as folk practices. (One can look at the invocation of sacred and profane space in Babytai's biography as well as the temple entry movement described by Guru in the next chapter.) Instead of purity and pollution, those problematic categories that were early on invoked by European scholars to describe Indian society, the notion of space offers a different set of conceptual categories to model Indian social experience. Thus, it should not surprise us that the ideas of purity and pollution are themselves crucially dependent on prior formulations of space.

Guru argues that ideas and concepts make sense only in the space which they belong to. In some sense, this is a Foucauldian move and might allow us to place the argument within a larger discursive space. Redefining experience through the idea of experiential space changes the traditional ideas of self and subject with regard to the category of experience. Even where Ambedkar uses terms like 'self-respect', Guru describes them in terms of experiential space.

What is the consequence of shifting the discussion from self/subject to space? Let me point to one interesting philosophical consequence. In the context of the self, the notion of 'I' was important to make sense of the fact that we seem to have ownership of our experience. My experiences are mine. And all my experiences are mine. The belief that there is a witness, a seer, to our experiences also led to the postulation of the self. In both the Cartesian and later theories of the self, the role of the self as a reflective agent, capable of judgement and action, gave a sense of autonomy to the self. However, shifting the locus from the self to space changes any naïve belief in the existence of the self. Moreover, in the context of untouchability and Dalits, as described by Guru in the next chapter, there is indeed a constant abrogation of my experience as 'mine'. The experiences of these communities illustrate the externality of experience, externalized in the various kinds of spaces around them. Thus, their experiences are driven by the external and they do not have the luxury of having private, subjective, 'internal' experiences. In other words, their sense of self is always mediated by a sense of self given to them by the spaces that they inhabit or that they are excluded from.

One could thus say that their sense of self is actually supplementary to the sense of self that defines others who inhabit the various spaces around them. Such a notion of supplementary self allows us to understand another important characteristic of untouchability which is the subject matter of the last two chapters.

4

Experience, Space, and Justice

Gopal Guru

> Wherever Gandhi is, it's the capital in India.
>
> —*Jawaharlal Nehru*

> Gandhiji, I do not have Homeland.
>
> —*Babasaheb Ambedkar*

In the above title, a claim is being made that these three terms in the title are deeply interrelated and make complete sense only together. It is also suggested that they also make sense only in the above conceptual sequence. The above title involves an epistemological claim in as much as it suggests a concept of space embedded in experience as the source both for the formation of thought and its articulation. By this I am not suggesting that other frameworks, for example, the idealist or the materialist, lack an epistemological capacity to produce thought. In fact, as we all know, they do produce and provide some of the epoch-making systems of thought.[1] But this universal character of thought is seldom capable of capturing a specific reality that exists in a complex particularity. For example, Marx—with his universal principles of understanding—tried to offer some explanation about Indian reality, and scholars from India did try to apply it to the Indian situation, and yet many of them do accept the limitations of Marx in terms of unfolding to us the Indian social reality in all its complexity.[2]

---

[1] See Heller (1989: 32–3); Seidler (1986); and Smith (1989).

[2] Chattopadhyaya (2002).

Theoretical representation of experience cannot be achieved in advance. The theory of experience has to wait for its reflective realization until the emergence of experience, which is produced by forces of domination and endured particularly in the first-person singular. To express this differently, a theoretician can proceed with doing theory but needs to be aided by the empirical evidence of the experience of an individual or a social group. Such reflective realization becomes a possibility primarily in the context of experience that provides necessary background conditions for doing theory. These conditions can be twofold: objective (material) and subjective (conceptual or epistemological). I argue in this chapter that experience, which is subjectively realized but objectively produced through the logic of space, finds its theoretical representation mediated by experiential space.[3] Let me then suggest here that reflective realization—which is achieved at the level of conceptual approximation, however—is contingent upon experience that acquires expression (sometimes violent) within a specific space. I further argue in this chapter that production of experience hinges on the reproduction of spaces. Spaces that are structured along different axes—economics,[4] colonial,[5] discursive[6]—tend to produce fragmentary forms of experience. In this chapter, I am therefore making a second submission: that ideological restructuring of spaces across time leads to the stability and continuation of experience in different forms. Although the adversary or a tormentor forms the constitutive source of experience, yet the former does not produce experience as she desires. In fact, the tormentor requires certain supporting conditions in order to produce tormenting experience, which in many cases is deployed as the weapon of the stronger. Thus, for the tormentor, experience acts as a political condition to maintain domination, while the theoretician uses it as a tool for theorization. Both these attempts, however, share one thing in common, in that both of them achieve their success based on the objectification of victim.

[3] See Lefebvre (1984: 184).
[4] See Harris 2003: chapter III.
[5] See Goswami 2004.
[6] Chatterjee 1986.

Taking a cue from Lefebvre, I argue in this chapter that space provides this necessary condition for the tormentor, who then uses these spaces for producing a particular kind of experience that can morally paralyse a victim.[7] The tormentor reconfigures spaces accordingly, so as to seek the ultimate regulation of the victim into hegemony and domination of the former. She defends domination, either using spaces to enact unprecedented violence or by using them for marginal cooption of the victim in the symbolic universe of the tormentor. For example, a tormentor may use a cultural space to accommodate either a Dalit or a woman by assigning the latter a symbolic recognition as a 'Goddess Laxmi' who has no hold on wealth (in the case of a Hindu woman) or an 'untouchable' as an enlightened consumer in the age of globalization but who is almost on the verge of starvation. Hegemony, which plays out through spaces as an effective form of power, thus depends on the objectification of a person as 'Uncle Tom' (servile) or 'Ghamdya' (a servile person in Marathi). The tormentor also uses spaces to seek the reduction of a human being to a repulsive object. For example, the middle class in Mumbai treats people staying in slums as walking dirt. The 'victim', however, does not remain eternally fettered to this servile condition. In fact, the victim seeks to reconfigure spaces with the purpose of divesting him or her off the tormenting or humiliating meaning that, as part of the hegemonic politics of the dominant, gets blamed on the victim. The victim is motivated to restructure and rearrange the space in favour of egalitarianism. The victim, as I will argue in the following section, uses the space-bound experience in order to throw up a radical language for the collective mobilization that is considered so necessary for altering, annihilating, and transcending spaces that are otherwise quite dominating and discriminatory.

However, in walking over, 'taking over', or walking out of the dominant spaces, which (as Lefebvre argues) are necessarily closed, it is necessary for the victims to not only grasp the experience that underlies these spaces but also to intensify it through an abstract language.[8] In other words, the victims come to terms with themselves through intensification and then they seek to transcend the servile

[7] Lefebvre (1984: 67).

[8] *Ibid.*, p. 58.

identity that is contained within the dominant spaces. Radically discovering oneself as an active or reflective agency presupposes the authorship and not 'ownership' of experience (see also the discussion in Chapter 1). For such self-discovery, the cultural and intellectual mobilization of those in question becomes necessary. These forms of mobilization become possible through implicating certain morally and politically motivating categories—dignity, self-respect, freedom, equality, and social justice—or a compelling sense of comparative worth in the politics of the reconfiguration of spaces.

SPACES AND THE LANGUAGE OF MOBILIZATION

As I will argue in the following sections of this chapter, those who are pushed into a servile experience are likely to adopt a language of self-respect and dignity. The ability to restructure and at times annihilate or liberate these spaces provides reason for the protagonist to deploy a new conceptual vocabulary that they find necessary to intensify the experience, both spatially and intellectually. The intellectual or political mobilization of Dalit masses by Ambedkar and peasantry by Gandhi testifies to this intensification. As we shall see in greater detail in the following section, in the case of Gandhi, reason (moral) is invoked internally from within the tradition, while Ambedkar seems to be invoking reason both internally (heterodox traditions such as Buddhism, Kabir, or Jotirao Phule) and externally (modern and perhaps Western traditions). Both these thinkers deploy experience as well as space in order to produce sets of categories that are morally (in the case of Gandhi) and politically (in the case of Ambedkar) motivating as far as the mobilization of the masses is concerned. Both these thinkers seem to be approaching their respective social constituencies with a different set of categories emanating from dif-ferential experience. Both of them, of course, confront the spaces that are hostile to their emancipatory project. Gandhi's project obviously involves the rectification and recovery of spaces while Ambedkar's seeks radical subversion of these spaces. We shall see how it happens in both the cases.

It is already clear from the above section that there is a particular epistemological claim that is involved in the title of this chapter. Here we argue that experience provides an initial epistemological condition for the creative reflection or theoretical representation of experience. Categories that emerge from the mediation between experience and space tend to empower a particular argument. Gandhi deploys the moral category of '*seva*'[9] in order to forge the intra-group solidarity that he thought was necessary for producing the conjucture, namely, 'India's independence'. Ambedkar, on the other hand, invokes the category of self-respect that signifies the transcendence of Bahishkrut Bharat (the India of the excluded—the untouchables) into PraBuddha Bharat (the India of the enlightened people). Gandhi's argument suggests a kind of reconfiguration of India that is arguably ahistorical and hence mythical in nature, (Ram Rajya) while Ambedkar's argument suggests a radically different kind of reconfiguration of India that is fundamentally historical in that it assumes that Bahishkrut Bharat is the result of the social processes that are historically produced and reproduced by the totality of social dominance and that PraBuddha Bharat emerges from the critical re-appropriation of heterodox tradition.[10]

Both Gandhi and Ambedkar share one thing in common: for both of them, experience provides the vantage point for making epistemological moves[11] and also for ideological or political mobilization of the masses. However, there is a fundamental difference between the two. Gandhi experiments with the experience of the self and others. Thus, the experience of Ambedkar and his community becomes an object of Gandhi's experiment. Ambedkar and his entire untouchable community do not have to experiment in order to produce experience— in fact, untouchables are born into it. (This is an instance of the lived experience that was referred to in Chapter 1. Both Ambedkar and Gandhi draw fundamentally upon lived experience in order to build theoretical insights and one could argue that it is entirely due to their different lived experiences that their theoretical formulations differ). To put it differently, Ambedkar gets ontologically related to

[9] Literally meaning 'selfless public service'.

[10] This tradition ranges from the Buddha in the ancient period, through Kabir and Tukaram in the medieval, to Jotirao Phule in the modern period.

[11] Trechek (1986: 316).

the experience that is deposited in him by the tormentors. It is for this reason that Gandhi very rightly chooses to work with the upper-caste tormentor. Both Ambedkar and Gandhi generate a set of moral or political categories that they deploy to motivate the masses for the purification of society in the first case and the purification of the soul in the second. However, both Gandhi and Ambedkar do not produce these motivating categories a priori. Both of them suggest, perhaps Ambedkar more consistently and forcefully than Gandhi, that an insight into social dynamics and examination of all the minute details constituting social reality at local level must form the basis of knowledge.

It could be argued that a universal principle in its abstract form does offer, at least to some, a tantalizing insight; but this particular quality of a universal principle was not favoured either by Ambedkar or Gandhi. Both these thinkers produced and shaped their categories through detailed knowledge that was produced not simply by reading texts but by experiencing the context in varying degrees. Both these thinkers of modern India gained an understanding of social nuances and an adequate understanding of India through voyages across Indian regions. The detailed investigation and incisive interrogation of experiential spaces both by Gandhi and Ambedkar did not force them to essentialize a universal principle. Commentators in contemporary India now seek to universalize the ideas of both Ambedkar and Gandhi, often forgetting the formative importance of that specificity of experience that got factored into the very formation of the ideas of the latter.[12] Ambedkar's categories are embedded in an agnostic territory, but they do not stay there. They move out into emancipatory spheres.

There are some scholars who have sought to address the deficiencies in the postcolonial framework and pointed out that this framework is lacking an account of its failure to invoke space as a category for the fuller understanding of nationalist thought in India.[13] Such a critical take on postcolonial thought no doubt acknowledges the usefulness of the postcolonial perspective for understanding the derivative impact of the European Enlightenment on Indian political

---

[12] Nagaraj (2010).
[13] See Goswami (2004).

thought during the nationalist era. Goswami, with specific reference
to an important work by Partha Chatterjee, makes a claim that such
intervention, though desirable, is not adequate as Chatterjee's critique of nationalist thought and its dynamics depends too much on
the discursive content of European tradition.[14] She, therefore, rightly
argues that for a fuller understanding of the colonial impact on India,
we need to take into account the concept of space.

Her critique of Chatterjee may in a certain sense be valid, but in an
instance of spiral logic, her framework also suffers from a limitation.
As I will show in my analysis of space and experience, Goswami's
use of space does not exhaust all the reference points that surround
the reality of experience. Secondly, while she is right in placing
emphasis on the need to bring in centrally the category of space in
doing so, she quotes only selectively from Henry Lefebvre's (1984)
widely acknowledged work on space.[15] But I seek to go beyond the
postcolonial take on nationalist thought and argue that 'space' as an
explanatory category is better equipped to understand adequately the
colonial impact on various aspects of Indian reality.

For example, taking her cue from Lefebvre, Goswami recontextu-
alizes space as a social relationship between the colonial state and the
Indian society. Again basing her import of space on Lefebvre's work,
she further states that space is at once a central field of action and
basis for action.[16] This conception is no doubt useful in understanding the action of nationalist leaders against the colonial state, but the
main limitation of such an import is that it seeks to challenge the
self-understanding of the colonial state as the 'benevolent lord' only
in the colonial configurations of power. It thus makes a huge concession to the local lords who adversely dampen several social groups
in local configurations of power. These local lords in Jotirao Phule's
language are 'Shetji & Bhatji'[17] and in Ambedkar's 'Brahmanshai and
Bhandwal shai'[18] (Brahminism and capitalism).

[14] *Ibid.*, p. 20.
[15] *Ibid.*, p. 23.
[16] *Ibid.*
[17] Phadake (1988: 30).
[18] Khairmode (1985: 105).

EXPERIENTIAL SPACES AND THE EMERGENCE OF SOCIAL THOUGHT

The dynamics of local configuration, which has a definite bearing on the formation of social thinking in India, can be better understood in terms of the experience that some of the social groups gain from their spatial location. This point can be elaborated further by taking another cue from Lefebvre.[19] For Lefebvre, and of course Foucault,[20] experiential space is a culturalized phenomenon and not merely the geography or an empty, socially neutral space. It is thus primarily about controlling people in finite, enclosed, and divided sites. It is this conception of space that has epistemological implication for the emergence of social thought in early twentieth-century India. I would like to substantiate my argument by taking a cue from scholars who consider space as an important category in understanding the link between liberalism and empire.[21] Both Uday Mehta and Raman Shankaran, for example, do provide necessary clues in understanding the link between territory and the liberal thought developed around the phenomenon of empire.

I am going to argue that spaces on their own do not offer epistemological conditions leading to the development of thought. In fact, spaces become available for creating epistemological promise only on the condition that they are aided by some element of experience. A particular thought acquires a specific nature and occurs in a sequence depending on the differential experiences embedded in varied spaces. For example, the spatial location of non-Brahmin thinkers like Jotirao Phule and Ambedkar from Maharashtra and Periyar Ramaswamy Naikar from Tamil Nadu would produce an experience of caste-based discrimination that in turn would prioritize social thought over political. Thus, experience introduces dynamism into the spaces. Dynamic spaces or dynamism of spaces brings into question the relationship between old and new concepts. This tension between the old and the new suggests that the old spaces normally put up stubborn resistance

---

[19] Gupta (2000: 104).

[20] *Ibid.*

[21] Mehta (1999: 47); see also Shankaran (2006: 276).

to the new concepts. The dynamic nature of space therefore suggests the normative limits of the static spaces and it also offers the theoretical promise to develop a new vocabulary of emancipation.

Therefore, it is the reconfiguration of old spaces affected by the force of reason normally brought from outside that engenders this new language. Taking a cue from the important work *Liberalism of Empire*, it is possible to argue that the liberalism of empire can provide a necessary condition that impregnates spaces for the multiple creation of concepts. Ambedkar himself is convinced regarding the intervention of liberalism that seeks to demobilize the Dalit masses from the truth that is given by tradition. It also promises to create a critical energy among the Dalits, who can then invest this energy in search of a new truth.[22] According to Ambedkar, since new truth does not have tradition, people normally take time to accept it. This is not the case with the truth that has tradition, especially truth that emerges through the social processes built around the caste system. The liberal spirit of inquiry and self-doubt motivates people to question their location in the hierarchical spaces and visualize new spaces that can guarantee their existence on a much more egalitarian basis.

This line of inquiry would look plausible particularly in the experiential context from India. I would like to take references from the western parts of India, with which I am a bit more familiar. While developing my argument I would also particularly like to draw some reference from the work of Uday Mehta and Raman Shankaran.[23] Both of them, in my opinion, do provide the necessary clues to understanding the link between territory and the liberal thought developed around the phenomenon of empire. This chapter, while drawing on these scholars and on Lefebvre's work, argues that ideas and concepts do not acquire salience on their own. In fact their reverberating power is contingent on the nature and dynamics of spaces. If the spaces are hierarchically ordered, particularly as in the Indian context, then the dynamic of such spaces would produce the concept of Sanskritization.[24] The social experience produced through

[22] Ambedkar (2002: 64).

[23] Mehta (1999) and Shankaran (2006).

[24] Srinivas (2009: 200).

the dynamic of such rigid spaces would form the subjective content of the concept of Sanskritization. If the spaces are relatively open, then they would produce different vocabularies, like individualism, civil society, dignity, and self-respect. If the spaces are the result of colonial construction, then the dynamics of such spaces would produce different vocabularies, such as self-rule and freedom within the nationalist framework. While the construction of spaces provides an initial condition for the emergence of a conceptual vocabulary, by itself, however, it does not have any control on the articulation of such a vocabulary. Authoritative articulation would establish sovereignty of some concepts. The privileging of spaces or rendering of spaces as sacred would also produce concepts that acquire a sovereign status. For example, constructing the nationalist space as 'Mother India' would make the former sacred and hence beyond any scrutiny and criticism. This construction would treat other vocabularies as hostile to the sovereign vocabulary of self-rule and freedom. Thus, the vocabulary of self-respect and social justice emanating from the Dalit perspective would be treated as inimical to such a sacred space.

Further, in the anti-colonial context, the concept of self-rule is raised to sovereign status. The twin processes—annihilation of traditionally dominant spaces such as (*agrahara*), which by definition are closed and rigid (reversal of the Platonic cave) and their conversion into open spaces—provide an epistemological precondition for the successful deployment of concepts that emerge as alternatives to the one that is treated as sovereign. At this point, it is also necessary to assert that the ideas do not sprout on their own just because they have been propelled by the unfolding of spaces. In other words, the hermeneutic capacities of categories do not expand solely on the basis of the discursive content that these ideas possess. In fact, an effective expansion of ideas rests on the fluidity and flexibility of spaces that are inhabited by people who are socially and culturally fragmented. The expansion of modern ideas therefore is coextensive with the expansion of spaces.

In the Indian context, Ambedkar's social and political movement sought to expand the spaces through counter-sterilizing them. These spaces stuffed with the ideology of purity–pollution are forced to undergo a counter-sterilizing in the sense that these spaces have already been ritually purified by the Hindu priests. Counter sterilization of spaces, according to Ambedkar, becomes a historical necessity for two important reasons: first to reach out to the sensibilities of a cross section of Hindu society and secondly to disrupt 'one dimensional imagination' through giving the high-caste Hindus a bitter dose of reason embedded in normative values: mutual respect, social justice, and equality.[25] In short, as has been argued by Benedict Anderson, modernity renders the closed society more egalitarian.[26] Ambedkar's adoption of a modern vocabulary (social justice, equality, self-respect, and dignity) was definitely aimed at making a dent in the local configuration that was built up around the two power axes of Brahminism and capitalism.

The dynamics of local configurations power and the resultant experience has a definite bearing on the formation of social thinking. This can be better understood in terms of the category of experiential space as suggested by Lefebvre. Lefebvre argues that space is actually experienced in its depths, as duplications, echoes, or reverberations. Lefebvre's argument further suggests that 'space is in my body and then it is my body's counterpart or "other" its my mirror image or shadow'[27] is relevant for understanding the shadow of an untouchable's body. As we shall see in greater detail, particularly in regard to the society and social disabilities of eighteenth-century Pune in Maharashtra, the untouchable's body as space doubled up as both corporal substance and its shadow. The untouchable's body and its shadow worked in tandem to produce a humiliating experience for the former. During the Peshwa rule, even the shadow of an untouchable was considered polluting. Thus, the real and the reflected did become equally powerful in mapping the space in favour of the socially dominant castes. It is in this sense that this chapter aims at extending Lefebvre's framework to India.

[25] Khairmode (1985: 134).
[26] Anderson (1991).
[27] Lefebvre (1984: 184).

SPACE AS A CULTURALLY CONSTRUCTED PHENOMENON

As mentioned above, for Lefebvre and Foucault, experiential space is a culturalized phenomenon.[28] It is primarily about controlling people in finite, enclosed, and divided sites. I argue here that it is this conception of space that has epistemological implication for the emergence of social thought in early twentieth-century India. Taking a cue from Lefebvre, I further argue that space is experiential in its depth when understood in its cultural manifestation.[29] Space is a culturally constructed phenomenon. Structuring and restructuring of a given space is the result of a specific action carried out by a historically dominant social group, which achieves its hegemonic purposes through a regulated exercise of civilizational violence against those social groups that are victims of this kind of violence. Violence in general would seek to restructure space in a specific way. Patriarchy, for example, constructs public and private spaces in a specific way, assigning a little domain of sovereignty to women. Women thus are restricted to enjoy their sovereign power only over the kitchen. In this regard, scholars often quote Tagore's *Ghare-Bahire*. The confinement to the private domain indicates indirect ways of inflicting violence on women through intimidation. Interestingly, patriarchy deploys its ideology to neutralize the impact of this violence.

Yet, I argue, these forms do not complete the definition of civilizational violence. Caste-based violence is primarily linked with the Dalit struggle to liberate the rigid spaces through transgression of boundaries. One could cite umpteen cases from the social history of India to prove this point. The most recent example that one could mention is the transgression of hierarchical boundaries by Dalits in the village called Khairlanjee in the Vidarbha region of Maharashtra. But the Dalits had to pay a heavy price for this transgression as four Dalits from the same family were killed by the middle castes from this village. The members from the middle caste did not like Dalits violating the social protocols that were arbitrarily decided by the former for maintaining their social dominance in the village. What defines violence is the simultaneity of both the 'presence' and 'absence' of the

---

[28] Gupta (2000: 104).
[29] *Ibid.*

victim of violence. Physical violence leading to the annihilation of a corporal being fulfils half the condition of the definition of civilizational violence. The elimination of certain groups like the untouchables from social and culturally active relations ironically provides the full definitional conditions of civilizational violence.

Let me explain this by drawing on Ambedkar's social understanding of the historical evolution of the untouchables in India.[30] Ambedkar develops the theory of 'broken men' in order to understand how a particular restructuring of social space has pushed a large section of the population beyond the pale of human interaction. Ambedkar argues that all human beings basically dwelled in the dense forests and hilly habitats. It is only through their settlement on the plains that they were fragmented into several caste groups, tightly organized around the ideology of purity and pollution. The discovery of agriculture on the plains led to the production of surplus grain. The surplus and control over it, in turn, led to its appropriation by a few, who had to defend the surplus either through physical force or by the force of an ideology. As Ambedkar suggests, the twice-born used Brahminical ideology first to create the category of untouchables and later used them as a shock absorber to defend the surplus from being plundered or destroyed by the barbarians.[31] As a part of the ideology of purity–pollution, the untouchables were pushed outside the main village. Ambedkar calls them 'broken men'.[32] Ambedkar's understanding of broken men gives us a clue to the argument that the village system based on a rigidly hierarchized social morphology came into being along with the emergence of a social surplus in grains. Broken men were pushed outside the main village and those who were more militant were pushed further into the forests. Those who stayed close— but not too close to the functioning village—were required to protect the main village from intruders by first warning the people about impending danger and then by physically protecting the main village

[30] Ambedkar (1987b: 80).

[31] During the seventeenth and eighteenth century in Maharashtra, the Mahars were pushed out of the main village, beyond the Gaothan (physical boundaries). They were called Veskar, who would protect the village from the bandits and the enemies. See Bhavare (2007: 116).

[32] Ambedkar (1990b: 274–5).

both from the wild animals and the 'barbarians'. Thus, the social and cultural distance was maintained through working out an elaborate ideology that was developed over time. The untouchables were required to enter the village only during a specific period of time. Most of the time, they were supposed to remain in their dark hole (their little ghettos) and ultimately remain untouchable, uncrossable, unseeable, unhearable (seeing and sensing human beings and offering appreciation for their creations also form a part of civilization), unapproachable, and uncommunicable (language provides the main energy for the continuation of any civilization). They had to be all this almost all the time to at least the top rung of the twice-born who were to use Plato's terms, the philosopher kings of India.[33] What was just for the untouchables, to use the Platonic and Aristotelian ideas of justice,[34] was to remain confined to their black hole and their only job was to provide free service to the twice-born caste in the main village by producing for the latter along with the other service castes. As seen before, in addition to the production of grain, the untouchables also protected the top rung of the twice-born from external enemies. To put it more sharply, the untouchables performed the job of a 'shock absorber' in order to protect the top rung of the twice-born, who were so completely 'self-absorbing', in the Aristotelian sense of the term.[35]

This confinement into the 'dark hole' was fully demonstrated by the Peshwa rule in eighteenth- and nineteenth-century Pune in Maharashtra. As has been well documented by several scholars,[36] the untouchables were pushed outside time and space or they were relegated to the fragmented time and space through restricting their movement across social space by using rigid ideological lines. During Peshwa rule in nineteenth-century Pune, orthodox Brahmin rule in Pune imposed severe social restrictions on the untouchables, thus rendering them socioculturally disabled in terms of normal interaction among several social groups. Thus, untouchables were restricted to walk in the streets of Pune only during noon and night-time but

[33] Heller (1987: 2).
[34] *Ibid.*
[35] Shields (2007: 10).
[36] Curtin (1992: 5); Ghurye (1965: 77).

not in the morning or in the afternoon. This was because it was not only their touch or sight that was considered polluting; even their shadow was considered to be a source of defilement for the upper castes.[37] Needless to say, in the nineteenth century, the untouchables were erased from human interaction. This civilizational annihilation enacted through the shadow of the untouchables in effect removed the possibility of a human being touching another being or being touched in turn by others. Thus the idea of the shadow as an effective means of protection from ritual pollution requires time and physical space as a precondition for its articulation. The shadow (of an untouchable) itself becomes not an empty but a powerful space that can conversely regulate the movement of an upper-caste body. The shadow then becomes a boomerang for the upper-caste Brahmin.

The shadow, in another context, plays an important role in defining the notion of authenticity and dignity or self-respect. Those who prefer to walk in the shadow of somebody do not find it necessary to discover themselves outside the shadow. The idea of the shadow is very interesting and requires a detailed treatment, but I do not intend to pursue it here except to mention that the shadow provides, at least at the discursive level, an opportunity for people to feel epistemologically superior.[38] For example, political thinkers in modern India such as Bhudev Mukhopadhya felt epistemologically superior in what they thought was the dark epistemological shadow of Western thought.[39] Conversely, as Uday Mehta has pointed out in his work, the Western thinkers also used Indian thought as the dark epistemological shadow to derive the satisfaction that their thought was on the right track and perhaps better than Indian.[40] The shadow in a metaphysical sense acquires a negative power, almost like the ghost or voodoo magic that is used to keep oneself—or the entire village, free from evil forces.

In the context of nineteenth-century Pune, one could conclude that in the reciprocal act of mutual constraints, the Brahmins forced

---

[37] Ambedkar (2005: 422). See also Russell (1916: 186) and Ghurye (1965: 72–3).

[38] Mehta (1999).

[39] Kaviraj (1995).

[40] Mehta (1999: 67).

the untouchables to tie an earthen pot around their neck and a broom around their waist. The pot was to spit in and the broom to erase their footprints that were also considered polluting. It is quite ironic to notice that Brahmins all over the country followed the footprints of British thinkers but within the local configuration of power, they forced the untouchables to erase the footprint. They did try to erase the philosophical footprints of Ambedkar too. Thus, the Peshwa rule seems to have developed the prototype of today's bio-metric techniques, which the state has developed for greater extensive surveillance of its population. During the Peshwa rule, the notion of space compounded the sense of humiliation of the untouch-ables first by seeking the confinement of the latter in a social space and later by rendering the bodies legible through grafting cultural symbols on these bodies. Thus, bodies are turned into cultural spaces that the Brahminical system could rule over, could write on, and could regulate. The Peshwa rule in nineteenth-century Pune follows the same path that the colonial state adopted for the upper-caste Indians.

The Brahminical rule not only controlled the social space but also turned the untouchable body into a cultural space that pushed the untouchable into shadow during the daytime. Ambedkar, therefore, argues that the untouchables were treated like 'hyenas', who, like untouchables, are '*nishachar*', and come out into the open from their den only during the night-time.[41] In terms of time, the untouchables could become sovereign during the night as the Veskar, the village watchmen. In terms of space, they could also become sovereign when they were within the confines of their dark hole: *hulgari* or *cheri*, *Mahar* or *Mangwada* or *Chamar Tola*. Thus, village India entailed the division of two mutually connected and yet culturally exclu-sive social spaces: agrahara (the puritan inner) and the cheri, the untouchables' ghetto (the impure exterior). This dynamic between the universal sovereign (agrahara) and the particular sovereign (*dalit-wada*s) is very effectively brought out by Baby Kamble in her own autobiography.[42]

---

[41] Ambedkar (2001: 203).

[42] Kamble (2000: 67).

Kamble's autobiography suggests that the ideological division of space into sacred (agrahara) and profane (untouchables' ghetto) was created and regulated over the body of her father.[43] Her father's body defined two mutually exclusive spheres of sovereignty—the agrahara and the Dalit ghetto, as mentioned above. Whenever he was walking in the main village, he would walk with a hunched back, eyes cast downwards. This body language certainly endorsed the universal notion of sovereignty as enjoyed by dominant castes within the village context. He had speech power but that was radically replaced by the noise of the bells that were tied to the top of the stick that the Mahars were supposed to carry with them whenever they were in the service of the village. The noise of the bell would communicate the undesirable arrival of untouchables in the main village. Thus a speech act with words got replaced with sign language. Whenever her father finished his job and entered the Dalit ghetto, his body language would radically change, thus making his body flexible, with a straight neck, chest ballooned, and eyes cast towards the skies. This body language would suggest that he enjoyed sovereignty over the ghetto. Within this sphere of sovereignty, he would not only 'enjoy' his freedom but also a 'superior' status over his fellow untouchables. This body language achieved the perfect definition of the servile who is too ready to obey the master and too quick to run down his own constituency. Ambedkar's struggle to annihilate these two spheres of sovereignty and to render Dalit rights universal was linked with the social movement aimed at transgressing the sacred spaces.

The predicament of Kamble's father thus suggests a complex relationship of space to subjectivity. The untouchables were caught up in their own subjectification as they responded to the social relationship that had a constraining impact on their subjectivity. If this was the nature of Indian civilization, which under the logic of the local configuration of power reduced a large section of people to the level of hyenas, then it becomes imperative on the part of the postcolonial theorists to give up their one-sided reading of civilizational violence[44] and take a historicized or *samayak* view that will make them accept

---

[43] *Ibid.*, p. 68.
[44] Fischer-Tiné and Mann (2004).

what Walter Benjamin had to say about civilization: that 'every document of civilization is a book on Barbarism'.[45]

HIERARCHICAL SPACES YIELD DIFFERENT CONCEPTS

Interestingly, it is this barbaric aspect of civilization that makes
Gandhi more self-reflective and therefore critical about his own tradition and Ambedkar his conscience-keeper. I am going to argue that
it is this division of space between the sacred and the profane that
plays a more important role in shaping Gandhi's and Ambedkar's
thoughts in twentieth-century India. Although both Gandhi and
Ambedkar are critical of tradition with different degrees of emphasis, this critique of tradition does not lead to the production of the
same set of categories. For example, in Gandhi, it is the category
of self-rule (both morally and politically) that becomes a sovereign
viewpoint and in Ambedkar, it is the category of self-respect and
social justice that acquires central importance. Ambedkar's conceptualization also indicates the limits of the Gandhian imagination.
The main argument in this chapter is built around the notion of
experience, which finds its expression in a cultural construction of
space by social and political forces. I, therefore, continue to argue
that it is the *achar* (practice) and *anubhava* (experience), mostly of
others, in Gandhi, and the authentic anubhava, in Ambedkar, that
have formative impact on their respective thought.

Gandhi's efforts to identify with others' experience leads him to
adopt different instrumentalities of thought. For example, Gandhi's
identification with untouchables forces him to generate moral categories, like seva (selfless public service), for example. Gandhi uses
these moral and hence non-cognitive categories such as seva, trustee-
ship, care, and cooperation to produce historical conjuncture. These
categories acquire their validity from the political practice of people.
The production and reproduction of experience leads to an ontological wound in Ambedkar and this in effect leads Ambedkar to develop
an entirely different set of categories, such as self-respect, social justice, and egalitarianism. In Ambedkar, it is the category of anubhava

[45] Baxi (1995: 142).

that becomes the primary epistemological source for producing a different set of categories of alternative imagination and the politics of emancipation. Thus in Ambedkar's thought, unlike in Gandhi's, we find a constellation of intersecting categories: *manuski* (self-respect), *mankhandana* (humiliation), *puraskrut* (harmonious), *bahishkrut* (socially ostracized), *adhikar* (rights), seva (service), *shram* (labour), *vethbegari* (unpaid labour), and finally social justice–injustice. Out of these sets of categories that constitute his thought, I am going to focus on only three concepts: social justice, self-respect, and nation. I have selected these three concepts as they offer a new reading of space and experience, and vice versa. Moreover, these are concepts that are determined by the notion of experience, which itself is embedded in socio-culturally constituted spaces. In the following sections I would like to elaborate on the interrelationship between the concepts of social justice, self-respect, and nation and the experiential space.

Ambedkar saw a great theoretical as well as political promise in the emergence of the modern social space that was unfolding due to the pressure of colonial modernity. Colonial modernity, despite its limitations,[46] surely involved rather different enabling processes of modernization—industrialization, urbanization, and modern education—that encouraged Dalits to question the social forces that produced their degrading experience for them. Ambedkar—along with other modernists, including Marx—believed that these spaces would produce a new experience for the untouchables where they would realize a genuine sense of justice and equal treatment once the hierarchical spaces were sterilized and streamlined into secular hierarchies based on capacity rather than caste.[47] Thus, from Ambedkar's perspective, it is the restructuring of spaces of opportunity that involved the possibility of restoring dignity to Dalits and securing justice that was to be defined primarily in terms of getting a fair chance to gain a new and liberating experience. Ambedkar also thought that along with other modernizing processes, urbanization would offer the untouchables a much-needed opportunity to walk out from the

[46] Many scholars have pointed out the limitations of colonial modernity. Prominent among them are Dipesh Chakrabarty, Ranajit Guha, Partha Chatterjee, and Nicholas Dirks, just to name a few.

[47] Heller (1989: 23).

constraining 'dark hole' (according to Ambedkar's view, the village system based on caste was a dark hole). As we have already noted earlier, in a face-to-face situation in the traditional village setting, the upper caste's social or cultural gaze did not fail to size up the untouchables as a 'moving moral plague'. Ambedkar thought urbanization would liberate the untouchables from 'quarantined' spaces. He believed that urbanization would positively destroy this face-to-face social interaction and make people strangers to each other. The option of anonymity, ironically, was considered desirable because it would offer untouchables a fair chance to become placeless individuals who then would organize their social protocols with others on an equal basis.

However, the patterns of urbanization even during his own time did not fulfil Ambedkar's dream, as he landed up in the same Maharwada (Dalit dwelling place) that he had left behind in the village. The social morphology of the villages was replicated even in most of the urban cities of India, including Bombay. The Bombay Development Department (BDD) cement *chawl*s (tenements) where Ambedkar and his family lived was occupied by the untouchables who had come from Konkan areas of Maharashtra.[48] These localities and even the labour chawls came to be organized around caste and even sub-caste lines not only in Mumbai but in many places, such as Kanpur.[49] As mentioned in the previous section, according to Susan Bayly, the process of urbanization rigidified the caste boundaries more than before.[50] Gooptu in her study of Kanpur shows that the untouchables who migrated from rural Uttar Pradesh to Kanpur somehow were pushed into the socially segregated ghettos, which were no different from the secluded settlements that they had left behind in their villages.[51] Those untouchables who migrated to other cities in colonial India, such as Bombay, also were pushed into slums such as Dharawi or the Matunga labour camps. These slums in Malabar Hill (a posh elite colony in Bombay) were perceived to be worse than a garbage depot. The elite from Malabar Hill did not

---

[48] Khairmode (1990a).
[49] Gooptu (2001: 146).
[50] Bayly (2001: 230).
[51] Gooptu (2001: 150).

distinguish untouchables from physical dirt. In their perception, untouchables were mobile dirt and dirt was mobile untouchability. This sense of repulsion was so deep in elite perception that it denied any legitimate advantage of odour to a scented body from the slum. Thus the continuous production and reproduction of mobile dirt suggests a spatial dimension of ontology. The untouchable's image as 'walking dirt' was chained to his or her physical association, and the experience of being 'a walking dirt', which of course was given to him or her, was sustained through the static nature of the space. Ambedkar, along with the other untouchables, was also the depository of this static experience of space. It was static in the sense that the urban space, like the village, was equally hostile to the dignity of untouchables as the latter could not appear in public without a sense of shame. The urban upper-caste bodies, with their minds stuffed with a deep sense of untouchability, did not offer the untouchables any moral advantage that would make them feel that there is more to the 'walking dirt' and that there is more to the body that exceeded beyond these static spaces.

My own study of early twentieth-century Bombay also shows that as a result of the political economy of urban capital as well as colonial capital, the working-class localities in the Lal Baug and Parel areas came to be organized around caste lines.[52] Thus, the colonial and local capital did not show any foresight in restructuring the urban spaces towards a more egalitarian social morphology. In fact, one finds continuity of caste right into the social space—the chawls and the sections of textile mills. These urban spaces became the major sources of the articulation of the deep sense of repulsion and revulsion by upper caste. Continuous denial of generic identity to untouchables and to Ambedkar was blatantly demonstrated by the middle-caste workers (the Marathas) in the textile mills in Bombay during the early 1930s. The Maratha workers opposed the entry of untouchable workers into the weaving section of these mills, as is well documented by Ambedkar himself.[53]

If the untouchable workers had traditional skills, why did the Marathas or Kunbis oppose their entry into the weaving section?

[52] Guru (1987: 67).
[53] Ambedkar (2005: Vol. I).

First, the Marathas also could not have tolerated a Mahar becoming culturally superior to them in the new setting. On the contrary, the Maratha textile worker desired that the Mahars remain culturally inferior to himself or herself, as was the case in the past. Ambedkar in this case treats untouchability as an ideology that was used by the upper-caste workers to protect their material interest. This analytical ability of Ambedkar to control a significant reference point has often been ignored by scholars who see untouchability as the only reality.[54] These scholars see too much of untouchability in this opposition. Certainly untouchability was one of the main reasons. But there were other material and cultural reasons behind this opposition. First, the Marathas—who, according to some studies,[55] were relatively few in numbers compared to the Dheds (Dheds are the Mahars in Bombay and Bunkars in Gujarat)—always felt insecure that they would be further marginalized by the Dheds, who were almost double the numbers of the Marathas (who were around three thousand in the 1930s).[56] This fear was further compounded by the fact that compared to the Dheds, the Marathas did not have past experience in weaving.[57] The traditional skill in weaving is also demonstrated in family names such as Bunkars that the Dalits from Gujarat seem to have adopted. In Hindi, *bunkar* means 'weaver'.

The Mahars and Bunkars, like other service castes, did develop skill in weaving in order to cater to the social needs of the upper castes. In fact, they were forced to weave cloth of some quality for their own use. The stigma of untouchability barred them from either buying new cloth or selling new cloth. The traditional weavers from other backward castes wove cloth for the so-called forward castes. Moreover, according to the dictates of Manu, they were not allowed to wear new garments made by traditional weavers from the service castes.[58] These social conditions forced the untouchables to use either the cast-off garments of their feudal lords or weave cloth for themselves. Most of the untouchables, including their women in some

[54] Omvedt (1996).
[55] Morris (1965).
[56] Lieten (1984: 84).
[57] Moon (1987: 3).
[58] Ambedkar (1987b: 230–8).

parts of India, were not allowed to wear upper garments, ever. Male Dalits used only the lower garments. (Actually the half-clad Gandhi looked more like an untouchable than a peasant).

The middle-caste mill workers, particularly the Marathas, found perpetuation of untouchability an effective force in achieving their desired end. What was their goal? Their goal was to use tradition to gain advantage in modernity, or conversely, they wanted to recover in tradition the confidence that they were likely to lose in modernity that was available to the Mahars.

Finally, the Maratha workers never wanted competition—particularly from untouchables—in the weaving section, which was a relatively well-paid section of the textile mills.[59] In this regard it is also interesting to note that the capitalist and the colonial states did not show any strong interest in shunting the caste-like social force out of the textile mills. In fact, they very actively promoted harmony between the functional hierarchies of industrial labour organizations and the social hierarchies—thus achieving a perfect blend of tradition and modernity.

All these related factors led the Marathas to oppose the untouchables on traditional grounds and not on rational, modern grounds. That is to say, financial space—of which Manu Goswami is so critical for its having a saturating impact on the local desi[60]—kept easy pace with the social space that permeated caste.

The share market in Bombay did not accommodate or appreciate Ambedkar's skill and expertise.[61] He was almost thrown out of this market because he was an untouchable. One of the Bombay-based Gujarati newspapers revealed his caste. The role of print media in India was significant not in terms of imagining the nation,[62] but in consolidating the hold of caste over financial spaces. The relevant question is what implication does this overlap between the financial and social space have for the emergence of normative concepts such

---

[59] Morris (1965:).

[60] Goswami (2004: 74).

[61] Rege (1991: 84).

[62] 'Sorry, Prof. Benedict Anderson, the caste system in India has abused your concept' (Khairmode, 1990: 118).

as social justice and self-respect, particularly in the social thought of Ambedkar.

MATERIAL SPACES AND SOCIAL JUSTICE

Why did Ambedkar think social exclusion of untouchable workers from the weaving section was unfair?[63] He considered the exclusion problematic particularly on two major grounds.[64] First, he put forward the principle of proportionality for making the justice claim on behalf of untouchable workers. This has to do with the size of the workforce in the Bombay textile mills in the 1930s. According to one estimate, Dheds constituted the largest chunk of the workers.[65] But most of them were employed in the manual sections, such as head loading and sanitation. Ambedkar gave a strong hint of the disproportionate distribution of the labour force in the mills and suggested a rectification of the imbalance.[66] Secondly, exclusion from the weaving section, in Ambedkar's opinion, resulted in the denial of cultural justice to the same untouchable workers. This was a denial of cultural justice to the extent that it involved the misrecognition of the weaving skill and traditional experience of untouchables in weaving. On the contrary, the claims by Maratha workers to self-certify themselves as the skilled weavers was also unfair because this claim was not supported by the necessary experience in weaving. This exclusion of the untouchables ultimately pushed them into unskilled sectors of the textile mills, thus leading to their deskilling. As a result, the untouchable workers suffered the loss of self-esteem and self-respect.

Ambedkar did not want to push unskilled untouchable labour into the weaving sections. He suggested that workers after training would be eligible for entry into weaving section.[67] He got a batch of 130 trained untouchable workers from the Vhrahad (now

---

[63] Ambedkar (1987a: 261).
[64] Ambedkar (1990a: 262).
[65] Lieten (1984: 84).
[66] Khairmode (1991a: 291).
[67] *Ibid.*

Vidarbha) region to train untouchables in weaving in textile mills. As Khairmode notes, even then the upper-caste workers did not allow these workers to join the textile mills and hence the training of untouchables could not take off.[68] In this regard it is pertinent to note Gandhi's notion of self-respect, particularly in regard to the textile-mill workers. According to Gandhi, the moral source that can result in the loss of self-respect is the workers' demand for wages for the days on which they did not work as they were on strike.[69] In the Gandhian framework of moral economy, it is the labour that is performed in an actual time and space that constitutes the source of self-respect. Commitment to moral duty is the guarantee for earning self-respect. Thus, for Gandhi, a free rider would have no claim over self-respect.

In Ambedkar, the idea of self-respect as part of the larger concept of cultural justice springs from another experiential space—sacred space (Hindu temple). Sacred space, according to Ambedkar, is the source of not only the struggle for equal entry but the moral struggle for recognition. The temple-entry movement led by Ambedkar was neither aimed at creating sacred space for spiritual satisfaction nor was it undertaken to achieve social elevation for the untouchables. It involved a higher moral purposes where he sought to invoke a sense of self-respect among the untouchables on the one hand and cultivate reason among the recalcitrant Hindus on the other. Ambedkar uses the principle of labour contribution as the rallying point in order to achieve this twin pedagogical purpose. Ambedkar argues that those untouchables who were responsible for constructing and later protecting the Hindu temple have every reason to feel the loss of self-respect as their labour contribution was not recognized by high-caste Hindus.[70] In his view, contribution generates the language of right to enter the temple.[71] If the untouchables failed to assert their right, then their self-respect would diminish. In Ambedkar's under-standing, the source of self-respect lies in the language of rights that

---

[68] *Ibid.*

[69] This is in contrast to Ambedkar's position. Ganguli (1973).

[70] Ambedkar (2005).

[71] Ambedkar (2003: 128).

emerges from the contribution made by untouchables in protecting Hindu temples.[72]

In other words, Ambedkar considers moral ability to assert one's claim over temple entry as the source of self-respect. He uses a double pedagogical move to generate the necessary political energy and urgency among the untouchables. First, he shakes the Dalits out of their objectification by raising an affirmative question: 'Would you not lose your self respect if you did not fight for the temple entry as a matter of right? How are you to validate your contribution made to the protection and construction of Hindu temples?'[73] It is in this sense that he deploys a pedagogical device to invoke an affirmative response from the untouchables in favour of the language of rights. Second, he also sees moral merit in pursuing the temple-entry movement just to bring out a sense of reasonableness, if not shame, within the upper castes who, according to Ambedkar, are stubborn in refusing the legitimate claim of the untouchables over the temple. Thus, in Ambedkar's framework of social justice, the temple as sacred space gets seriously implicated in the radical politics that is aimed at creating a kind of negative consciousness among the untouchables.[74] As we know, Ambedkar successfully uses this temple-entry movement to the extent that it is necessary for pushing Dalit consciousness to higher levels where its political articulation foregrounds the notion of justice—social and cultural. In Ambedkar's understanding, the contestation of the temple as sacred space militates against the mainstream Hindu imagination where the temple as sacred space is intensified through the cultural construction of India as 'Bharat Mata' (Mother India). We shall discuss this point in greater detail in the last section of this chapter.

There is one curious similarity between Gandhi and Ambedkar. Gandhi differs from Ambedkar to the extent that he does not deploy the modern language of rights while advocating temple entry for

---

[72] *Ibid.*

[73] Khairmode (1991b: 67). During the seventeenth and eighteenth century in Maharashtra, the Mahars were the traditional security guards whose duty was to protect the village and the temples that gave shelter to high-caste Hindu pilgrims. See Khatare (2009: 99).

[74] Guru (2007b).

the untouchables. On the contrary, he puts emphasis on the moral duty of the high-caste Hindus to allow the untouchables to enter the Hindu temples. For kindling an element of reason within the high-caste Hindus, he puts tradition to critical use. In his efforts to cultivate moral reason within the upper caste, he appeals to them: 'If in your own belief temples are the sacred spaces to wash the sin of this birth or previous birth, and if you think that untouchables have committed sin in their previous birth, is it not your moral duty to give them chance to wash their sin in the sacred space?'[75] Here Gandhi does not take into consideration the principle of 'contribution' and thus deviates from his earlier position, which he took with regards to textile workers in Ahemdabad. As we know, on moral grounds, he linked actual labour with justice and self-respect.[76] Ambedkar, on the other hand, tries to reason with the caste Hindus by deploying disembodied universal reason based on the notion of 'entitlement', which itself emerges not out of inherited social property or assets but from the actual contribution made.

In this regard, we have to remember that Ambedkar uses the temple-entry movement not for lending legitimacy to sacred space but to tactically use it for generating negative consciousness, which forms the precondition for the political articulation of the concepts of social justice and self-respect. Thus, here it is the temple entry that forms the basis of creating a subversive cultural consciousness among the untouchables. But in a different situation, he uses the idea of exit from the temple as the basis of creating cultural consciousness as the background condition for the articulation of the concepts of social justice and, particularly, self-respect.

SEXUAL LABOUR AND SELF-RESPECT

Ambedkar, like many other untouchables and non-Brahmin leaders from the south of India, considered the devadasi system as a source of humiliation. According to these thinkers, the system withers the

[75] Tendulkar (1968: 230).
[76] Nagaraj (2010).

sense of self-respect within untouchable women.[77] These untouchable women are tied to the Hindu temples occupied by gods and goddesses through the system of 'sacred marriage'. While these women are married to the gods and goddesses, for all practical purposes they become available to the local lords. The devadasi system, which is found in the temples in Puri in Orissa and in Saudatti and Chandragutti in northern Karnataka, is the source of these untouchable women's sexual exploitation. These women are considered a moral plague in the society. Ambedkar addresses the question of devadasis very centrally and makes several appeals convincing them to give up this system and walk out from the temple into civil society. For him the temple as sacred space is not only the source of exploitation but its also terrible source of collective shame and humiliation.[78] Ambedkar suggests marriage as the resolution of the devadasi problem. He argues that the marriage of devadasis, not with the mythical entity but with living human beings, is the source of self-respect. Thus, it is not the sacred space but spaces in civil society that can provide the context for the gaining of self-respect. (This for radical feminists, that is, those against marriage would be a highly objectionable proposition). The codified rationality in the Buddhist marriage system as suggested by him thus was the ultimate source of human dignity.

But devadasis also entered in the same profane space.[79] In the case of devadasis, the static experience and the experiential space converged on to each other. The devadasis left the temples and landed up in Kamathipura (a sex workers' locality) in Mumbai. Ambedkar treats this area as the source of indignity for untouchable women in particular and the entire untouchable community in general.[80] He initiated a conversation with these women in the 1930s. The main plank of this mobilization was to acquire a social good, namely, self-respect. He addressed a meeting in Kamathipura and made a sincere appeal that they should give up this work and take up some other more dignified work that would guarantee them manuski (self-respect). His idea of social freedom is tied up with the liberation of

[77] Geetha and Rajdurai (1998).
[78] *Ibid.* p. 210.
[79] Profane space in the present context refers to the red light area.
[80] Khairmode (1985: 130–8).

Dalit women from the stigmatized places that are the source of a preceived moral plague.

Ambedkar argues that it is not the space that is the source of humiliation; it is just the manifestation of indignity.[81] *Space is mere existence of humiliation.* My work is an extension of Ambedkar's concept of space. It treats space as active and productive. The moral quality of labour is the real essence of self-respect. The suggestion made by Ambedkar involves an alternative notion of labour that has a positive implication for self-respect. The terms of trade in the 'flesh market' might assign some autonomy to sex workers and the logic of the market would introduce some hierarchy among the sex workers. Does it mean that we endorse their freedom to 'choose' who they should have sex with in the market place? Ambedkar's answer to this question is categorically 'no'.[82] Perhaps he is not in favour of mixing physical labour with sex workers. Perhaps he is suggesting a proper marriage as the dignified route to the satisfaction of physical needs. Thus he does not at all endorse the idea of untouchable women becoming sex workers and being reduced to mere commodities only to produce pleasure for exchange in the flesh market. Ambedkar therefore suggests that self-respect fundamentally emanates from the process where untouchable women would mix their labour with material properties such as nature, land, and industry. In Ambedkar's view bodies are an embodiment of labour power. They should not dissolve themselves into mere symbols of pleasure. In Ambedkar's opinion do such bodies contribute to the production of a primary good such as self-respect. But bodies with the same labour power that are responsible for making a contribution to the moral economy of untouchable households through the mixing of their labour with sexual labour objects, in his view definitely earn respect for themselves and for society at large. Taking a cue from Ambedkar, it could be argued that human bodies with working hands have a contradictory aspect in that they contribute to the realization of social good but at the same time jeopardize their physical well-being. He concentrates on a specific need of the Dalit household, particularly the moral economy, that constitutes the moral source of self-respect.

[81] Khairmode (1990b: 67).
[82] Ambedkar (1989: 373).

Similarly, Ambedkar defines self-respect in terms of the capacity to exercise autonomy over the distribution of value produced by one's own social labour.[83] In an equivalent fashion, a free rider or a parasite is one who exercises the power to distribute the fruits that occurred from another's labour and hence loses his or her self-respect.

The idea of self-respect in Ambedkar is clearly demonstrated in his critique of Tamasha folk theatre as the profane space that, according to him, provided an opportunity to the upper caste, who used Dalit women as objects to achieve their personal ends.[84] Patthe Bapurao, a Brahmin balladeer, eliminated the distinction between the agrahara and the Dalit colony, and married Pawdabai, an untouchable woman with spectacular skill in Lawani and a stunning beauty. Here Tamasha, a folk theatre (both settled and mobile) does provide a social space for the cultural performance, mostly by untouchable women. (One might argue that Tamasha may be providing a liberating space for those whose body is already liberated like upper castes). It seems Bapurao mixed his love and literary imagination with the skill of Pawda, which made Tamasha a very popular medium of entertainment as well as a source of social mobilization in the first half of the twentieth century.[85] But viewed from Ambedkar's perspective of dignity of labour, both Pawda and Bapurao lose their self-respect. Pawda's loss, according to Ambedkar, corresponds to the loss of autonomy as she fails to exercise distributive power over her body and the fruits of her labour.[86] First, Patthe Bapurao loses his self-respect because he, according to Ambedkar, is a free rider who uses untouchable women as a commodity to get wealth and glamour for himself. In Ambedkar, self-respect emerges from an affirmative link between the moral quality of labour and the claim that can be made over the distribution of the fruits of that labour.[87] Secondly, the money that is raised through the Tamasha also lacks moral calibre because it is not the pure aesthetic appreciation of the skill that motivates people to pay, but it is the objectification of the physical

[83] *Ibid.*, p. 258.
[84] *Ibid.*
[85] Achalkhamb (2006: 120).
[86] Ambedkar (1989: 256).
[87] *Ibid.*, p. 258.

body as a commodity meant for satisfying sexual urge that motivates people to pay. It is for this reason that Ambedkar rejected the offer of a donation that Bapurao made which Ambedkar could have used for his social movement.

Thus, for Ambedkar, Tamasha—a cultural space—formed the primary source of producing free riders, who in turn caused indignity to themselves and others.[88] According to Ambedkar's reading, the 'Kushal Chendu' (free riders) are devoid of self-respect, and so is the system of vethbegari (free or unpaid) labour, for it constitutes the moral degradation of the untouchables who have been, by and large, the *vetbegars*.[89] This continues even today in some parts of the country. (I would guess that most of the temples in India are constructed out of the contribution made by untouchables through their unpaid labour.) Ambedkar expected the untouchables and also employers of such vetbegari to account for such humiliating work by changing the conception of labour from vetbegar as selfless duty into a moral claim that would be valid on the basis of the contribution that untouchables had made in the construction of a temple. Ambedkar thus locates self-respect in making and asserting this claim by way of temple entry.[90]

FOREGROUNDING NATION IS SPACE

The idea of temples in the Hindu cultural imagination offers a defining condition for India as a nation. This is demonstrated in the idea of the *char dhama*s (four Hindu pilgrimage centres) that completes the religious and cultural imagination of Hindu India. (Nehru's use of the metaphor of temple for the contemporary projects that represent/typify secular and modern India is well known.) How do Gandhi and Ambedkar name India? Or what is their idea of India? The two of them differ in their approach to this issue. Gandhi imagines India as Ramrajya and Ambedkar names it *Bahishkrut harat*.[91]

---

[88] Khairmode (1985: 113).

[89] Achalkhamb (2006: 124).

[90] *Ibid.*

[91] Published by education department, government of Maharashtra, 1990.

Ambedkar, however, subsequently moves from Bahishkrut to PraBuddha Bharat.[92] The two of them follow different spatial trajectories for their respective conceptual productions of India. Gandhi produces his India primarily by identifying with the experience of '*daridarinarayan*', the peasant, and mobilizing the latter for producing historical conjuncture through the mass mobilization against the British rule.[93] Thus one can notice the shift in his adversaries. In the local configuration of power, his adversaries are the upper-caste Hindus, both men and women. But in the colonial configuration of power, for Gandhi, it is British rule in India.[94] Ambedkar, on the other hand, remains consistent in terms of locating the adversary primarily in the local configuration (not that he makes a concession to the British state) of power.[95] For Ambedkar, this configuration is important because unlike the colonial, it—through tightly organized spaces—produces convergent experiences combining untouchable and his master social experience across time and space. (Here space is taken in its territorial sense). As a result Ambedkar opens up primarily in the social imagination of India a '*Bahishkrut Bharat*', the India of the ostracized.

Ambedkar is forced to imagine India in a language that may sound quite negative to many.[96] This imagination would not fit into the framework of Benedict Anderson.[97] The imagination of nation is triggered off in universal conditions that need also to be the dominant conditions at the same time. For example, the successful imagination of nation is based on the uniformity of social and cultural conditions. In territories where such conditions do not exist, they need to be created by deploying subjective resources such as ideology, for example. Ideologies for nation do not become articulable on their own. They also require space as the necessary condition for their articulation, for spaces provide a necessary background condition for the comprehensive representation of ideologues and their ideas. Along with the expansion of social space, there is also the expansion of

[92] Khairmode (1985: 147).

[93] Tendulkar (1968: 230).

[94] Goswami (2004: 265).

[95] Ambedkar (1990c: 111).

[96] Ambedkar (1989: 363).

[97] In Anderson's framework, the imagination of a nation is positive.

conceptual space, entailing the transformation of a particular person into an universal idea. For example, Gandhi, through a favourable social space such as the public maidans ceases to be a *bania* (trading caste) or a Gujarati, and becomes a Mahatma[98] for a majority of people residing in India. Gandhi feels encouraged to take a voyage and concretize his imagination of India through the voyage because he finds sociological similarity to be the most favourable condition for imagining India. He discovers sociological similarity in the village system with peasantry as the core of this system. In order to share the experience of the peasantry, he symbolically (through his bio-politics) transforms himself into a peasant by putting on a peasant's attire. In order to discover similarity in experience and share it for pedagogical purposes, Gandhi undertook extensive travel before he launches his project of 'producing village India'. What he discovers through the voyage are not just the spiritual boundaries but most importantly the sameness in the experience of the peasantry. This experience of exploitation, which the peasantry gains primarily from the colonial state, constitutes the major source for the Gandhian imagination of India. It is due to this given historical situation that it becomes easy for Gandhi to 'occupy' the central spaces that he uses so tactfully for the political mobilization of the Indian masses, basically the Indian peasantry. Thus, he could easily use the centrally located open space in Kanpur in the United Province to organize a rally; or he could an be the guest of Rohatagi, a well-known upper-caste personality of Kanpur. These examples could be multiplied into a huge number, depending on the Gandhian voyage across several regions of early twentieth-century India, thanks to the British railway that made the Gandhian voyage possible. It is therefore no wonder that Gandhi does not discover India as 'Bahishkrut' because his voyage makes him open up in a kind of sameness where he, by and large, finds himself in the midst of peasantry but residing with the families of the feudal lords and the emergent industrialist. Occasionally, as politics demanded, he also stayed for a brief while in the hut of the scavenger. Gandhi thus had a choice to 'transgress' spaces vertically.

Ambedkar did not have this choice. He and his social constituency open up only horizontally, moving from one dalitwada to another

---

[98] Amin (1984).

across the region. Thus when he went to Kanpur, he stayed with a person of his caste, Sonkar, and addressed the assembly of the untouchables only in the untouchables locality.[99] His voyage across the country landed him in different Dalit colonies in Kanpur and Agra in the north, and Belgaum and Kolar in the south. It is this discovery of sameness (his and his people's) in experience, sustained by spaces, that leads Ambedkar to imagine India differently.

This mode of imagining India is further accentuated in the context where Hindu public spaces such as *sarai* (public dormitories) were closed to the untouchables.[100] As noted by Pandita Ramabai through her voyage of India covering more than four thousand kilometres' travel in the nineteenth century, such spaces did not entertain the lower-caste people.[101] It is due to this restriction on the untouchables from central India that a Dalit leader had to bring to the legislative council the issue of liberating such sarais from upper-caste restrictions.[102] Ambedkar criticizes the notion of the dharmashala (sarai) because it is very much hostile and humiliating for the untouchable pilgrims going to Pandharpur in Maharashtra. Thus, it is very likely that the discriminatory nature of the serai discourages untouchables from taking all-India voyages requiring them to pierce through the rigid Hindu public sphere. The all-India voyage could become a possibility for Dalits mainly through the military route, either of local rulers or the British army. Dalits could not have imagined India into a 'char dhama' as the Adi Shankaracharya did.

It is also significant to note that the early Dalit leadership, at least in Maharashtra, emerges from the military sphere.[103] It is the arrival of the British railway that makes it possible for Dalits and for Ambedkar to undertake all-India travel. Through this voyage, Ambedkar finds similarity in experience.[104] It is also through this convergence of experience that Ambedkar privileges self-respect and social justice over self-rule and over the idea of the incredible India

[99] Interview with Sonkar in Kanpur, 9 April 2010.
[100] Dyer (1900: 24).
[101] *Ibid.*
[102] Moon (1987: 87).
[103] Zelliot (1992: 38).
[104] Ambedkar (1987b: 239).

of Gandhi, Patel, and Nehru. Care was taken by the upper-caste leaders and social elite to see that Ambedkar did not transgress the social spaces whenever they had to play host to him. For example, the four-wheeler helped to deflate the intention of a judge based in Dhule (a district in Maharashtra and an important centre of colonial state activities in the early twentieth century) and perhaps his wife's intention of humiliating Ambedkar as an untouchable. This judge found it difficult to invite Ambedkar to his *pathshala* (a Sanskrit school). Thus he decided to converse with Ambedkar in a moving car.[105] The cost of the fuel that was being burnt in the process was much less than the social cost that the judge would have suffered had he taken Ambedkar home. Those upper-caste individuals who showed this courage and took Ambedkar home had to pay a larger social cost.[106] This included men like Panwalkkar of Panwel, near Bombay. The domestic was very safely guarded, this time not by the upper-caste males but by the upper-caste women. This was clear from the predicament of none other than Ambedkar's own teacher. His teacher wanted to invite Ambedkar to his place but could not do so, fearing possible opposition from his wife.[107]

Such kinds of containment at Baroda[108] and Daultabad[109] forced Ambedkar either to take shelter in a dalitwada or in a government bungalow whenever he was on a government assignment. Modernization and the colonial policy of creating dak bungalows saved Ambedkar from crushing humiliation and his upper-caste hosts from complete ostracism. It is this experience that led Ambedkar to prioritize the idea of self-respect and social justice over self-rule. This language of dignity and self-respect survives and remains relevant even after the

[105] Ambedkar (2005).

[106] Surbha Tipnis and Panwalkar from Panwel had to face social boycott from the Brahmin community on account of their being hosts to Ambedkar. Sreedhar Balwant Tilak, son of B.G. Tilak, had to suffer the wrath of a section of orthodox Brahmins from Pune.

[107] Khairmode (1991a: 94).

[108] Ambedkar was thrown out of a lodge by a Parsi owner.

[109] Ambedkar, along with his colleague, was humiliated by a security guard at the Dalutabad fort, which is on the way to the world-famous Ellora Buddhist caves near Aurangabad in Maharashtra.

emergence of the nation. And yet such ideas do not become dominant. Why? This is because these ideas are ontologically related to the social existence of a vast number of people whose problems acquire only the rhetorical and not the regular attention of the social elite who are the ruling class of India.

In the case of Ambedkar, conceptual space discursively collided with social space. Experience sought to regulate the overlap. Unlike other categories, social justice and self-respect in the upper-caste imagination remain bracketed within the ignored social condition of the Dalits. It is very ironic that Dalits then are condemned for being obsessed with a narrow identity politics for which they are not responsible but which they are constantly pushed into by the state on the one hand and the upper caste intellectual on the other. Within the moral framework, is it not unfair to blame Dalits for parochialism when those who sit in judgement are also responsible for creating and sustaining the link between their ideas and his/her identity?

5

Experience and the Ethics of Theory

Gopal Guru

The relationship between experience and theory has always been a complex one, particularly in the field of scientific and systematic thinking. It has been argued by some that 'knowledge, strictly speaking, was scientific knowledge, the fruit of non-subjectivist theoretical labour upon the heterogeneous data of experience, that is ideology'.[1] It can be argued that experience at its best can provide a background condition for making poetry or writing autobiographies. But it may not contribute to the creation of stable and absolute knowledge. As a result, experience as an epistemic source has been ruled out by scholars both from the West and the East. However, in recent years, there have been scholarly attempts by some sensitive scholars not only to bring discussion on experience into focus but also to elevate the idea of experience from its mere literary or metaphorical articulation to the level where experience can provide an epistemic resource that is necessary to propose a serious and sensitive theory. However, efforts to forge complementary links between experience and theory have been comparatively a recent development as far as scholars in India are concerned. On the other hand, the West has a long and strong tradition of debate around the relationship between experience and theory in the social sciences.[2] In India the response of Indian scholars to the debate has been belated but it is desirable. The

[1] Mulhern (1960: 160).
[2] Fay (1996: 9).

initiative taken by Sarukkai[3] and the scholarly responses offered by Raghuramraju to this debate assume importance.[4] It is thus quite encouraging to see that the debate around experience is reverberating in the academic circle as well.

However, in this regard it is necessary to mention that although the West seems to have paid early and timely attention to assessing the role of experience in formulating and orienting theory, these efforts tend to escape the question of evaluating the doing-of-theory on an ethical basis. In this regard the observation made by Sarukkai (in this volume) is worth quoting here. He says that 'although theory claims to be ethically neutral it is nevertheless necessary to pay attention to ethics while doing theory'.

As we shall see in the following sections, there are some scholars who have expressed their scepticism about the link between experience and theory. This scepticism has been expressed in terms of the incommensurability between experience as the realm of emotion and theory as the realm of reason. Someone may want to further argue against experience as an epistemic source on the grounds that since the content of experience is fluctuating and hence short-lived, therefore it is not available for any standardization of meaning and knowing. This thus flouts theory's fondest hope, to standardize reality, which as experience either operates in a discrete form or remains opaque. Hence it is necessary to try and sort out this problem of foregrounding the role of experience, both in the production of theory and also in assessing the ethical calibre of theoretical practice.

Let us address the question of incommensurability between experience and theory by putting forward the following sets of questions.

First, what has been the epistemic status of experience as an analytical category? Which is to say, does experience provide epistemic conditions for producing knowledge and understanding? What decides the order of the intelligibility of experience? Do we require concepts beforehand to render the experience intelligible? In other words, can experience on its own explode into systematic understanding, without the support of theory? Or do we require theory to *intensify* experience? What does experience do to theory and vice versa?

---

[3] Sarukkai (2005; also reproduced in this book, Chapter 2).
[4] Raghuramaraju (2010).

Second, does mere availability of experience at the concrete or particular level provide a sufficient condition for experience to acquire intelligibility at the universal level? Will simple translation of some literary text into a global language be enough for experience to become universal? Can experience without theory acquire wings so that it may fly all over the globe and make a particular experience universal? Thus, is it necessary to deploy theory for making unified and universal sense of experience that otherwise seems to be discrete and particular?

Third, what is important for doing theory: ownership or authorship of experience? For theorizing experience, is it necessary to possess a particular experience? Can one become the subject of experience without becoming an object of it? What is important: the possession of experience or the conceptual tools?

This set of questions becomes important in the context of the central objection that Sarukkai has raised about my argument that the practice of social science in India is not egalitarian (Chapter 1). First of all, it will be naïve to think that the fragmentary nature of experience is internal to a particular group that 'gains' the experience. In fact, the politics of the dominant produces the differentiated experience within the social groups that otherwise can become quite dangerous to the former, if experience becomes unitary. While the continuous fracturing of unitary experience poses a serious challenge to the emancipatory theory of the protagonist, the politics of the adversary also make the possibility of counter-hegemonic politics difficult. It is in this context that the following question needs to be posed: Under what condition does the experience of a victim become transformative? At what level of its articulation is it available for the unification of consciousness, ultimately triggering off transformative politics?

These are some of the leading questions that form the central concern of this chapter.

EPISTOMOLOGICAL TERRAIN OF EXPERIENCE

As discussed in the earlier chapters, defining experience is not an easy task. This is because there are several meanings that are associated with the phenomenon of experience. Some leading thinkers have sought to assign different meanings to experience. For example, John Dewey

defines experience as the principal medium and means whereby the
world is encountered, enjoyed, appraised, and transformed into
a human habitation.[5] Experience, Dewey further explains, must
be treated as a way of conceiving what our contact with the world
must be, if experience has to serve as an incorrigible foundation of
knowledge.[6] For Dewey, experience is not just content; it in fact
includes context as well as the many dimensions of meaning—such
as the political, moral, religious, and aesthetic—in which the content
figures.[7] For Price, on the other hand, experience has an element of
shock and surprise.[8] Those who are the recipients of these shocks and
surprises tend to become more careful so that unpleasant experience
does not get repeated in the future. It is in this sense, as Price suggests,
that experience is our teacher.[9] The role of experience, according to
Price, is to participate and filter off the false ideas, largely in the form
of surprise, that occur in the course of experimentation.[10] For Levinas,
meanwhile, the experience of others 'to be close' is shattering.[11] Let
me explain this very pertinent observation made by Levinas by
citing some illustrations that are unfortunately available in my close
vicinity. The experience appears to be shocking in the context where
one does not expect offensive treatment or a hostile attitude from
one's very 'close' friends. The shock produces a much harsher moral
impact when such an attitude, assaulting one's dignity, comes from a
friend who never tires of claiming authorship of writing about Dalit
experience. For example, there are many in the teaching profession
who also deliver this shock.

The tormenting self can be kept under control through deploying
a fuse conductor for moral monitoring, which keeps the overflow
of emotions under control. Whenever emotions override reason, it
leads to a volcanic overflow that produces a shattering experience for
a person who does not anticipate this experience. One would not be

[5] Smith (1978: 145).
[6] *Ibid.*
[7] *Ibid.*
[8] *Ibid.*, p. 92.
[9] *Ibid.*
[10] *Ibid.*
[11] Wesleyan (2002: 89).

shocked if the right-wing ideologue attempts to humiliate a Dalit person. This is because such an ideologue is expected to humiliate a victim—either a Dalit or a minority-group person. But a Dalit would certainly feel deeply shocked when an ideologue having Left leanings and 'normative commitment' to the issues of egalitarianism and human dignity seeks to discriminate and humiliate a Dalit on unreasonable grounds. Such an attitude also demands an explanation on moral grounds. The explanation of experience, when thought of in terms of the moral framework, then assumes a particular ordering of values. This order includes those who occasion our admiration, those who do not lead a Janus-faced life, and those who do not allow prejudice to overwhelm good passion. That is, the truth of commitment to the dignity of an individual is as important as the discovery of the truth of knowledge. When prejudice based on 'one dimensional or closed ideology' motivates the 'cadre intellectual' to inflict insult and create a painful experience for others, it militates against the revolutionary need to produce collective experience, as suggested by one of the more sensitive subaltern thinkers, James Scott. He says that 'experience is a middle term between social being and social consciousness. Experience gives colouration to culture, values. In this sense every thing becomes a class experience. It is by a mode of collective experience that the mode of production exerts a determining pressure on other activities'. He further says that 'to omit the experience of human agents from the class relation is to have a theory swallow its tail'.[12]

Although experience becomes demonstrative and expressive at the local level, yet this local expression is the condensation of the much larger universe, which is phenomenologically reduced to the local level. As we shall see in the following section, the experience of caste discrimination in India, in a different social context in Britain, gets reproduced at the local level. What is local is elevated to the transnational or universal. And yet this local, which is basically understood as the field of emotion, creates difficulties for doing theory according to some.[13]

[12] Scott (1990: 42).
[13] Mahajan (2009).

Let us look at some of the scholars who tend to argue that the attempt to privilege experience over theory is not without problems. For example, Gurpreet Mahajan, while endorsing experience as the possible epistemological source of doing theory, also alerts us against an element of essentialism that is associated with experience.[14] She seems to be suggesting that a victim may treat experience more as a regular source of emotional and material patronage rather than as an opportunity for intensifying it (experience) at theoretical level. Therefore, she rightly suggests that while dealing with experience, one need not focus on the content of experience but only on the structure of experience.[15] She further argues that in comparison to the content of experience, the structure of experience is more important, for the reason that the latter is more stable while the former is fluctuating. So what are we theorizing: content or structure? According to her, since the content is inherently fluctuating, it can promote a tendency whereby experience can be individualized for narrow purposes and not for its theoretical significance.[16] Thus, individualizing experience does lead to distinctiveness and hence can pose difficulties for its theorization. Openness is a strength of experience and hence it is unavailable for producing absolute knowledge and ultimately theory. This formulation poses a challenge to the position which suggests that for doing informed and sound theory, one requires experience. Since experience is subjective and forms part of the fluctuating content, it poses a problem for doing theory.

How does one face this challenge? Is it possible to accommodate experience as an initial condition for theorization? There are think-ers who have suggested certain important steps in this regard.[17] The first step that one needs to take for making experience available for theorization is deploying a method that can forge unity in experience through concepts and categories. Foremost among those who suggest the unified sense of experience is Francis Bacon, who says that 'every-day experience stands on loose faggots with no internal or unifying order and hence no certainty and is itself an inaugurating moment

---

[14] *Ibid.*
[15] *Ibid.*
[16] *Ibid.*
[17] Scott (1991).

of a broader doubt in which sensory impressions are suspect, unless governed by a strict regulatory method'.[18] Thus Bacon does rule out the role of experience in the production of knowledge and assigns primacy to method.[19] In order to further emphasize the importance of method, he says that 'experience as chance is based on disorder, it is unreliable and subject to the vagaries of ungoverned perception. It is in contrast with the continuous and repeatable chain of axioms leading to well regulate [sic] experiment'.[20] Bacon thus suggests that experience be subjected to experiments. The founding moment of philosophical modernity does not lie in experience but in method and experiment. Bacon suggests a particular sequencing, putting method before experience.[21]

Experience suggests moment in which the subject and object are united. Reflexive consciousness of one's own experience creates a separation between the object and subject, and unites one with experience at a higher level of theoretical sophistication. Revisiting one's own experience through theory would help one avoid an undesirable danger. Experience left to itself remains mired in confusion, compounded by emotions expressed through crying, screaming, and even violence. Keeping in mind this possible danger that is involved in raw experience, scholars therefore suggest that one requires a faculty of reason before one acquires experience. That is to say, for intensification of experience, only the possession of experience is not enough. It is only through 'clear' experience that we can then produce 'clear' concepts. For getting a clear view of experience one needs to deploy reason. Reflection on experience, according to this view, one does not have to be a knowing subject.[22] It is not for such a person to hold an analytical power to establish a casual relationship with the help of available insights. One might have no difficulty in accepting this line of argument but in 'making theory', it is necessary to reflect and not merely react to experience. The recipient of experience carries a special responsibility to reflect on experience for larger theorization.

[18] Scott (1991: 202).

[19] Ibid.

[20] Ibid., p. 203.

[21] Ibid., p. 208.

[22] Fay (1996: 10).

What are the apt forms of reflection of experience? Can autobiographies be an adequate format to achieve this perfect reflection? Autobiographies might target a few persons and produce a moving description of a particular experience. But theories do not target individuals and seek to focus on the structures that produce this moving account of experience. Theorizing experience in terms of its structural essence rather than its varying content forms the basic object of any theory. Theory thus targets social relations and tendencies that operate through patterns and structures that inhabit relations and tendencies. Thus, there can be a theory of individualism and not of an individual. Theories target the structures of thinking and make a claim for paradigmatic replacement of the old ones. Sandra Harding, another leading scholar, mounts her objection to experience on the ground that it can lead to debilitating relativism.[23] According to G.C. Pande, the very word 'experience' is objectionable.[24] For him this word is questionable because all experience appears relative to a particular subject and object.[25] It is always subjective and cannot provide raw material for doing theory.[26] Finally, someone may argue that experience can lead to reification through autobiography or through policy regime. It could be called the politics of experience in the sense that people develop vested interests in using their experience for personal gains, or they may use somebody else's experience for their personal interests. Some of the non-governmental organizations (NGOs) are apt examples of this act of reifying experience. In this narrow context, experience gets treated as a fixed asset.

Keeping in view these objections, can we still argue for experience as the starting point for doing theory? What are the possible grounds on which the idea of experience could be defended? Sarukkai, in his contribution to this volume (Chapter 3), has already provided very convincing grounds for engaging with experience in theory. Let me add some more points.

---

[23] Harding (1992: 186).
[24] Pande (1994: 440).
[25] *Ibid.*, p. 400.
[26] *Ibid.*, p. 448.

EXPERIENCE AS INITIAL CONDITION OF ITS THEORIZATION

First, reference to experience is important for disputing efforts that seek to assign discursive treatment to theoretical concepts. In such efforts, concepts progress only with reference to other concepts, and rule out any possibility of reference to concrete experience as a necessary epistemic resource for the progression of these concepts. For example, there are scholars who would try and argue that in precolonial India, caste did not acquire an unique status in the social understanding.[27] This line of argument suggests that since there was no caste in this period, there was no caste-related experience as well. They would make this discursive move and dispute the very existence of caste by invoking multiple vocabularies that would deny caste its centrality.[28] Thus, they would say, caste as jati and its significance as an unique social phenomenon is undercut by parallel terms such as *manush* jati, *stree* jati, or *manav* jati. Since caste is used in a generic form, it does not have any specific existence in itself. Thus the discursive take on caste essentially renders the latter as ambiguous and not less than even an embattled category. Such discursive attempts achieve two objectives: first, they introduce flexibility into concrete categories and, secondly, they convert flexibility into a virtue for its own sake. Conceptual flexibility, entailing a variety of possible meanings, seeks to debilitate both the moral and political force of the categories with unified meaning. Thus caste loses its hermeneutic and political power to interrogate Brahminism. Such arguments empower scholars with alienated cognitive sovereignty. This suggests one needs only other rather loosely associated, argued, and conferred concepts (manav jati, stree jati, *purush* jati, and so on) in order to question the existing one (caste as jati). Secondly, in a certain sense, such discursive reading acquires an ahistorical character. It denies the historical production and reproduction of experience that is associated with caste.

In fact, the history of caste and the experience of caste oppression cannot be denied by simply making these moves. The ontological dimensions of these three competing terms (manav jati, stree jati, and purush jati) cannot account for the social specificity of local caste

---

[27] Smith (1978: 146).
[28] Samrendra (2011: 52).

oppression. The treatment meted out to an untouchable saint, Chokhamela, in the thirteenth century would debunk this discursive move. As the social historians of medieval Maharashtra have shown, Chokhamela was treated as a part of manav jati at the ontological level, but was treated as a despicable being at the social level.[29] Thus, it is evident from the social history that the caste practices have been produced and reproduced by the socially dominant castes.

Second, reference to experience becomes important to fight the regressive arguments that normally get associated with the notion of 'authentic experience'. Authenticity, is what one may choose to regressively define as the essentialization of particular experience. In the present case the experience is of being an untouchable. The more radical argument would be to assign more subversive content to untouchability through the act of re-signification of what is condemned as inferior. For example, the upper castes deploy untouchability in order to give Dalits an experience that pushes the latter beyond the pale of social civilization. That is to say, they are treated worse than animals. The Dalit writers re-signify this at another level so as to assign inverted power to what is condemned (reference to sun) as useless or worthless. Thus, in the positive re-signification, the Dalit writers would seek to compare untouchables with the sun on the ground that both the sun and the untouchables share the essence of being untouchable (see Chapter 7 by Sarukkai).

The Dalit writers would thus argue that untouchables are like the sun, which cannot be touched.[30] In the negative mode they would identify the untouchables with death, which living creatures take every care to avoid. However, there is a limit to this re-signification of experience. Such literary efforts seek to resolve the problem only at the symbolic level. This is because the tormentor, who is the source of this experience, does not find any moral merit or social reality in re-signification and hence refuses to take a trip into this imagination. On the contrary he or she keeps producing this experience even across time and space, as in the case of England, where some white British

[29] Zelliot (1992).

[30] This statement was made by Baburao Bagul, one of the leading Dalit poets from Maharashtra.

people create forms of torment for the brown and dark Asians.[31] The experience, which is encapsulated into an idea, gets exported abroad. The only difference between the experience in London and that in India is that in England, the social base of experience gets expanded so as to cover the entire South Asian population. The idea of oppression thus produces a much wider category of population moving from the specific lower-caste self to the wider racial self. Thus, this ideology has the power to transmute caste into race or elevate caste to higher levels of social existence.

Third, experience and the idea of experience that have been produced historically become important in order to understand both the philosophical foundation of emancipatory movements and also to measure the moral personality of a tormentor. The experience of victimhood provides a negative vocabulary that tends to define the philosophical background condition for the emancipatory movement of those who have been the recipients of this experience. This has been demonstrated by the social movements led by Jotirao Phule and later by Bhimrao Ambedkar.

It becomes the moral responsibility of those who are the recipients of torment, crushing experiences to vocalize the experience of past silence. The tormentor avoids writing the history of social evils for which he or she is responsible. It becomes the added responsibility of the tormented to resurrect the history of experience, reflect on it, and use it radically for the political and intellectual organization of masses who then would be ready for the annihilation of the structures of domination that underlie and renew this experience. Thus, reference to experience becomes important in order to detect the absence of the ethical principle of co-responsibility within the tormentor. How does the victim access the historical experience? What prompts him or her? History that moves through thought and concepts makes sense to Dalits only through the experience that stands behind these concepts. It is in this sense that a priori principles get embedded in experience. My argument closely follows that of Collingwood, who

[31] Interview with Prakash Gyanam, National Centre for Advocacy Studies, Pune, 23 March 2002. Caste is still present in England; especially as its confirmed by a layer of racism.

observes that 'history, according to Hegel, consisted of empirical events, which were the outward expression of thought and thought behind the events formed the chain of connected concepts'.[32] It is in this sense that one can argue that behind every experience related to untouchability, there is a Brahminical thought (Sarukkai raises similar points in his chapter on untouchability [Chapter 7]). This raises a question: Do you need to subject your experience to concepts? Well, the realist would answer this question in the negative on the grounds that primacy of private data or experience can help one to escape the dogmatically imposed interpretation of a particular world view.[33]

Some idealists would insist that this real life is ultimately mediated or conditioned by ideas.[34] In idealism thus the 'real' is given through ideas. However, Deleuze is against the mediation of real.[35] For him, life is lived directly and immediately.[36] In this regard M.N. Srinivas also takes a position that is similar to Deleuze since Srinivas argues that empirical reality does not require theoretical representation. However, Dewey does not take this either/or position. Instead, he suggests that experience on its own does not communicate itself to the world. It requires concepts and theoretical language.[37] In a Deleuzian sense, ideas extend experience but they do not organize or construct experience. However, both Dewey and Deleuze suggest one thing: that concepts and theory seek to intensify experience and experience in turn seeks to force theory to moderate its claim of being absolute.[38] Experience can also help trigger ideas. However, both Deleuze and Dewey assign primacy to experience over ideas.[39] In the language of empiricism, in contrast to that of the idealists, ideas do not order experience but, on the contrary, ideas are the effects of experience.

[32] Collingwood (1994: 118).

[33] James (1990: 46).

[34] *Ibid.*

[35] Colebrook (2002: 79). M.N. Srinivas made this point in one of the conferences in Delhi in 1985.

[36] Smith (1978: 146).

[37] *Ibid.*

[38] Smith (1978) and Colebrook (2002).

[39] *Ibid.*

In this regard, in my view, it is difficult to take a third position except to align with the position that Dewey has already taken.[40] I would like to argue that transformative politics demand that if experience has to become a social force for radical mobilization against those dominant forces that are responsible for the creation of experience, then it is important to communicate the unified nature of the social experience. This can be done only through the theoretical mediation of the differentiated experience. That is, one has to start from immediate experience to understand the real world.[41] Thus, for understanding the external world, one has to start from one's own experience. The connection between the abstract and the immediate takes place primarily through theoretical mediation between the particular and the universal. The description of a particular experience in the form of an autobiographical account may not be a sufficient condition to radically connect the particular to the universal. Here I would like to impress upon Sarukkai (in response to his argument in Chapter 2) that while autobiography is important to open up dialogue with those who are not part of the experience, they can merely share that experience through sympathy with the authors. This is insufficient. Moreover, humiliating, degrading experience narrativized through autobiographies might prompt some to notice the details of the painful experience and develop the moral stamina not to repeat the act that would produce such a morally objectionable experience for others. However, this access to somebody's experience through autobiographies may not create the need to have everybody's cognitive apparatus restructured. If one fails to restructure the cognitive apparatus, one might develop the moral capacity to repent on past experience but not the cognitive capacity to reflect on present experience. Without this restructuring, the autobiographical reading would make the unity of mind possible but only at the moral-ethical level and not necessarily at a level where the unity of experience could grow stronger within the field of contestation of not just the discursive but also the practical and the political. This unity is important for both theory and practice. It is for this reason that Gramsci placed an emphasis on the need to forge an organic link between

---

[40] Smith (1978).
[41] Eagleton (2000: 48).

the immediate experience and differentiated social position.[42] There is a need to develop an organic link between the social position and the experience of a person who is writing an autobiography. This is a Gramscian challenge, which seeks to rule out the notion of parachuting into somebody's experience. This ethical challenge of doing theory, can further be substantiated by taking a cue from Gellner, who said that 'epistemological principles are basically normative or ethical. They are prescriptions for the conduct of cognitive life'.[43] Before we elaborate on this point, let me focus on the debate relating to the sequencing of experience and theory.

I would like to suggest that immediate experience has to be treated as initial epistemic grounds that would ultimately provide a vantage point for the immediate experience to unfold itself into a much larger unified experience. That is to say, immediate experience that is cast into an abstraction or formulated into abstract ideas would help those in the primary experience to move out into a much larger unified sphere of experience. The immediate experience does provide epistemic grounds for such a move, primarily because this particular experience is the result of the larger structures that shape and orient this experience in the first instance. That is to say, such experience does not come from nowhere. It is produced and handed down by those who deploy it as a part of their politics of domination. Thus, experience creates categories that find their meaning and essence against these larger structures of domination. The political need to fight these larger structures also creates the corresponding responsibility to fight the reification of experience into a particular identity. It is in this sense that the epistemic grounds produces an universal category to confront the larger structures depart from the standpoint epistemology, as suggested by Sandra Harding.[44] According to Harding women's experiences can contribute to the creation of knowledge without becoming centralizing categories in a conventional sense of the term.[45]

---

[42] Gramsci (1996: 65).
[43] Gellner (1984: 34).
[44] Harding (1992).
[45] *Ibid*. p. 186.

EXPERIENCE AND ITS EPISTEMOLOGY

I would like to argue in the following sections that the Dalit experience in India has the ambition to produce centralizing categories that would seek epistemic departure from the existing centralizing categories that are inadequate in understanding the Dalit experience. In fact, it is part of a larger experience waiting to explode into an oppositional consciousness. This dissolution of particular experience into a unified experience depends on theoretical intervention. For example, to convert individual experience into the social is basically the job of a theorist who would clear the ideological layers that deny the possibility of the merging of different levels of experience. It is the social nature of experience that anticipates subversive theory and transformative politics. Other kinds of experience do not motivate a theory to acquire a subversive nature. For example, the experience produced through the reciprocal touching of the skin of the body of two differently constituted bodies (a Brahmin male and an untouchable woman in the novel *Sanskara* of Ananthamurthy or a Brahmin woman and a lower-caste man in the play *Hayavadana* by Girish Karnad) would no doubt lead to a local subversion but it would not explode into a radical annihilation of caste structures (refer to the untouchability debate in this book).[46] This is because such an experience would invoke the response of people only at the moral level, which would eliminate the need for wider political mobilization as it would rest on the possibility of personal initiative. Similarly, the experience without theory that is produced through self-inflicted injuries by, for example, the Potraj (a male person from the lower caste) in Maharashtra would not provide background conditions for the possibility of subversive social theory. In fact, it does produce a sense of amusement among the general public. For example, in recent times a Scheduled Caste legislator chose to become the Potraj in order to protest against the relative backwardness of one of the sub-castes of Dalits from Maharashtra.[47]

[46] Phenomenology and archaeology debate between Gopal Guru and Sundar Sarukkai in *Economic and Political Weekly*.

[47] Potraj are those cultural identities who belong to Dalit state and exist across several states from the west to the south. They earn their living by flogging in the public.

In social experience, on the other hand, there are no boundaries. That is to say, experience of the other at the same time is my experience as well. The running thread that connects different social groups through common experience, however, is not easily discernable. Social experience becomes significant only in the condition that it has to pass successfully through two routes that could be called objective and subjective. The first route is marked by unity and continuity of social experience. The subjective route is marked by the unity of mind. Both these routes, in a radical condition, should not run parallel to each other. In fact, the objective route is immanently a primary condition to get on to the other route. Ideas are the reflection of experience as they are formed from experience. Hence the subject, in some sense, is not the author of ideas. Rather, experience takes place in the mind and forms into a series, thus producing a subject. That is to say, the subject gets formed through the series of experience. Thus the mind is the site of experience.

Unity of experience can be explained in terms of its historicity. Historicity foregrounds it in two ways: (i) an inclusion of a wide range of social categories that feed into this experience and (ii) the configuration of power. For example, an experience of untouchability as produced by the top rung of the twice-born would lead to the emergence of social categories such as Shudra-*Atishudra* (Phule), touchable–untouchable (Ambedkar), or, in the material realm, ShetjiBhatji (Phule), or such as capitalism and Brahminism (Ambedkar).[48] These social categories acquire their essence and purpose in the context of a specific configuration of power. For example, the categories produced by Phule and Ambedkar take shape in the local configuration of power. They represent a particular social experience relating to caste and untouchability that is produced by the social relationship dominated by Shetji and Bhatji in Maharashtra or the *bhadralok* in Bengal. These categories suggest a unity of social experience that is shared by the Shudra-Atishudra castes. Thus, Phule experienced maltreatment from the upper-caste person in nineteenth-century Pune who threw Phule out of the upper-caste marriage procession while Ambedkar was thrown out of a lodge in Baroda.

[48] Phadake (1988: 30).

On the other hand, the colonial configuration of power produces certain political categories that suggest the unity of experience that implicate the bhadralok[49] castes. For example, the colonial power sought to marginalize the upper castes in terms of the time–space dynamics. Europeans threw Bankim Chandra Chaterjee and Gandhi out of the railway coaches. The upper castes produced different categories in order to capture their common political experience. To put it succinctly, the local configuration of power produced the experience that came to be expressed around the question of caste and untouchability while the colonial configuration of power produced the social experience that got articulated around the category of nationalism and race. Thus, the upper castes would emphasize the category of self-rule or freedom.

The unity of experience suggests a broader range of shared universes of social experience but along the vertical (Bankim Chandra Chaterjee and Gandhi) and horizontal (Phule and Ambedkar) axes. However, social experience that takes shape within the local configuration of powers generates cracks in unity and continuity in the social experience of the Dalits and the Bahujan castes. In the above pages I have tried to replace the dichotomy between experience and theory and argued that experience needs to be treated as the *initial condition* and theory as the *essential condition* for producing unified knowledge.

EXPERIENCE: OWNERSHIP OR AUTHORITY

Let me in the remaining pages of this chapter offer a response to Sarukkai's argument regarding the ownership and authorship of experience (see Chapter 2). Who can have an exclusive right over theorizing experience? Whose experience and whose theory are they? These are questions that become important in the context of the ethics of doing theory. Is it ethically correct to parachute into somebody's experience? This question gets further validated in the context of the warning given by Gadamer. He says, 'The case where

[49] A group of people who have produced certain cultural standards and share these standards collectively.

one's claim to know the other serves to deprive other [*sic*] of his/her legitimacy, just as one can when helping or caring for someone ends [*sic*] up simply dominating them.'[50] Sarukkai notes that ownership involves the element of authenticity. If social experience is given by others, how can it be authentic? Yes, I can still argue that somebody can still claim to have ownership of this experience for the simple reason that it is embedded in this person and someone is the carrier of this experience. Somebody has deposited that experience in me. Do I have a special access to theory just because I am the owner of a particular experience? An answer could be given by citing a negative example. Since somebody is the repository of a social experience, this somebody can become available to anybody to deposit their experience in this somebody.

Let me give another example other than the ones that Sarukkai and I have given in the earlier chapters. An upper-caste woman undergoes the same experience, as a Dalit woman, of sexual violence in the bedroom situation. Excitement and amusement constitute into a mixed psychological experience in which a male/female feels excited and also amused at the same time about the actual or possible physical intimacy. But such women refuse to articulate this experience in the first-person singular. These women treat this self-representation as an embarrassment, if not taboo, which they themselves would not be able to describe. Instead they choose to communicate their experience through translating the similar experiences of Dalit women. They do not feel awkward while translating this experience from the vernacular into English. They somehow refuse to own and author their experience. On the contrary, they try hard to become the author of somebody else's experience. How ethically sound is this position? If their experience is no different from Dalit women's, why cannot they claim their own experience? Why should they hide behind somebody's experience? This act of surrogating one's experience has to be understood as a move to escape the embarrassment that is likely to be caused by the first-person literary representation. This is ethically objectionable on another ground as well. The act of depositing one's own experience in another's experience amounts

---

[50] Gadamer (1960: 383).

to the objectification of the other.[51] (This analysis can be compared with the idea of supplementation inherent in the act of untouchability as discussed by Sarukkai in this book). The act of surrogacy also undermines the much-celebrated slogan 'personal is political' through privileging what Gellner calls 'referential' over personal language.[52] The first-person singular accounts given by Dalit women not only validate the slogan but also carry moral significance with them. They are morally significant in the sense that opening up the 'delicate details of personal life' in public is morally risky and yet Dalit women take this risk through writing their own autobiographies.

On the other hand, many Dalits who are the regular recipients of humiliating experiences may find it morally embarrassing to make their experience public. This is borne out by the fact that some of the middle-class Dalits take serious exception to Dalit autobiographies that tend to bracket or fold them into the Dalit experience.[53] In this regard, it is worth remembering a story related to Charlie Chaplin. In a contest where there were three contestants acting as Chaplin, the 'real' Chaplin was also one of them. It is ironic but extremely insightful to note that the 'real' Chaplin came third in this contest of representing himself on stage![54]

The contrast between the subjective representation of experience and its object can very well be seen reflected in the distance between the stage and the audience. The upper-caste person representing Dalit experience on stage would do it with a freely flowing or relaxed body language, but the body language of those Dalits who are the part of audience would shrink. The transposition of experience or the reminder that the performer is sending to Dalits would lead to this kind of withdrawal in an embarrassing situation. Similarly, an upper-caste woman does not acknowledge that her dance originated and developed in the Devdasi (temple dancer) tradition. Instead

---

[51] Joan Cox (1989).

[52] Gellner (1984: 22).

[53] Pawar (1978: 102).

[54] I thank Atul Tiwari, a leading theatre and film personality, for sharing this valuable information with me. One version of this story can be found in http://www.livingworkshop.net/chaplin.html (last accessed on 2 June 2011).

they merely spiritualize it, de-contextualize and de-historicize it to a 'Krishna-Gopi' version. Her body language on stage perhaps would be free but her access to the devadasi experience would be limited. It would be partial because it is completely alien to her lived experience. She has a pragmatic choice to walk into and walk out of the experience whenever she wants. She, unlike the devadasis, has a choice (refer to Sarukkai's response in Chapter 2). The non-Dalit seems to be acting to get the pure experience of being a devadasi through access to the concept of a devadasi and her narratives and the truth that is rendered visible only through textual material. Since this person lacks the direct experience of being a devadasi, her understanding remains self-aggraddising and appropriative in character. A theory, in this case, thus violates the subjective conditions of its own possibility as a theory. In the absence of an inner evidence of being a devadasi, she fails to distinguish herself from a parachute, who lands in somebody's experience with the help of theoretical tools. On the other hand, the conversion by a devadasi of her experience into merely an ontological wound would certainly obstruct experience from exploding into shared public affirmation. The insulation of experience from collective affirmation or treating it as strictly personal would lead to a loss of inter-subjective public. Both these moves, of parachuting and personalizing experience, would lead to the elimination of the possibility of wider universality, which serves as the basis of doing theory.

Collective self-realization based on the rational sharing of experience certainly provides the basis for theory. Sharing thus involves an ethical challenge that many do not want to accept. For example, upper-caste women somehow refuse to accept that their experience is similar to the social experience of an untouchable woman. The social patriarchy has devised certain social norms that render upper-caste women untouchable at least for a brief 'period'. During this period of menstruation, these women are treated as untouchables, like the other untouchables. But these women offer a novel interpretation so as to distinguish their experience from the experience of those who are still treated as sociological untouchables. Their temporary exclusion from normal interaction within the upper-caste household has nothing to do with either norms or the ritual power of the patriarchy. In fact, they argue, it gives them an opportunity to enjoy freedom from the domestic drudgery and other pressures.[55] They claim it is a freedom from routine work. Although the lived untouchability of these women is shorter, or they live little of untouchability as reality, this experience as an inner evidence or insight into the awareness of repulsion should provide them the necessary grounds to connect with the experience of the untouchable women and men. They need to realize that, after all, the experience of untouchability is the product of an abstract process regulated by larger forms of social patriarchy. Although this forms the regular experience of these women, they do not treat it as a context within which a unity of social experience can be achieved.

For socializing experience, it is necessary to remove it from the realm of the purely personal private. It can be done basically by adopting two ways. First, the de-subjectification of experience or its unification into common experience depends on the inability of the system to produce differential experience. The social forces whose very survival depends on the production of differential experience and the resultant impossibility of solidarity would never allow the deprived to expand and stabilize their consciousness based on an unified experience. These upper-caste forces, in order to accumulate more power, are compelled to dilute the accumulation of crises that look imminent in the unification of the experience of those who are on the margin. This increases the responsibility of the marginalized to produce a moral hegemony that would make the marginalized look beyond a relative advantage, which is promised by the system to a selected few, and aspire for a more universal egalitarian alternative. Second, the task of social experience is to inter-subjectify experience through debate, persuasion, and public exchange of arguments where individualities are transcended and transformed into a collective but subversive subject. In order to achieve this rather complex task it is necessary to assign due consideration to experience while laying down the metaphysics of emancipation.

[55] My experience with upper-caste women who participated in an annual conference held at Panjim, Goa, 15–19 May 2007.

6

Ethics of Theorizing

Sundar Sarukkai

At various points in this dialogue, ethics has been invoked in the context of describing experiences. Our contemporary understanding of theory would find a fundamental contradiction in raising the question of ethics in the act of theorizing. After all, theory is about rational inquiry, one that is done for the sake of knowledge and understanding. How can such an act be judged to be good or bad? Social theory is about describing, explaining, and ordering social structures and social experiences, and one believes that there is really nothing ethical or unethical in this process per se. In other words, if a major task of social sciences is to describe social 'facts', then, following the well-entrenched opposition between fact and value, it would be a mistake (the naturalistic fallacy) to invoke ethics (values) in the description of facts.

However, there are some aspects of doing theory which are indeed related to ethics. For example, there are ethical considerations on how one can generate data from the field. There are also certain ethical stances that are required when studying communities and societies. One would hope that some ethical considerations play a role when social scientists formulate policies based on their research. However, all the above cases only illustrate the possibility of ethics in 'experimental' or 'applied' work—namely, fieldwork, collection of data, intervening in certain contexts, policy making, and so on. These ethical issues do not seem to arise in the act of theorizing, if by this we mean merely thinking about an issue. Data may be used to establish a theoretical point of view; but in the act of theorizing, there seems to be no place for ethics. A simple analogy might perhaps make this point forcefully: One's moral code might inhibit one from performing an immoral action, but there is nothing to really stop one from *thinking* any immoral thought.[1] It is widely believed that theories, associated essentially with thinking and imagining, cannot be good or bad but can only be right or wrong, or empirically adequate or not.

Such a well-entrenched belief about thinking and theorizing did not arise naturally. It is a product of a long historical attempt by some communities, particularly those of science and arts, to reassert the primacy of thinking without constraint and with uninhibited freedom. In what follows, I will restrict myself to the issues surrounding some early ideas of theorizing. In particular, I will argue that the idea of theory in social sciences is much indebted to a particular formulation of theory in the natural sciences, and the origin of theory in the modern sciences was possible only when ethics was removed from the domain of knowledge. This also meant that the moral status of the knower became independent of the knowledge held or created by the knower. One can understand the discussion in Chapter 2 on ownership and authorship in this context. In erasing the intrinsic relation between the knower and knowledge, experience is distinguished from the content of that experience. Since what matters in modern theoretical knowledge is only the content of that knowledge and not the ethical or cultural characteristics of the knower, ownership does not really become a significant issue, thus enabling the removal of the subject from experiential knowledge.

THEORY AND ITS PROBLEMATIC RELATIONSHIP WITH ETHICS

While there are many aspects to the act of theorizing, let me focus on one of its most fundamental aspects—namely, thinking. While all thinking is not theorizing, there is a particular mode of thinking that characterizes the act of theorizing. Some of the characteristics of

[1] Theology's concern with thinking 'wrong' thoughts has been a long and enduring one.

theory, such as subsuming particulars under universals, unification of diverse phenomena, description (thick description, mathematical description, and so on), or explanation (particular structures of explanation) are all illustrative of this particular mode of thinking. One could view theorizing as a particular 'style' of thinking. Independent of how a theory finally comes to be, it is the act of reflection that is the originary impulse to theory. This theoretical act is an 'Extraordinary' one in the platonic sense. Where theory is a shift from the ordinary to the extraordinary realm mediated by Eros. Modern imagination (fuelled further by theories in natural science) continues this kind of fascination with theory as something 'extraordinary'.

So the real ethical challenge to theorizing has to be found in this original act of thinking theoretically. Indeed, there are many such questions that we can pose to this act of reflection. For example: What gives me the right to think about something? Do I have a *right* to think of, and reflect on, any subject and any problem? Just as there should be some prerequisites and qualifications that are necessary to do certain acts, are there some prerequisites and qualifications for thinking about certain issues? Are such prerequisites ethical in nature? Moreover, once a person begins to think about a problem, are there certain avenues that that person should *not* follow? These are problematic questions, primarily because our understanding of theory is so much based on the belief that we have a *right* (moral right?) to think, even if we do not have a right to always act in ways that we might desire. This capacity to think what we want, in contrast to doing what we want, defines the modern self and the very idea of the human will. In bringing the question of ethics into the very act of theorizing, we are challenging these fundamental presuppositions about the modern self.

Let me list a set of problems to motivate a sympathetic view of the above issues. Suppose a person has no idea of how poor people survive in a society. Suppose this person has a superficial exposure to the world of the poor as well as little understanding of the complexity of poverty. Moreover, suppose this person ends up making policy decisions that have a direct impact on poverty. Let us even grant the possibility that this person's decision, through some fortuitous circumstance, is actually a good policy. Is there anything intrinsically wrong in this process? One might say that there is a great danger that the policies could turn out to be 'epistemologically wrong' but the real question is whether it is also ethically wrong for such a person to be involved in making policy decisions on poverty. Similar issues resonate through the feminist discourse, as also the Dalit discourse.

Consider another example. A scientist, in the process of thinking about various kinds of viruses, thinks of a method to develop a most dangerous virus. This scientist knows that this virus has the capacity to eliminate the world's population very rapidly. Should the scientist even consider the possibility of creating this virus, knowing well the potential cost? Here the problem is that the scientist knows in her mind, through her thoughts, that the virus is extremely harmful. But she might also be aware that a discovery of this magnitude might get her great recognition. One ethical question here is whether her ideas should be converted to reality, but yet another ethical question is whether she should have spent her energy and time thinking about this possibility at all! What reasons can one give to justify thinking about the possibility of finding the most dangerous virus? Thus, the ethical challenge is not as much to stop the production of the virus but to stop thinking about such matters.

One can immediately see how problematic the above assertion is. How can one stop thinking? Who can regulate what an individual can and cannot think? In traditional discourses on morality, one can find similar arguments about not just not doing evil but also not thinking evil. Our thoughts are so much out of our control that it seems we cannot control what and how we think. Since thoughts are essentially private, the acts of theorizing can only be *self-regulative*. It is indeed possible to impose ethical constraints on what we think, how we think, and how we relate these thoughts to the activity of theorizing. Very good examples of systems that are based on the constraint of thought are the meditative traditions, as also the Gandhian one.

The last example I will use is one that problematizes the modernist assumption of separating the knower and the known. Such a division is essential to scientific and, in general, 'rational' knowledge. After all, why should the particularities (or, as some would have it, subjectivities) of the author matter to the scientific description of nature? In the social sciences, one naïvely extends this view to claim that the particularities (including the historical and cultural particularities) of the author cannot matter as far as theorization is concerned. All these specific characteristics of the author are replaced by some other prerequisite for doing theory—and this prerequisite is primarily couched in the language of merit. But it was not always so. For a long time and in different cultures, the moral status of the producer of knowledge influenced the way that knowledge was viewed. Consider a well-known example: Dr Mengele was the notorious doctor of the Nazi regime and he performed experiments on the Jewish prisoners in the name of medical science. Now, should the knowledge generated by his experiments be accepted by the medical community? Just as we have a problem with ill-gotten wealth, shouldn't knowledge that is also ill-gotten be rejected?

These are fundamental questions of theory's relations with knowledge. Compared to the role of theory in other disciplines, these questions are for more relevant to social theory, more than any other discipline. When Guru framed the problem of theory in Indian social science, he was asking a question about the basic ethical prerequisite needed to do a particular act of reflection (Chapter 1). In other words, what he was asking also is this: *Why* does a non-Dalit want to study Dalits? Why does a person who does not share the lived experience of one community want to say something about that community? This is an ethics of choice and not of method. This is equivalent to the ethical choice scientists have to make in choosing research problems. When some scientists refuse to work on projects supported by defence funds, they are doing something similar. Their refusal need not be because they are averse to the end product of their research; it may well be an assertion of their ethical right in choosing a research problem. In a similar manner, what is the ethical stance towards theorizing that social scientists can take?

In the context of natural science, it is possible to deflect questions on the ethics of theorizing by placing the problem of ethics in the domain of technology. This misdirection of ethics has been so successful that today it is generally believed that ethical issues in science arise only through its applications, most often through technology. The common argument that underlies this belief is that any scientific or technological object is both good and bad: a knife is used for cutting vegetables as well as people and the scientist should not be blamed for how the technology is used. It is remarkable how much this simple argument has become entrenched in the public discourse of natural science.[2] Similar arguments are invoked in any discussion on nuclear bombs or fertilizers and in general on the harmful impacts of various technologies. This argument places the blame of unethical action not on science or technology per se but on the human agents who 'use' these products. Another way in which this myth gets reinforced repeatedly is by dividing science into two parts: pure and applied science. Technology is placed within applied science, and ethical issues in science are often discussed within the ambit of this domain.

The distinction between the pure and applied is not present as clearly in the social sciences. While some might argue that social work and the domain of policymaking within the social sciences constitute the 'technology' of the social sciences, there is something fundamentally different between the technology of the natural sciences and these interventions in society. Surprisingly, in spite of this ambiguity, ethical concerns in social theory have been ignored, although such concerns are sometimes voiced in the context of social policy and interventions based on academic social work. The reason for this is clear: We have bought into the presuppositions underlying the theoretical act, particularly the cleavage between the subject who is involved in producing the knowledge and the content of the knowledge one produces, the ethics of choosing any research problem one desires, the absence of critical engagement with what kind of theoretical structure one decides to use for what problem, and so on. Most importantly, these issues reflect ethical problems inherent in the act of theorizing and are not just epistemological problems. That is, these are not about whether a particular theoretical approach is 'correct' or not, whether it leads to 'true knowledge' or not. Instead, they are primarily about the ethical stance one needs to have in the very act of theorizing, in the very act of reflection about the human community.

A major reason for believing that there is no ethical question as far as the basic act of theorizing is concerned has to do with a carefully constructed view of theory and knowledge and their relation

[2] Bunge (2007) and Sarukkai (2009b).

to the scientist. The way this construction unfolds historically is fascinating and filled with lessons for the practice of social science. How do scientists justify the choice of their research problem? How does one explain to another why one is working on a particular problem? In the narratives of science, we find a common denominator among many of these descriptions. Scientists tend to say that *curiosity* drove them towards thinking about a particular problem. Scientists are curious about a whole lot of things: what will happen if a nucleus is split, DNA is cloned, if life could be made in the laboratory, and so on. The way the scientists escape ethical challenges to their practice lies in this cocoon of curiosity that they build around themselves.

What is most remarkable about this cocoon is that it is one carefully constructed over a few centuries. The beginning of modern science is as much indebted to the construction of a new image of curiosity as it is to method and new experimental discoveries. For science to be liberated from ethics (particularly religious ethics), it had to liberate curiosity from its negative connotations. The way this was done is a fascinating story that shows how, step by step, curiosity was legitimized as the prime mover of scientific thinking while at the same time releasing the bond between the ethical status of the scientist and the status of the knowledge created by that scientist.

Early views on knowledge in the West did acknowledge a relation between the knower and the known. Curiosity was seen to be a catalyst for generating knowledge but since curiosity was related to the 'sins' of pride and vanity, the knowledge created through curiosity was also contaminated by these sins. Modern knowledge needed to break this link and the way modernity dealt with it was to isolate curiosity and make it a natural, human act that has a high value. The way curiosity was rehabilitated involves a long story from Bacon to Hume.[3] In the late sixteenth century and in the seventeenth century, there was a concentrated effort by scientists to attach positive virtues to curiosity. Part of the argument was to make curiosity a natural act and moreover to make it a *duty* to be curious in order to attain knowledge. Curiosity was also legitimized by arguments that there were many curious things in nature and since God created nature,

[3] Sarukkai (2009b).

God must have meant curiosity to be a positive trait. In fact, the Royal Society in Britain in the early eighteenth century emphasized the value of curiosity as the most important characteristic of a scientist. So much so that certificates given to elected members of the Society declared these members as embodying curiosity. The Society moreover made the exhibition of curiosities an important part of its function.[4]

This is the inheritance of social science when it borrows the notion of theory from the natural sciences. Unfortunately, among other things, it also borrows this septic notion of curiosity without recognizing the historical and constructed origins of the same. Just as scientists can 'play' around with the world and attempt to discover for the sake of discovery without concern for the impact of such an action, social scientists too believe that one can be curious about any social issue and that curiosity is enough of a prerequisite for doing theory or at least attempting to theorize. But if unbridled curiosity is ethically problematic for natural science itself,[5] then one can imagine how much more problematic it will be for the social sciences. The ethics of research is not only concerned with the methods and practice of research but also with the research problems one chooses. Curiosity has often validated the choice of research problems but ethical responsibility (knowing well that the end result might get published and thus become a valid document of an event) must begin at the point one chooses to work on a particular problem.

Social scientists can choose any problem to work on. Why? Because they are curious about or 'interested' in that problem. In principle, there is nothing problematic in invoking curiosity or interest to legitimize exploration, but there is an ethical cost to this 'free' curiosity. Where the curiosity argument really fails is when it is confronted with the category of experience. One's experience is not outwardly open to another's curiosity and thus is fundamentally insulated from the intrusive tool of curiosity. Following the development of the theoretical stance in the natural sciences, social science can decide to ignore the experiential and the subject as integral components of theorizing or it can create its own style of theorizing by building

---

[4] Fontes da Costa (2002), Harrison (2001), and Peters (2001).

[5] As argued in Sarukkai (2009b).

upon these as the core elements. On following the latter path, there will be a different set of problems for social theory, such as the following: who has the originary right to theorize; the distinction between authorship and ownership; the belief in the universality of theories that makes it possible to describe Indian social reality largely through the vocabulary and framework of European and American theories of societies; linking the moral position of the social scientist with the knowledge he or she produces; and, perhaps most importantly of all, generating a set of norms of accountability to decide the merits of a theory. The last point is merely the expectation that theory is judged not only with respect to certain epistemological expectations but also to ethical concerns. It might be useful to remember here that epistemology was earlier intrinsically related to ethics. The dissociation of ethics from epistemology is at the root of the modern stance of theorizing. It is the power of theory as also the bane of it.

But how does one go about doing all this? It is easy to give prescriptions but, in the context of social theory, how do we actually go about incorporating these and related questions? I will discuss these issues later in this chapter, but first we need to begin with understanding the first steps of theorizing, namely, the act of thinking about experience.

THINKING EXPERIENCE AND THE EXPERIENCE OF THINKING

Experience is automatic. One just feels. This instantaneity may seem to be contrary to the process of knowing. Rarely do we think that 'one just knows'. To know is to indulge in a process of judgement, to be reflective about something and then arrive at a decision. Philosophers are aware of a species of knowing, self-knowing, but it has always been difficult to adjudicate on what constitutes self-knowledge. Part of the reason is that self-knowing is fundamentally an experience that is accessible only to the subject who experiences it. This is why a major problem in self-knowledge is related to the legitimization of such knowledge.

Moreover, just because we have new experiences all the time does not mean that we have new knowledge all the time. However, this does not mean that knowing is beyond experience. In fact, the very act of knowing is itself a particular kind of experience. It is an experience that is perhaps best known as the 'Eureka' moment. There is an experience of knowing when we suddenly get an insight or when 'things fall into place'. Often, in these cases, the content of that experience is seen as knowledge and the experience of knowing is often dismissed as 'mere' experience. However, many psychological accounts of creativity try to recapture experiences related to the eureka moment and I believe that these accounts illustrate the importance of these experiences.[6]

What can one say about experience? Granted that we have our own individual experiences, it is nevertheless the case that we talk about these experiences. We communicate them to others or at least try and communicate them. If experience is so private, what are we doing when we are talking about it? We could rephrase this question by asking: What is it to *know* an experience?

Knowing experience (and equivalently, theorizing about experience) is to reflect upon an experience, to think about that experience. This is a standard model for understanding knowledge that arises from an experience. In this view, we have the experience first and then we think about it. We reflect upon it and learn lessons from it. This idea that we first have experience which is followed by thought can be problematic, particularly if it leads to the belief that thought is 'outside' experience—that is, if it is believed that once we have had an experience, we can extract it and then apply thought to it. Often this confusion between thinking and experience gets reflected in the conceptual problems of the experience–theory relation.

What is it to think about experience? First of all, it seems that thinking about an experience is to think about the memory of that experience. Thinking and experiencing cannot go together, cannot be instantaneously present. So if thinking comes after experience, then it can *never* reflect on the experience per se. Thinking can only reflect on a memory of that experience, a memory of how it felt and not what it meant to feel in a particular way.

However, thinking is essential in order to grasp our experience. This is the conundrum: to know something about an experience, I have to reflect on it after it has happened. Although this act of

[6] Csikszentmihalyi (1996).

reflection is itself an experience, it is a different experience. For example, suppose I had the experience of tasting the sweetness of a banana. Reflection on the content of this experience of sweetness is a different experience—that of the act of reflection or thinking. The conundrum is precisely this: I cannot think or know about my experience without thinking or cogitating about it. Even if experience is self-knowledge—that is, just by having the experience I know that I have had a particular experience—the awareness of knowing often arises after having the experience.

Therefore, any attempt to understand experience has to be in relation to the act of thinking. This relationship leads us to consider the inherent relationships between experience and language, experience and reason, and experience and perception. This is because thinking is essentially concerned with language, reason, and perception. While earlier theories on thinking and thought were related to ideas, later there was a shift to making sense of them in terms of language. One expression of this is the claim that there is no thought without language while another strain of this is the argument that thought is structured like language. Similarly, we can ask whether experience is available only through such categories. That is, is experience structured like language? An immediate answer to this is that experience is not so structured. In fact, the quality of experience is that one has it independent of any articulation of it. The language argument for thought is also based on the observation that we do not seem to have any thoughts that are not constructed like language—whether it is verbal language or even visual language. But experience is quite different. We have experiences, the feeling of something. Thinking and thus the linguistic expression of this experience comes after the experience.

Similarly, thought's essential relationship with logic and reason, and its essential relationship with experience, creates a space where experience and reason co-inhabit. Logic is primarily about the structure of thoughts and making connections between thoughts. The expression that logic is the 'laws of thought' captures this intrinsic relationship. Now, experience has often been understood as being contrary to logic. The notions of first-person subjectivity, as well as the relation between emotions and experience has led to the removal of reason from the world of experience. But rethinking experience's relation with thinking allows us a way to reclaim the essential relation between experience and reason. This reclamation has consequences for the larger question of the relationship between experience and theory.

Finally, thought's relationship with perception reminds us once more of the intrinsic relation between experience and perception. In fact, the idea that thinking is like a sense has much to do with the way experience is related to the senses. In the context of making theories, 'thinking' acts as a sense whose function is to create theories. Thinking functions like perception, a perception through the 'mind'. The mind 'sees' more than what the senses perceive—no wonder some philosophers think of logic as the seeing of the mind. In fact, I believe that one could make the argument that the relationship between experience and the senses is analogous to that between thinking and the mind as a sense.

It is in this context that I would like to view thinking as a 'sense for theory-making'. Thinking has often been understood as an extra sense to perceive more of the world than is available to the five senses. If we see thinking as a specific 'sense' used for theorizing, then we can grasp yet another argument relating experience and thinking. Experience is primarily associated with sensations, with the five sensory organs. If thinking is a sense, as described above, then experience is automatically related to thinking.

One could make a reasonable argument that thinking is intrinsically related to experience. Viewing thinking as a sense makes this claim much stronger. There is a very interesting phenomenon that is relevant in this context. It is commonly thought that the five senses of the body are independent of each other but it is not necessarily the case. Philosophers like Merleau-Ponty argue for the unity of the senses and the need to see the senses as functioning as a unity. But independent of these positions, there is the unique condition of synaesthesia where the senses do not exhibit this independence. When we extend this to the question of experience, we confront this possibility: Experience is not related to the individual senses alone but can be presented in the mode of synaesthesia. Thus, one's experiences are an intrinsic combination of the experience of bodily senses and the experience of thinking. This view can also explain how experience and knowledge can be instantaneously available.

There is a profound consequence of this intertwining of experience and thought: Experience is fundamentally structured by thought. Thus, there are really no innocent and naïve personal experiences. Most importantly, we have no self-knowledge of our experiences. Our experiences have to be taught to us—we learn how to recognize our own experiences in particular ways. Let me illustrate this with an example.

The example has to do with two individuals who had never taken a folk 'drug' called *bhāng*. This is an organic product that is publicly consumed in various states of northern India. It causes certain kinds of hallucinogenic experiences. The two individuals took bhāng for the first time and for quite some time insisted that they didn't feel anything out of the ordinary. They went on insisting that there was no effect on them until another person who was experienced in the ways of bhāng explained to them *what* they were experiencing. The moment this person told them what they were experiencing, the two individuals suddenly started experiencing the same! In fact, their experience became so pronounced that one of them couldn't handle the feeling arising from the consumption of bhāng. The point of this example is that until these two individuals were told what they were feeling and how to understand their experience, they had no way of understanding what they were feeling. The moment they were told, they began to *feel* their experience completely differently.

This example shows how we do not always have direct and immediate access to our experiences. We have to be taught to recognize our experiences, including our emotions. Anger therapy is very much based on how we can reinterpret what we have been earlier taught to recognize as anger. While I am not negating all possibility of 'brute' experiences, I do not think that they are significant in any sense. Our experiences of the world are mediated and thus are not purely subjective.

For example, we are taught to categorize primarily through the use of concepts. We, most often, recognize an experience for what it is primarily through conceptualizing it. This is true even for the most basic experiences of pain and emotions. One can immediately see a parallel between this view and a related view that thought is always conceptual or that thought is always linguistic. While I do not intend to get into this discussion, I am presenting this argument primarily to emphasize the point that this mediation of experience is the space where an ethic of theorizing can be situated.

DIRECT PERCEPTION AND DIRECT EXPERIENCE

One can detect an immediate problem in the above discussion on the relationship between thinking and experience, and this has to do with the way we understand experience. Experience is seen to be immediate; it just happens in the same way that perception 'happens'. As much as perception is passive (in the sense that in our normal perception we are just passive viewers of what appears to us), so also is experience. We eat a fruit and experience the taste: this experience is passive in the same way that seeing the colour of the fruit is passive. (In contrast, thinking is active in that it supposedly involves volition and will).

However, this view of perception has been challenged on various grounds. The challenge occurs in ancient philosophies as well as in contemporary philosophy of perception. When we see an object, 'information' about the object is processed by the eye and then finally by the processes of the brain. It seems obvious that somehow the mind reconstructs the object from the 'images' of the object within our consciousness. This is the reason why some philosophers invoked the idea of a mind's eye. If we do not subscribe to the idea of the mind's eye, then we could consider the sense-data theory, which suggests that an object is reduced to a set of sense data and that the real object of perception is not the object in the world but this sense data.

In the long history of perception, the question of direct perception occurs repeatedly. Direct perception is a claim that we are directly aware of the world that we perceive. This means that there is no intermediary between our perception of the world and the world as itself. The problem here is whether we directly see what we see or whether we actually see something else. As Smith[7] describes it, direct perception means that these objects of perception are 'not perceived by proxy'. Indirect realism argues that objects can be perceived only

[7] Smith (2002: 6).

through 'perceiving something distinct from them'.[8] For example, for many indirect realist accounts, 'perceptual sensation' is our immediate perception. These sensations are described in terms of awareness and feelings: we can see an immediate connection to experience here. If we follow this line, then it would seem that we first have experiences because of which we think we perceive the objects of perception. Thus, 'perceptual experiences, rather than giving us an immediate awareness of our physical environment, are *themselves* our immediate objects of awareness'.[9] Perhaps the strongest reasons supporting indirect perception are the ones relating to illusion and hallucination. In these two cases, it seems as if one is perceiving sensations that have no correlate with the real world. From this one could argue that all perception is of these intermediary sensations and not the object in the world in any direct sense.

It is important to note that critiques of direct realism needed to 'accept direct experiences', if not direct perception of physical objects. But why would we believe that experience is itself immediate? Cannot there be a mediatory state through which we experience? For a proponent of direct realism, as Smith is, it is important to distinguish 'perceptual consciousness' from 'merely having sensations' since it seems obvious that sensations are indeed 'objects of awareness'.[10]

One standard method of distinguishing objects and sensations is based on our naïve belief that objects are outside us in a way that sensations are not. These objects, unlike sensations, are also objects of perception for others. These simple distinctions influence a long tradition of philosophers who distinguish between sensation and perception. As Smith points out, this distinction is often grounded by viewing perception as sensation supplemented by 'an additional, distinctively cognitive, act of the mind'.[11] This extra supplemented term is thought or concepts. Thus, what is special to perception in this view is that it is sensation along with concepts. There is another distinction, following Reid, between sensation and perception in that there is an object of perception but the sensation is itself its object.

[8] *Ibid.*
[9] *Ibid.*, p. 8.
[10] *Ibid.*, p. 66.
[11] Smith (2002: 67).

This view, with variations, has been held by a large number of philosophers, including Reid, Kant, and Sellars. Belief and conception have been seen as constituting perception over and above sensations. So perceiving involves belief and concepts, and is also accompanied by the experience of that perception. For a proponent of direct realism, the idea that concepts are essentially involved in perception is a 'misguided' one.

There are good reasons to believe that perception is necessarily accompanied by concepts. This view seems to explain the way we make perceptual judgements, the way we recognize certain objects. Once we possess certain concepts, we recognize objects as falling under those concepts. Smith argues against mistaking these judgements as perceptions since even when two individuals do not share concepts, they will have the same perception of an object that they perceive. Smith describes three good reasons for believing that perception essentially involves concepts: it describes the intentional character of perception; it explains perception as judgement—perceiving something *as* something; and it gives an account of the identity of objects, in that we think we see the same object even though their presentation may be different in different contexts.[12]

Smith offers arguments that weaken the above claim that all perception is conceptual. One argument draws on things that can perceive but that does not have concepts, such as a baby or an animal. Another argument involves a critique of what concepts really are. The biggest challenge to the conceptualist view is that we do perceive a variety of entities without having any concept of what they are. Although Smith's arguments are largely about objects, the discussion can be extended to perceptions of processes such as motion.

However not having a particular concept, or having a particular 'correct' concept, is not reason enough to deny conceptualism. The point is that we may already be suffused with concepts, whether they are the right ones or not for a particular perception. In fact, we learn concepts through such mismatches that occur through perception. Moreover, the difficulty, if not the *impossibility*, of recovering perception-without-concepts once we know the concepts makes it difficult to accept direct perception. That is, once I have a concept

[12] *Ibid.*, pp. 97–8.

under which I can place my perception, it is impossible for me to
see that object in any other way. Until I know what a chair is, it
is possible that I see the 'chair' without knowing that it is a chair.
But once I have that concept, then why is it impossible for me to
see that perception as anything other than a chair? Moreover, it is
not necessary that a particular perception has to have a particular
concept associated with it. It is enough that there are always concepts
that underlie perception. Knowing *what* the object is only refines the
conceptual scheme.

Since my aim in this chapter is to explore the relation between
experience, theory, and ethics, I draw upon the above discussion in
order to make two points: one is to recognize that there are other
traditions in philosophy, notably the debate between the Buddhists
and the Naiyāyikas, which deal with conceptual and non-conceptual
perception, and the other is to critique the conceptualist viewpoint
from another entirely different direction, namely, the belief that
sensation is immediate and non-conceptual. The consequence of the
latter is that experience itself can be seen to be mediated by concepts.
The example of bhāng that I discussed earlier in the chapter illustrates this possibility that experiences are themselves 'immediately'
conceptual.

There is an interesting and long debate in the Indian philosophical traditions on whether perception is immediate or whether it is
mediated by concepts. The Buddhists hold the view that perception
is immediate and direct whereas the Nyāya tradition holds that
perception is conceptually mediated. For the Buddhist logician
Dignāga, perception is related to experience in the following manner:
In perception, one perceives *svalakshanā*, a self-characterizing entity
that is 'unique, singular' and 'momentary'.[13] One can immediately
note how this description is very close to experience. Experiences
are indeed unique, singular, and momentary. (I believe that it is far
more useful to look at experience in terms of singular and plural,
and not in terms of subjective and objective). For Dignāga, the word
pratyaksha, which is translated as 'perception', is itself indicative of
immediate experience, since 'pratyaksha' means 'before the eyes'. It
is this immediacy that makes it possible for Dignāga to argue that

[13] Lysenko (2007: 20).

concepts do not occur in perception. For the Buddhists, the means of valid knowledge are perception and inference. It is only in the case of inference that language and concepts are used. For Dharmakīrti, seeing something and seeing it as something are two different cognitions. He also offers a way to counter the point about perception having external objects, for he argues that it is only because of concepts that a 'cognitive image appears' as an 'external thing'.[14] In fact, there is a rich debate on conceptual and non-conceptual perception between the Naiyāyikas and the Buddhists that can illuminate some of these contemporary issues on experience and concepts.[15]

The second problem with conceptualism is that perception is seen as sensation along with the application of concepts (that is, perception = sensation + concepts). In so bifurcating perception, there is the underlying belief that sensation, which is the experiential mode, is accessible immediately. This has led to the commonly held belief (one that I have repeatedly invoked through this book!) that somehow experience is given to us in its immediacy and only higher-order cognitions need concepts and beliefs. The Indian philosophical arguments on determinate and indeterminate perception give us an inkling of how to understand the possibility that experience is itself mediated. (This might explain why many Indian language terms for experience already have the connotations of knowledge within them: see Chapter 3). The detailed discussion on this aspect of experience and perception allows us to understand how ethical considerations enter into the act of theorizing, as I will discuss in the next section.

CULTURAL ORDERING OF EXPERIENCE

If we follow the basic credo of empiricism that knowledge follows from experience, then we can see the inherent tension that is at the heart of theorizing. It is that experience and knowledge are described in very different, and contrary, ways. Experience is seen to

[14] *Ibid.*, p. 21.
[15] See Chadha (2001), Chakrabarti (2000), Phillips (2004), and Siderits (2004) for one such debate.

be 'subjective', private, and internal. Knowledge is 'objective', public, 'external', and justified. Theory is associated with knowledge and not with experience. This shift from this private, singular experience to the public, pluralistic theory is not merely a matter of 'objective' method but also a matter of ethics. Let me illustrate this claim with some specific examples.

In Chapter 2 on experience and theory, I made a distinction between ownership and authorship in the context of experience. Let me come back to this idea by rephrasing this issue as follows: How much of our experience is really ours? How much of my experience is really *mine*? If we understand these questions in the context of ownership, our experiences are entirely ours. We believe that we own our experience in the sense of the meaning of ownership described in that chapter. However, we hold this belief primarily because we think experience is immediately available to me and only to me, and that there is no mediation to experience. This means that concepts play a role when we want to understand the experience or make sense of it. The dominant belief about experience is that it is direct and unmediated.

However, our most primal experience—sensation, if you like,—is already formed and ordered in some way or the other. The example of bhāng discussed above illustrate the problem in believing that we cannot recognize our experiences without being taught how to recognize them as such.[16] What I am arguing for is the impossibility of having an experience, of being aware in any sense of the term, without it being influenced by certain beliefs and ideas (if not 'concepts'). It is not just our perception that is 'concept-laden'— or, as an extension, 'theory-laden'—but also our experience. This claim does not imply that there is no unmediated experience; there could be, but they will have to be a small set of 'brute experience' in a manner similar to 'brute facts', which are seen as pre-theoretical or prelinguistic facts. Perhaps such brute experiences are part of our childhood experiences, but the moment we consciously acquire concepts and the capacity

---

[16] Jefferey *et al.* (1989) describe the difficulty in easily finding 'experience' of childbirth in rural Bilaspur. I am thankful to Rakhi Ghoshal for directing me to this point and for suggesting that these women had to be 'taught' the 'experience' of childbirth.

to 'apply' concepts, we lose the capacity to have this unmediated experience.

This claim necessitates a modification to my earlier description of experience in terms of ownership. We can now ask whether we actually own our concepts. Suppose we accept the argument that experience is always mediated and ordered by concepts. Then, are these concepts 'mine'? Do I own these concepts? Are these concepts immediately accessible to me?

Those who claim that some concepts are innate are committed to our possession of these concepts. But most often these innate concepts are very few in number. One is in general suspicious of innate concepts since this seems to be an easy path to explain difficult phenomena. There are many problems in the ideas of innate ideas and innate concepts, including the influential a priori concepts described by Kant. But we do not need to invoke innate ideas in the argument that follows. I only want to show how the mediated view of experience brings with it the possibility of ethics within the act of theorizing.

First of all, concepts are essential to the act of theorizing. When we describe a theory of society or of individual experiences, we invoke different concepts. The beginning of modern science was indebted to the notion of measurable concepts. For Galileo, the task of science was to describe the world through a special set of concepts, those that are measurable: that is, quantifiable and mathematical. Concepts other than these had no place in the description of the phenomenon. This distinction between the kinds of concepts that are necessary for a discourse to be called scientific has also greatly contributed to the continuing distrust between the qualitative and quantitative in social sciences.

Thus, the act of theorizing is an act of judging what kinds of concepts are needed to describe phenomena. In the case of experience, it is the act of deciding what concepts are best applicable to the experience. Saying this does not necessarily imply that there is experience independent of concepts. As I mentioned before, once we have concepts in our possession, we seem to automatically apply them to experiences. Our recognition of most of our experiences is thus mediated. This means that the way we recognize what our experiences are depends on the concepts we deploy to make sense of these experiences. The choice of these concepts is not 'natural' in that there is nothing in the experience per se that will dictate what concepts are to be deployed. The choice is both epistemological as well as ethical in that we not only choose certain concepts to make sense of our experience in a particular way, but there is also an ethical component to what kind of concepts we use to describe these experiences. This is particularly so in the case of social and individual human experiences.

Here are some examples. Let us consider the most basic physical experiences, such as pain. Consider the experiences of headache or stomach ache. One might argue that there is nothing conceptual about these types of pains. Everybody recognizes these pains naturally and immediately. In fact, these could be considered examples of brute experiences. However, even in these examples, we can see how concepts work to order our experiences. If we consider the discourse on healing pains, we can see how conceptual reordering of the same experience gives us another way to experience these phenomena. Healing and managing these pains illustrate how conceptual reordering can help change the nature of the experience itself. Meditative healing, in particular, works to get rid of the pain not by ingesting analgesics but by cognitively reordering the way we experience the pain. For many non-allopathic traditions, pain is as much mental as it is physical and thus one can negotiate pain by learning to 'apply' different conceptual frameworks. This implies that the first experience of pain itself is based on a particular framework and these methods of healing only change the prior framework by which we experience pain. Even in this brute experience of pain, we can see that it is not a simple matter of saying that all of us experience pain without any conceptual mediation. This is also perhaps the reason why different people have different thresholds of pain.

If a biological experience like pain is itself mediated, then consider how much more difficult it will be to isolate unmediated 'social' experience. Consider a person who is working under 'inhuman' conditions. This person has a particular experience of participating in that kind of labour. However, an enduring paradox of this condition is that the labourers do not themselves seem to recognize certain aspects of this experience. Labour unions and others take on the job of 'educating' these labourers about the nature of their experience by supplying them with concepts that will illuminate what they are themselves undergoing. We might interpret this act by saying that the labour unions give concepts to these people to help them understand the nature of their experience, and the 'first' experience is outside these concepts. However, this misconstrues the nature of the experience of these labourers. They are already 'labouring' under concepts that might not make them recognize these experiences as being inhuman. For example, when these labourers are told about concepts such as exploitation, human rights, humiliation, oppression, and so on, they seem to recognize the same experiences in a difficult way, so much so that many descriptions of their experiences after being taught these concepts is filled with this vocabulary. They tend to use these conceptual descriptions across a wide range of experiences. Not only is this a different description of their experiences but it is also a cognitively different experience. It is well recognized that such a reordering of conceptual categories is central to many revolutionary movements.

Perhaps popular self-help books have understood this process far more successfully than academicians have. For example, a very popular book called *Feeling Good*[17] advocates cognitive therapy, which is primarily a method of understanding our experiences in an entirely different manner. What is significant about this approach is that it is directed towards our most 'basic' experiences, those which we think are completely natural and unmediated. Experiences of anger, joy, sadness, and pain can all be reorganized by cognitively looking at them in other ways. The most important aspect of this 'therapy' is that once we look at these experiences differently, it becomes a matter of habit. The success of this and similar methods clearly illustrates how it is so difficult to actually have experiences that are completely personal and singular.

The reason why experiences are therefore in principle not subjective and private is that concepts are not private and subjective. A similar argument about cognition is offered by Naiyāyikas when they point out that language is public: the moment one uses language to talk about one's experience, that experience automatically becomes part

---

[17] Burns (1980).

of the public.[18] Consider a person who has a particular experience. Once this person is told that there are experiences that are humiliating, it allows this person to use this concept to describe her own experiences. This means that she might actually experience the same experience she had been having earlier but now filtered through this concept of humiliation. This radically changes her perception of her experience as well as her actions. Feminism has shown how powerful these concepts can be to re-describe experiences. Dalit movements have also shown how various concepts have been powerfully used for social mobilization and action towards social change.

Thus, if concept acquisition is so important to re-cognizing our experiences, then we can understand how ethics comes into the picture: by making the choice of concepts an ethical decision and not merely an epistemological or political one. Oppression is possible—as is well illustrated in the history of human societies—by not allowing certain kinds of conceptual reordering of experiences. One can continue to subjugate people if certain kinds of concepts are not chosen and made available to those who are subjugated. Labour struggles as well as social reform movements make available a different set of concepts for those who are oppressed and subjugated. Given this power, it is ethically necessary to choose a proper set of concepts to describe experiences of the individual and society. Here is where social theorizing, particularly in India, faces a great challenge.

How does a social scientist make sense of the experiences that she has of the Indian society? How does she understand them and theorize about them? In the context of Guru's original argument, which problematizes the belief that anybody can theorize about anything, we can ask: What does she need for the capacity to theorize?

Indian society has been described by a large number of scholars, both from within the country and outside. In the theoretical tradition, it is still the case that social theory is influenced by theories from the Anglo-American and the Continental traditions. The conceptual vocabulary to describe 'Indian' experiences is often derived from theoretical traditions that have been used to describe other societies. Much of this act of borrowing is based on the belief that concepts

[18] Matilal (1986).

and theories are universal. So what holds good for one description is potentially usable for a description of another society.

There are two aspects to this borrowal of concepts: one is that there is a very easy appropriation of theoretical structures from the 'West' and the other is that there is a general neglect of concepts derived from Indian contexts. That is, not only is there an excessive dependence on the conceptual world arising from and developed in the West but, at the same time, there is also a neglect of the use of theoretical categories from India and the non-West. While the former is legitimized by the story that theory is universal, the latter is explained by saying that theories arising from Indian contexts are specific only to that context! In a sense, this is an extension of Guru's argument about theoretical Brahmins and empirical Shudras.

But this is no longer an epistemological issue; it is primarily an ethical one. The ethical issue is not with respect to the neglect of the Western academia to Indian theoretical attempts, but it is about the practice of Indian social scientists who continue the myth that theoretical structures from the West have as good, if not better, a capacity to describe Indian experiences as compared to 'indigenous' concepts, histories, and narratives.

This argument may seem like one about theories but it is essentially about experiences. As we saw above, experiences are themselves mediated through concepts. One is not in a position to access experiences 'innocently'. We are always in the midst of conceptual ordering at the experiential level. As we also saw, concepts are acquired in various ways. We acquire concepts through other theories and then use them to understand our experiences. In the Indian social theoretical context, the major influence seems to be 'universal' concepts starting from the early Greeks to contemporary Continental thinkers. Look at how much European writers like Marx, Weber, Durkheim, Dumont, Foucault, Derrida, Habermas, and others have influenced a disproportionate amount of theorizing. Look at how much Aristotle and Plato are invoked either directly or through these thinkers in order to understand social experiences in India. To understand the structure of Indian society, kinship relations, or even the theoretical aspects of untouchability (as I myself have done in Chapter 7 on the phenomenology of untouchability), one tends to look to European sources as a default mode. And the limitation of this looking outwards is that, first, it ignores the possibility that these writers may have little understanding of the complexity of what they assume to be describing and, secondly, it stops the growth of fertile theorizing at the local level. At the same time, there is a serious lacuna in engaging with the theoretical structures offered by various Indian classical and folk traditions. Very few of these traditions, if any, have been taken up to understand non-Indian societies. This hegemony and asymmetry is not special to India but is endemic to non-Western intellectual contributions.

Is this act of appropriating the conceptual world of Western theories, under the misguided belief that such concepts are universal and best describe Indian experiences, legitimate or not? Moreover, if we acknowledge that such theories arise in response to the historical and cultural contingencies of the Western world, how would that modify the answer to the above question? Let me illustrate this argument with an anecdote of my interaction with a famous French theorist who is very popular in India. I asked him whether he was surprised at the popularity of his theories among Indian students who use his work to describe innumerable situations in Indian social and cultural contexts. He replied that it didn't really matter to him whether his work was of interest in India because for him his work was driven by his deep desire to understand the society he lived in. He believed that contemporary Europe was wrongly understood and it was his task as a theoretician to find ways to correct this misperception. The fact that his theories are so uncritically appropriated in various Indian contexts was more a source of bemusement for him.

The point is merely this: Much of this uncritical appropriation of theoretical concepts and structures happens only because of the myth of the universal in social theories. This is a model that is conveniently taken over from natural science. Theories in natural science, like other aspects of these disciplines, simulate universality by claiming that the personal, historical, and the cultural find no place in justifications of these theories. While there is nothing intrinsically wrong in Indian social theories basing themselves on theories derived as a response to other civilizational experiences, it is wrong to ignore the hegemony and the politics of theorizing inherent in this naïve assumption about theories. There is a double move that characterizes this process: one is to make theories universal and at the same time make experience private, and the other is to decouple the two in some essential sense in the name of objectivity.

Thus, an ethical stance towards theorizing can programmatically be defined as a stance that acknowledges a 'critical universality' of theories from other cultures and societies but which, at the same time, draws upon a culture's own historical and intellectual capital. In concrete terms: To do theory is to choose certain kinds of concepts and structures, and this choice cannot be legitimized on an epistemological basis alone but should also be ethically answerable to what is right and wrong in talking about certain experiences. Thus, the chosen concepts are not only judged on whether they are 'correct' or not but whether they are also 'right' or not. One might argue that this is a regressive view that will drive theory back to the days before the origin of modern science but this would not be a fair criticism. Many theoretical interventions, particularly from the Continental tradition, can be seen to encode these and more complex ethical imperatives in their theoretical formulations. Guru's worry that non-Dalits are appropriating the discursive space of the Dalits is one aspect of this ethical imperative on the activity of reflection. We can also see an immediate connection to the politics of curiosity discussed earlier in this chapter.

Among the questions that will arise when the act of theorizing is put under the scanner of ethics are the following. Instead of hiding under the convenient veil of the objective, can theory explicitly incorporate the subjectivities of the author, negotiate between irresponsible curiosity and justified interest, establish the relation between the life practices of the author and what the author says (a Gandhian stance of theorizing), and factor in the relation between experience and theory once more—this time not as subject/object but as singular/plural?

It is not that our current practices are completely divorced from such ethical considerations. The incorporation of subjectivities has long been a part of one branch of social philosophy. The emphasis on scholarship is as much ethical as it is part of a grammar of academic writing. Citation and proper referencing are protection against plagiarism, which is often seen in ethical terms. Intellectual virtues such as honesty and open-mindedness, which are ideally a part of the activity of theorizing, have ethical correlates. But at the heart of theorizing, there is no ethical imperative that regulates what we can *think* about and *how* we can think about it. Ethical issues surrounding citation and plagiarism, for example, are primarily seen to belong to the activity of reporting theoretical results. As we discussed earlier, natural science escapes ethics by hiding behind curiosity. As I have argued elsewhere,[19] curiosity is not really an individual virtue but a *social* one. Scientific curiosity often tends to follow social modes of curiosity. So, placing the burden of ethics on curiosity, interest, and motivation allows us to recover ethics as a fundamental element of thinking, reflecting, conceptualizing, and theorizing.

Intrinsic notions of ethics should be accepted as an integral part of theorizing in the social sciences. For example, what should the ethical stance be towards studying people and communities? Should the people who are the subjects of theory also become 'authors'? Similar exercises have been attempted in ethnographic writing. Van Maanen discusses the attempt at joint authorship of work done by researchers along with the subjects of their research.[20] Is it possible to have an ethics of democracy in the circulation of theories around the world? In other words, is it an ethical duty for a theorist to consider theories and traditions from around the world more equitably? Or will theory continue in its historical trajectory of exclusiveness, where communities and cultures have been kept away from the ambit of theorizing, where non-Western cultures have been denied the capacity of theorizing?[21] Will questions of language be accepted as ethical questions and not merely as instrumental ones? This issue becomes very important for many social-science communities in the non-Western world where mainstream social science has been reduced to a community of English speakers and writers. In a place like India, with its multiplicity of languages, isn't it the ethical imperative of the community to develop and integrate writers in languages other than English? (I am not considering the other problematical question related to the use of another 'language', mathematics, in the social sciences). This is an ethical problem because it is not *right* that a society is only represented and described by a small group of people

[19] Sarukkai (2009b).

[20] Van Mannen (1988).

[21] Gadamer (2001).

drawing upon conceptual categories that may be alien to the experience of the society.

Some might want to rephrase these questions within the frames of sociology and politics of knowledge instead of ethics. Accepting these possibilities, I would still like to suggest that these questions about theorizing are essentially about ethics for two fundamental reasons. The first reason has to do with the *excessive* dependence on theoretical structures produced in the West for theorizing the non-West. Excess is the problem and not the use of ideas from all around the world. And excess is an ethical issue, whether it is the excess of consumption or excess in any human action. (We need to only remember Gandhi at this point). The second reason has to do with representation. As we pointed out in the Introduction, it is the case that there is a great asymmetry between the representations of the non-West by Western scholars and the representations of the West by non-Western scholars. Asymmetries of representation are an ethical problem and have direct consequences on cultural confidence, on pedagogy, on making sense of oneself and one's community, and even on social policies. These consequences have a deleterious effect on a society. Thus, one has to necessarily invoke ethics in the domain of theorizing as a way of responding to the problems of excess and asymmetries.

A final point about these contentious claims: It may well be the case that there are no conceptual and theoretical resources available in the non-Western traditions. Or, worse, it may well be the case that Indian conceptual frameworks, for example, may actually inhibit social theory, particularly critical theory, where one hopes for social transformation along with 'understanding'.[22] This may be true, but sufficient reflection on these possibilities has not been internally generated and thus it would be hasty to come to such conclusions. For instance, this view is often based on the claim that many 'modern' concepts such as democracy, secularism, human rights or even rationality, do not have conceptual correlates in Indian languages. This argument is unfortunately based on a misunderstanding of what it means to translate concepts as against translating words or sentences. It is really not correct to ask what concepts exactly mean;

[22] I thank Uday Kumar for raising this issue, although the way I have expressed it may not reflect his exact sentiments.

one can only ask for the meaning–bearing capacity of concepts.[23] So what is needed is not a search for exact matches but a creative and deconstructive exploration of the capacity of concepts drawn from different cultures. It is after all this very strategy of appropriation and misappropriation of concepts that makes possible the rich theoretical imagination of the academic West.

[23] See Sarukkai (2012).

7

Phenomenology of Untouchability*

Sundar Sarukkai

For many social commentators, the practice of untouchability characterizes the Hindu civilization. But what exactly constitutes this practice? Interestingly, while there have been tomes written on the sociology and politics of this practice, there is little of significance on its philosophical foundations. Such a philosophical reflection is made all the more urgent given the magnitude of the problem and its direct impact on modern Indian society. It is also essential to inquire into these philosophical foundations because once we look at this notion carefully, we find that there are various levels of complexity hidden within it.

Untouchability as a social practice is simple enough to describe. It refers to certain practices of 'higher' castes such as refusing to touch or share water and food with people who have been called the 'untouchables' and who are today collectively called Dalits. These sets of practices involve not only proscriptions on both groups of people but are often justified through notions of purity and related concepts.[1]

---

* A shorter version of this chapter was previously published in 2009 as 'The Phenomenology of Untouchability', *Economic and Political Weekly*, XLIV (37): 39–48.
[1] It is difficult to summarize the characteristics that would define an 'untouchable' in its full generality. The standard accounts that use pollution–purity to define this class run into trouble with many exceptions, both from within that class and outside it. One classification that is more

But what are the philosophical ideas related to the specific practices as also the conceptual world of untouchability? This chapter explores the philosophical foundations of untouchability through an analysis of the phenomenology of touch. The sense of touch is unique in many ways. One such is the essential relation between touch and 'untouch'. Drawing on both Indian and Western traditions, I begin by analysing the meaning of touch and then go on to explore some meanings of 'untouchable'. I will conclude by arguing that since the notion of untouchability is an essential requirement of Brahminhood, the displacement of this characteristic to the untouchables illustrates not just the 'outsourcing' of untouchability but also a philosophical move of supplementation. It is through this process of supplementation that untouchability becomes a positive virtue for the Brahmins and a negative fact for the Dalits.

This chapter can be seen as illustrating, however imperfectly and incompletely, some of the ideas and strategies discussed in the earlier chapter.

THE SENSATION OF TOUCH

To understand the notion of untouchability, it is first necessary to inquire into the nature of touch. Touch is one of the five senses of the human body. While it is often believed that sight is the dominant sense, ancient traditions in different cultures emphasized touch as the most important sense. In particular, and of special importance in the context of untouchability, the Indian traditions considered touch as an important sense; in some schools, touch was the most important sense.

Montagu, in his influential book on touching, considers the importance of the sense of touch, both biologically and culturally.[2] He begins by agreeing with writers who viewed touch as the 'greatest

---

inclusive is as follows: The untouchables in Indian society are those who are '[1] economically dependent and exploited, [2] victims of many kinds of discrimination, and [3] ritually polluted in a permanent way' (Deliege 1999: 2). See also Béteille (1992).

[2] Montagu (1971).

sense' in the body. Touch is what 'gives us our knowledge of depth or thickness and form; we feel, we love and hate, are touchy and are touched, through the touch corpuscles of our skin' (quoted in Montagu 1971: 1). Also, it is the sense that continues to operate even when sight (and the other senses) shuts down during the process of sleeping.

Montagu points out that after the brain the 'skin is the most important of all our organ systems' and the sense of touch is the 'earliest to develop in the human embryo'. Before its eyes or ears are formed, the embryo can respond to touch on its skin. Even in terms of weight, the weight of the skin as a percentage of the total weight of the body is about 19.7 per cent in a newborn and about 17.8 per cent in the adult. If we accept the observation that the earlier a 'function develops the more fundamental it is likely to be', then the skin and the sense of touch are the most basic.

Paradoxically the skin was not studied in great detail until the middle of the twentieth century. Montagu also notes that there is a surprising lack of a role for the skin in poetry, and when found in prose, most often it is associated with pathologies, such as blotches, pimples, and so on. However, there are many metaphors that we commonly use that draw upon the image of touch—such as having a 'touching' experience. Nevertheless, it is true that our common discourse about the skin is most often about its relation with sweating, with images of becoming patchy, peeling off, having pimples, and so on.[3]

Montagu reminds us of another important characteristic of the skin: While we can conceivably learn to live without our other senses, such as seeing and hearing, it is impossible to live without having the sensation of touch. Drawing upon the experience of Helen Keller, he points out that 'when other senses fail, the skin can to an extraordinary degree compensate for their deficiencies'.[4] Even for those who have not lost these senses, there are nevertheless states, such as sleep, where these senses are not involved in conscious acts. However, in sleeping, the skin is constantly in touch with the brain.

[3] For some recent literature on the various aspects of the skin, see Classen (2005) and Connor (2004).

[4] Montagu (1971: 7).

Experiments on animals have shown that newborn babies who are not touched or licked by their mother have a greater mortality rate. As Jablonski notes, the special significance of skin, fingers, and touch was not just to help animals and humans find food but also in creating social bonds.[5] She points out that '[s]ocial animals like primates reinforce bonds between individuals through touch'.[6] Although it was well known that touching nurtures infants, it is also the case that loss of touching can often be fatal for a newborn animal. Infants, including human infants, who are deprived of touch seem to exhibit 'behavioral inadequacies in later life'. It also seems to be the case that for psychological as well as social well-being touch is very important. As Jablonski notes, 'Put simply, the absence of touch equals stress'.[7] Almost any notion of care involves touching. Studies on deprivation of touch in children again illustrate the importance of touch not just in the infant stage but also in childhood. In the case of primates, the sense of touch also plays an important role in conflict resolution. Following conflicts, most communities of animals indulge in ritual touching and this act of touching reassures the individuals involved in the conflict as well as 'restore[s] the social bonds'.[8]

Different cultures have different codes of touching. Jablonski considers the American society an example of a touch-averse culture. One consequence of such aversion is that 'older children and adults suffer from awkwardness in demonstrating physical affection and ineptness in body relationships with others in general',[9] thereby leading to social anomaly and psychological disorders. Thus, it is clear that in both animals and humans, the process of touching is of great importance to their well-being and perhaps even to their survival. Consequences of the process of touching and its primary importance in the development of a human being are often neglected when touch is understood primarily as a sensation. It is here that we see the impact of particular philosophical world views on the significance of touch. Both in the Western and Indian traditions, touch as a sensa-

---

[5] Jablonski (2006).

[6] *Ibid.*, p. 103.

[7] *Ibid.*

[8] *Ibid.*, p. 108.

[9] *Ibid.*, p. 110.

tion has evoked serious discussion. In what follows, I will discuss a few of these ideas briefly in order to set the stage for a more serious engagement with the idea of untouchability.

Aristotle's views on touch have been influential. Aristotle's view on the senses is based on defining senses by reference to sense objects, and in so doing, he follows Plato.[10] As Sorabji points out, while the stress on sense objects is useful, it is not enough. For Aristotle, all objects of touch are reducible to four basic ones: dry and fluid, hot and cold. First of all, Sorabji notes that the objects of touch cannot help us in distinguishing the nature of touch for these objects are varied. Moreover, the objects of touch are often the objects of other sensations also. He then offers two criteria that were used to characterize touch: one is the 'contact criterion' and the other is the 'non-localisation criterion'. Direct contact with a body characterizes touch. In fact, as Sorabji points out, the word for touch in use even now—namely, haptic—carries the meaning of contact and thus touch is through direct contact. In the *De Anima*, Aristotle says that 'all things that we perceive when in contact with them we perceive by touch' and 'what is perceived by touch is directly contacted'.[11] The other senses, such as seeing, hearing, and smell, 'are *never* exercised through direct contact', whereas taste is only exercised thus. Therefore, for Aristotle, taste is a form of touch.

The other criterion of non-localizability can be found in Plato when he classifies objects of touch as those that are 'common to the body as a whole'.[12] Here, contact is not the defining criterion and is reflective of the fact that the organ of touch is spread through the body instead of being localized in the way the eyes, ears, and nose are localized in the body. Sorabji believes that the non-localization criterion continues to influence the popular understanding of touch even in present times.

Paterson makes the point that touch, for Aristotle, was the most basic sense, without which animals would not be able to survive; but Aristotle believed that sight was the most superior sense.[13] Given that

[10] Sorabji (1971: 58).
[11] Quoted in *Ibid.*, p. 70.
[12] *Ibid.*, p. 73.
[13] Paterson (2007).

there is no localized organ like the eye for the sense of touch, Aristotle places the sensory faculty of touch 'within' in the sense of an internal organ.[14] Because of the non-localization of the sense of touch, flesh is considered not as the organ of touch but as the medium, in the way that air is seen as the medium that enables us to hear sound. This is why it seems to be the case that touch is an unmediated sense and that there is really no medium between the senses and the object of perception.

Chrétien also accepts that the sense of touch is the 'most fundamental and universal of all the senses' because the other senses not only depend upon it but the very idea of life is based upon this sense—thus, we have the Aristotelian belief that when an animal is deprived of touch it is also deprived of life.[15] Even the 'first evidence of the soul is the sense of touch'.[16] The living body is primarily a tactile body, and other senses belong not just to the body, but to the tactile body. The Aristotelian idea of the primacy of touch as the central sense in the body means that touch is not only what defines the body but also the very nature of life. Thus, 'through touch, life as such, in its totality, opens itself to the dimensions that constitutes corporeity'.[17] Touch is also connected with intelligence and sensitivity, a point that Aristotle seems to explicitly make.

The distinction between the other senses and touch is based on the observation that the sense of touch is coterminous with the act of touching. This means that there is a particular sense of 'action' associated with touch that is not present, for example, in seeing. Seeing an object in front of me is different from touching it. Obviously the sensations are different as they are different experiences, but more than that, there is a fundamental difference as far as the body is concerned with respect to these two experiences. The other senses might be spectatorial in character whereas touch immerses us in the world, makes possible our very existence in this world.

Aristotle was aware that the sensation of touch hides its essential nature. Contact is one phenomenological experience of touch. We

[14] *Ibid.*, p. 17.
[15] Chrétien (2004).
[16] *Ibid.*, p. 85.
[17] *Ibid.*, p. 93.

touch things when we are in contact with them. The moment of contact is also the act of erasing the distance between us and the object. Touch could be seen as something that erases the distance between the subject and the object, but as Chrétien points out, 'as Aristotle shows, the interval is never abolished, only forgotten'.[18] This means that the interval continues to persist even in the act of touch. This ever-present intervening 'body' constitutes 'an *untouchable* element in touch, a skin or membrane that separates the skin from things but cannot be felt'.[19] Although we might accept that there is a minute layer of something that separates even in the moment of touch, does it really matter? For Aristotle, it does, for it allows him to replace the contrast of contact–distance (which is one common way to describe the nature of touch) with a new set of contrasting terms: near–far. As Chrétien notes, near and far are phenomenological experiences belonging to a subject, unlike categories such as contact and distance.

The most important consequence of this argument is that if we understand touch as contact, we forget the continuing presence of the medium that is essential for any idea of touch. To touch is to move towards an object, to bring surfaces into contact. Therefore, 'to touch is to approach or to be approached'.[20] In the sensation of touch, the distance that characterizes the objects of touch is forgotten and so also the ever-present minute distance between surfaces of contact. Not only is this forgotten, but without the constant recreation of the distance, there is no possibility of sensing touch. We can understand the phenomenological significance of the act of touch in this context. What is the difference between touching a thing and being a part of that thing? Is my hand touching the shoulder joint that it is attached to? Does it touch in the same way that one hand touches another or one hand touches an object? The question of the touching of a part to another part (both of which compose a whole) is different from the touching between two objects. What characterizes this difference—the ever-present space or medium or body between the two objects that are in contact? Touch is more than contact because

[18] *Ibid.*, pp. 87–8.
[19] Chrétien (2004: 88, italics mine).
[20] *Ibid.*

of the ever-present, ineradicable space between the objects of touch. It is this manipulation of this intervening medium that constitutes the different textures of touch. It is also this ever-present medium that is *untouchable* in the act of touch. Thus, the idea of untouchability is always present, always contiguous to the act of touch. The notion of untouchability is all the more interesting because we are always in the process of touching even when we do not act to touch. Even in sleep, as mentioned earlier, we are constantly in touch.

But is the notion of contact so clear? Do we know really what we mean by contact? Should contact be defined as physical contact? The Indian views on contact and touch offer a different set of possibilities to understand these terms. First of all, there is in general a clear distinction made between touch (*sparśa*) and contact (*saṁyoga*). Moreover, touch is a quality of substances.[21] What is the nature of qualities? Qualities are those that inhere only in substances, are not in contact with anything, and have something inhering in them.

Material substances have finite dimension, are capable of motion, and are defined in terms of contact. One standard classification of the nine primary substances includes five that are material and four that are not. The five are earth, water, fire, air, and the internal organs; the four immaterial are time, spatial direction, *ākāśa*, and selves. Touch is a quality of substances; contact is another quality. Each of these four substances—earth, water, fire, and air—has its own unique qualities. Earth is the unique locus of smell and water of cold touch. Similarly, fire is the substance whose quality is hot touch.

The Nyāya-Vaiśeṣika[22] categorization views the body as an entity, excluding the sense organs. The body is seen as the 'locus of the sense organs'.[23] The body is the locus of motions caused by the self (in that body). Also, pains and pleasures associated with organs are experienced in the body and not in the senses.[24] Each sense organ is composed exclusively of one of the five elements: smell of earth, taste of water, touch of air, sight of fire, and hearing of ether. Because of

[21] Datta (2008: 130).

[22] Vaiśeṣika is a philosophical tradition closely aligned with Nyaya but distinct from it also.

[23] Datta (2008).

[24] See also Bhattacharya (2008: 165).

this unique constitution, the objects of perception have to be those that are either entirely or mostly composed of the element associated with that perception—so we need fire (light) to see, and so on. Furthermore, for the Naiyāyikas, the sense organs are the ones that are found on the body, but they are imperceptible.

Touch is a *guna*, a quality, like taste, smell, and contact.[25] What is the difference between touch and contact? One is locus-pervading and the other is not. When a monkey is in contact with a tree it is in contact only with those parts of the tree and those parts of itself which are in mutual contact. (The idea of touch seems to be locus-pervading in that all parts of the locus are pervaded by the sense of touch, although this comment should be qualified). Touch is a quality only for earth, water, fire and air whereas contact is a quality for all the nine substances including ākāśa, time, place, self, and internal organ. Furthermore, touch is perceived only through one sense organ but contact can be by two sense organs. Also, contact produces a variety of qualities including pleasure, pain, aversion, merit and demerit. However, touch does not produce these which contact does.

In the context of untouchability, what exactly is the role played by these two different qualities of touch and contact? The notion of contact is much broader than that of touch. Contact is a quality that inheres in a pair of substances. This means that contact is a quality that is present in the 'toucher' and the 'touched'. If two bodies are in contact with each other, then that contact is a symmetrical relation—each body is in contact with the other. However, in the case of touch, there seems to be an asymmetry since the person who touches is at the same time not being touched by the object. So when I say I am touching a chair, I do not at the same time say the chair is touching me (although Merleau-Ponty would disagree!). Touch in this sense is a specific human sense, unlike contact, which is a specific kind of relation between any two entities.

Indian philosophical schools clarify the relation of sense to the objects of sense in various ways. Vaiśeṣika classifies qualities into twenty-four kinds: touch and quality are among them. But there is one fundamental difference between them. Contact is a quality that

---

[25] Guna as 'quality' is one imperfect translation of 'guna', imperfect since gunas are not repeatable like qualities are, for example.

belongs to all kinds of substance, both material and soul substances.[26] Touch is a quality that belongs only to material substances. Touch is perceived by the tactile organ and is found in four of the five primary substances, namely, in earth, water, fire, and air. The differentiation of touch into cold, hot, and neither cold nor hot helps to distinguish the kind of touch in these substances. A response to the question as to whether rough and smoothness are also kinds of touch illustrates the difference between touch and contact: The response is that hardness and softness 'are not varieties of touch' but of contact[27], and they are varieties of contact because they are perceivable by the visual organ also, in addition to being perceived by the tactile organ. So in this example we can see that touch is a limited form of contact, one that is detectable by the tactile organ alone. As we saw earlier, contact belongs to all substances and is perceived not just by the tactile but by the other organs also. Another difference is that contact is a relation and needs at least two substances whereas touch is a quality that is present in an individual substance.

Moreover, there are many different types of contact—the Advaitins describe six types of contact.[28] First is saṁyoga, contact of an object with the sense organ. Visual perception of an object arises from its contact with the sense of sight. The second is samyuka tādātmya, 'contact with an object that is in contact with the sense organ', for example, perception of the colour of an object (the colour that is in contact with an object, which is in contact with the sense organ). Another type is the 'identity of generic nature of colour with the colour itself', which is about the nature of colour in the colour of an object, and so on.

Given the semantic complexity of contact and touch, we can see a potential problem in the use of the English word 'touch', which in common usage often refers to some idea of contact. In our understanding of untouchability, the contact with a person who is untouchable is what is seen to be defiling. But for this to be possible touch becomes a *quality that inheres in the object*. This means that the untouchable manifests the sense of 'untouch' within the person,

---

[26] Datta (2008: 123).

[27] *Ibid.*, p. 131.

[28] Gupta (1995: 223).

whether or not the person comes in contact with another person. We can thus begin to see how the notion of untouchability gets carried into the ontology of a sense because of these different interpretations of contact and touch.

Moreover, the physiological description of the body and the senses in these traditions should make us question any naïve reading of touch. For example, for a medical tradition like Āyurveda, the model of the body was much more complex than understood now in biology. Suśruta, the famous surgeon of ancient times, classified the body into seven layers of skin. If the skin is the organ of touch, as we understand it now, then which of these layers of skin are actually involved in the experience of touch? To compound this problem further, proponents of Sāṁkhya and Advaita Vedānta, describe the body in terms of both a gross body (*sthūla śarīra*) as well as a subtle body (*sūkṣma śarīra*).[29]

Even the sense organs are not to be taken in the way we understand the biological eye, tongue, skin, and so on. In Āyurveda, the sense organs—which are the usual ear, nose, eye, tongue, and skin—are only 'external appendages' and are merely the 'seats of organs and not the subtle organs themselves'.[30] That is, the sense organs are themselves made of 'subtle material' and the visible skin is only the seat of the cognitive sense organ corresponding to touch. Since the sense organs are subtle, in death they leave the body and it is the gross material body that decomposes. This means that the qualities associated with these sense organs are not restricted to the gross physical body, because of which these characteristics continue to endure with the subtle body. The implications of such views should not be forgotten. For example, belief in the continuation of characteristics in the subtle body would explain the hereditary nature of untouchability. What this discussion alerts us to is the need to employ much wider categories in order to make sense of the notion of untouchability. Given that Indian philosophical views were reflected in social order in various ways, it will be useful to first of all interpret untouchability through categories specific to Indian cultural and philosophical traditions.

[29] Bhattacharya (2008: 165).
[30] Gupta (2008: 211).

INTERPRETING UNTOUCHABILITY IN THE INDIAN CONTEXT

The senses, the body, and their relation to the world are described quite differently in the many Indian traditions. To engage with the phenomenology of untouchability, it is necessary to explore the various nooks and corners of these discourses. In so doing, various interesting possibilities arise. In the earlier section, we saw how the view of the body, including the seven layers of skin, the distinction between gross and subtle bodies, the different qualities of touch and contact can all contribute to a more complex understanding of untouchability. I will discuss some of these possible approaches in this section.

Let me first begin with the skin, since the skin is seen as the organ of touch in both the Western and Indian traditions. The first problem arises when we consider the nature of the skin. How is the skin described and understood in classical Indian traditions?

The skin has an important function, that of encompassing and enclosing. It is intrinsically related to boundaries and surfaces. Glucklich uses these characteristics to make an insightful reading of dharma. He finds an inherent relation between dharma and skin since both of them have been symbolically conceived as a boundary, with dharma as a 'fence of propriety, or a boundary for proper conduct'.[31] The fact that the boundaries are sensed by the body in a particular way—namely, the way the body recognizes what constitutes a boundary—implies, for Glucklich, that 'dharma can actually be touched'!

The above narrative about the skin illustrates the complexity of its relation with touch. As mentioned earlier, there are seven layers of skin (although it is also said that there are between three to seven layers) that 'are replicated in Hindu mythology and in village folklore, with the seven layers of the earth'.[32] The symbolism and mythology surrounding the skin, along with the theory of karma, suggest a reason for the view that the 'skin is a primary register of the fruition of sins committed in previous births'.[33] Glucklich identifies two fundamental metaphors related to the human body: one of the

[31] Glucklich (1994: 90).
[32] *Ibid.*, p. 98.
[33] *Ibid.*, p. 99.

body as a 'microcosmic reflection of the world' (*Suśrutasaṁhitā*) and the other as a 'self-enclosed space' in an antagonistic relation with the world (*Rg Veda*). The first conception considers the skin in a spatio-cosmological sense. Along with this is the 'temporal metaphor of the skin as a map of character and moral disposition'.[34] While Glucklich considers these views as explaining certain traits of treatment in the Indian medical systems, I want to explore the relevance of these views to the question of untouchability.

When looked at from the point of medicine and cure, there are rich interpretations of the body and the skin, particularly the belief that health and disease reflect a balance between the exterior and the interior. The organ that makes possible this differentiation of the interior and exterior is the skin. Thus, the skin 'becomes the primary organ of relation, and touch is its principal action'.[35] The influence of the symbolic understanding of the skin and the various narratives associated with it should not be underestimated. Tactility is not just a sense of the body but a way of being in the world. It allows us to orient ourselves in the world in very specific ways. The skin is the literal way into the world. Thus Glucklich's observation that the 'experience of the skin in the world simultaneously places the world—experientially, not symbolically—upon the skin'.[36] This is much more true in the Indian cultural experience, based partly perhaps on the way that skin and tactility are understood. The example of river bathing and the analyses of some central myths all suggest this possibility.

There are myths that suggest that the skin actually captures the essence of the individual. The myth about the exchange of skins between cows and men shows how the mere exchange of skins allows a complete reversal of action—in this case, reversing the skins allows men to eat cows. So when men and cow exchange skins, they are not only exchanging their 'outer wear but also their places in the food chain—a clear mark of identity' leading to the observation that 'it is almost as though the skin is the source of the animal, its defining quality (more than its flesh or bones)'.[37] Another interesting aspect

[34] *Ibid.*, p. 100.
[35] *Ibid.*, p. 107.
[36] *Ibid.*
[37] *Ibid.*, p. 110.

of the skin is the independent force it stands for when used in an instrument like the drum: the skin 'takes a life of its own' when used in this manner.

One way to understand the significance of the skin is by realizing that the way we move in the world, the way we relate to it, makes us what we are. But how we relate to the world is mediated by the gateway of the skin. The skin is literally a boundary. The importance of the idea of boundary in Indian thought is manifested in the narratives of frames, doors, walls of homes and temples, and so on. In this context, walls function like a boundary and doors are a way to move from the inside to the outside. Glucklich explicitly notes the connection between skin and wall when he notes that 'walls, much like the human skin, possess reflective, transitive, and temporal characteristics'.[38]

There are some important insights regarding untouchability that we can draw from this brief encounter with the complex narratives of the skin, the senses, and the body. The practice of untouchability has to do with a boundary that cannot be crossed. The interpretation of dharma as boundary allows the Indian mind to invoke the idea of dharma in the context of untouchability. Most importantly, it is only the skin that can do this job. That is, if morality in some sense is to be ascribed to untouchability, then it can only be done if they share a common characteristic—in this case, the character of a boundary. In other words, it could be because of these complex world views underlying body, sense, world, and dharma that untouchability is chosen as the vehicle for transmitting specific moral or dharmic dictums. The many different properties of the skin cohere together to establish the nature of untouchability: The skin as the defining quality of a person means that a person whose skin is untouchable is himself an untouchable (note the change from an adjective to a noun in this process, the creation of a kind of people from an adjectival property of skin); the skin as a 'map of character and moral disposition' again illustrates how an untouchable's skin embodies certain moral properties; once untouchability is inscribed on an individual, then the impossibility of crossing the wall of untouchability. All these explain why it is touch that is chosen as the primary sense in any such act of

[38] *Ibid.*, p. 131.

exclusion and proscription.[39] Proscribing touch is not only biologically and psychologically the most damaging but it is also the only way that matches a much larger narrative of untouchability and this narrative, contrary to most accounts, is not really about the pure and impure as much as it is about the metaphysics of the body.

We have already seen one aspect of this metaphysics. The Nyāya view that the body is the locus of the senses means that the body feels through the senses. The Buddhist view of the body is also important here, especially in the context of untouchability. One reason is that the Buddhists were the ones who rejected the Brahminical outlook towards individuals, society, and gods. The other reason is that, following Ambedkar, Buddhism has become the shelter for many Dalits. As mentioned earlier, the body has often been used as a metaphor for the world. For the Buddha, the body was indeed the world, in that it is within the body that there is the arising and ceasing of the world.[40] The belief in the impurity of the body in the Buddhist tradition seems to be all-pervading. Right from birth to death, the body is the site of impurity of various kinds. For example, in the *Ta-chih-tu Lun*, a compendium of Mādhyamika philosophy, most attention is given to the application of the mindfulness of the body.[41] Five impurities of the body are identified: the womb, the seed, the body's nature, the body's characteristics, and the corpse. Right from birth to death, impurity is what characterizes the human body.

As Lang notes, for the Buddhists, understanding the body is important because it also helps to understand 'how human beings remain trapped within them'.[42] One way to understand the body is to focus on the body during meditation: for example, to focus on the activities of breathing. Lang points out that such a meditative dissection of the body, being mindfully aware of the body and its constituents, eliminates the belief in self-identity. For example, meditation on a corpse will illustrate the nature of impermanence, impurity, and pain associated with the body. In such practices, two

---

[39] Although there is also the unseen (see Ambedkar 1979), the force of untouchability lies specifically in the act of touch.

[40] Lang (2003: 24).

[41] *Ibid.*, p. 27.

[42] *Ibid.*, p. 25.

important things happen: one, the negation of the self and, two, the recognition that one's own body is the site or locus of impurity. In a world view such as this, it is impossible to place the burden of impurity on another human body while appropriating a discourse of purity for one's own body. There is no possibility of supplementation that becomes the hallmark of untouchability (more on this later). In this sense, the metaphysics of Buddhism is indeed one that negates the metaphysics of untouchables.

A phenomenology of the body makes us realize that the body is conceptually grasped by us not in terms of experience such as inner and outer but as something enclosed by a skin, as a unity and as 'ours'. As Glucklich notes, the presence of pollution entails that the body has first of all been 'self-appropriated'—this means that ideas of pollution, sin, and defilement are to be understood within this self-understanding of the body, that is, the 'existential conditions of perception and basic cognition' are required to understand these terms.[43] In the case of the untouchable, if the skin is what is defiled, if touch is defiled, then the impurity is not just in the body but it is the body itself. What the phenomenology of untouchability tells us is that this unity of the body is what is lost to the untouchable when shunned by the touch of others.

One of the most important consequences is the recognition that the body is the site of ethics as much as it is the site of action. Glucklich argues that the narratives about boundary crossers, such as thieves and lovers, are understandable if we recognize that the 'very nature of dharma as a worldview [is] built by means of the body'.[44] This, along with ideas of the self, creates an ambiguous response to boundary crossers. There are two issues that should interest us here: the encoding of ethical action (although note that Glucklich does not use dharma as synonymous with morality) and the relation of ethics to the body. The latter is reflected in embodied cognitive accounts, particularly those of Varela, who argues that ethics consists not in reflection but in action.[45] His exemplar of such ethical action is the

---

[43] Glucklich (1994: 20).

[44] *Ibid.*, p. 9.

[45] Varela (1999).

Buddhist one, where again the issue of dharma is central. In the context of untouchability, the relation between ethics and the body becomes very important. The above discussion might also help explain why there is so much ambiguity about the untouchables in literary and other narratives. For example, there are examples of untouchable saints even in orthodox traditions. The ambiguity about these people is the ambiguity towards boundary crossers, the ambiguity that arises when morality is always viewed in contexts (as Indian ethics is often seen to do).

In fact, I believe that it is possible to interpret this complexity by considering touch not as a mere physical sense but as a *'moral sense'*. This might sound a bit odd in the first instance, but we need to look at our categories a bit more carefully when we consider concepts in Indian philosophy. It is well known that the categories of Western thought are not isomorphic with Indian ones and that distinct Western categories do not remain so in the Indian view—note how categories such as logic and epistemology, metaphysics and epistemology, metaphysics and ethics do not remain distinct and separate in the Indian systems.[46] So when Glucklich makes the important point that natural and moral concepts are interrelated (if not identical) in Hinduism, it should be of no surprise. The implication of this is that natural 'dirt' gets related to moral 'dirt'. Or those who are morally 'impure' also embody this impurity in their natural body. Thus, in literary descriptions of the Candālas, they are described as 'deformed, foul smelling and ugly',[47] these are characteristics that reflect and add to the notion of impurity associated with that community.

Something as universal as 'water' has different significations in these traditions. Glucklich notes that in the Western tradition, water was seen to be associated with 'dissolving', but in Indian traditions only hot water is dissolving but cold water is 'form-giving' and not 'form-dissolving'.[48] It is important to reflect on these differences particularly because cold and hot are sensations of touch. Such complex readings have to be extracted if we want to understand untouchability in the Indian context. Continuing with water, we

[46] See Sarukkai (2005).
[47] Glucklich (1994: 66).
[48] *Ibid.*, p. 70.

can note other important ways of understanding common acts such as bathing. First of all, there are three different types of bathing—obligatory, occasional, and voluntary—and in all of them there are two dimensions of bathing. One is physical cleaning, which is utilitarian and 'visible', and the other is 'invisible' and has a transcendent dimension.[49] In other words, the physical act of bathing and pouring water on oneself is completely endowed with various hidden symbolisms and these symbolisms should not be read on the surface. For example, the use of mud and cow dung to clean the body would not be seen today as an example of having a clean bath but these are the prescribed norms of bathing in the classical texts as well as folk practices.

In this example, there is another hidden significance about touch itself. Bathing is to be in contact with water but the act of touch is not circumscribed by this physical contact. Contact is always more than the physical one. There are different modes present in every single physical contact—one that is the physical, of course, but one that is more, a transcendent dimension. The use of language and the invocation of words and chants as part of the bathing process suggest the transcendent contact of the body and words (or sounds, or language). This means that the perpetual gap characterizing touch that leads to the aporia for Aristotle is also the one that causes complex theories of perception, touch, and action in Indian thought. Given that the touch or contact of a body with something else has more than the physical dimension, we can consider the possibility that untouchability is not really about the physical touching but is part of the other sphere inherent in touch. Given that the semantic world of 'water' is also correspondingly rich, it should not be a great surprise to note the organic relation between untouchability and water.

UNTOUCHABLE IN THE TOUCH

The idea of the untouchable is essential to the notion of touch. Through the many traditions, whether Greek or Indian or contem-

[49] *Ibid.*, p. 72.

porary Western philosophical ones, we are often confronted with this paradox of the sense of touch. To understand the nature of untouchability, we first have to begin with this paradox.

There is something special to the activity of touching and being touched, both as actions of the body as well as the experiences associated with them. One can take the view that being touched is fundamentally different from touching another object. In the first case, being touched is about the body-as-object, as Sartre describes in his *Being and Nothingness*; and touching is an act of the body-as-subject.[50] For Sartre, both these modes are fundamentally different. Such a process is common to other senses: Seeing and being seen are two different modes; similarly, smelling and being smelt.

Merleau-Ponty critiques Sartre's argument that these two modes are 'two essentially different orders of reality'. Sartre's view continues to maintain the duality between body-as-subject and body-as-object. For Merleau-Ponty, there is something special about touch that negates this duality. In his earlier formulation, he argues that there is an 'essential ambiguity' in which the 'touched hand feels itself touching and *vice versa*'.[51]

Merleau-Ponty introduces the new idea of reversibility in his *The Visible and the Invisible*.[52] As Dillon notes, 'the basic model of reversibility is that of one hand touching another'.[53] In the case of one hand touching another, there is a unity in touching and touched. Although there is no identity of the touching and the touched hand, this process 'opens' the body 'in two'. Merleau-Ponty uses this analysis to argue for the notion of 'identity-within-difference' in the sense that the touching hand is different from the touched hand (although both 'belong' to the same body).[54]

The process of touching an object 'outside' the body is to be understood on similar lines as the touched–touching hands. This model of identity-within-difference is essential for making sense of the process of touching the objects in the world. First of all, we can

[50] Sartre (1993).
[51] Dillon (1997: 158).
[52] Merleau-Ponty (1968).
[53] Dillon (1997).
[54] See Sarukkai (2002).

touch other objects because we share with them or can be identified with them because of the fact that we are corporeal, like the objects. The experience of being touched while touching—as it occurs in the case of one hand touching another—is not restricted to self-touching. Such an experience occurs even in the case of touching the objects in the world. Merleau-Ponty moves to the position of saying that when I touch a tree, I am also touched by it. This reversibility is not the same as the experience of one hand touching another, but nevertheless it describes the fundamental phenomenology of touching.

Merleau-Ponty considers seeing as being similar to touching: 'Since the same body sees and touches, visible and tangible belong to the same world...'[55] This does not imply that sense and touch are the 'same'. The essential implication of such a view of reversibility of vision and touch is that we can touch what we see and vice versa. It does not mean that one sense can replace another. The implication of this thesis as far as touch is concerned is the insistence that 'to touch something is also and necessarily to be touched by it'.[56]

Merleau-Ponty extends this touching–'being touched' to sight, thus suggesting that to see is also to be seen. Seeing a tree is to be seen by a tree. On the face of it, this claim might sound absurd but it is not so when we understand what we mean by saying that we are seen by the tree. As Dillon points out, the model for being seen by the tree is akin to the way a mirror sees the object. When I see a tree, I am at the same time being seen by the tree. When I stand in front of a mirror, I am at the same time seen by the mirror in the sense that the mirror makes me visible. It is the mirror that renders my visibility to my perceptual sense; without this I do not see myself. The mirror allows me to see myself in a very specific manner. It is this manner that explains how the trees see me when I see them or, in fact, how I am touched when I touch an object. Thus, 'the trees and the mirror function as Other'.[57]

This notion of reversibility makes it possible to understand the relation between the self and the other. Just as much as there is a

---

[55] Merleau-Ponty (1968: 177 fn).
[56] *Ibid.*, p. 161.
[57] *Ibid.*, p. 162.

reversal in the roles of touching and touched, so too is there a reversal between the self and the other. In that sense, the 'Other functions as my mirror', which means that the self can take up the other's vantage point without coinciding with the other.

Merleau-Ponty moves towards the idea of the untouchable following the analysis of touching and touched. Consider the example of my right hand touching my left. My body is involved in two processes simultaneously in this case: it is touching as well as experiencing the feeling of being touched. We might think that this is so because we tend to believe that there is a unity to the body, that the same body experiences both these acts of touching and being touched. However, for Merleau-Ponty, these processes cannot be coincident. Nor does it mean that they coincide in the mind or consciousness. What and where does this possibility of this simultaneous experience reside, if not in the body or in consciousness? For Merleau-Ponty, it resides in the 'untouchable'.

To touch and touch oneself... They do not coincide in the body: the touching is never exactly the touched. This does not mean that they coincide 'in the mind' or at the level of 'consciousness'. Something else than the body is needed for the junction to be made: it takes place in the *untouchable*. That of the other which I will never touch. But I will never touch, he does not touch either... it is therefore not the *consciousness* that is the untouchable... The untouchable is not a touchable in fact inaccessible—the unconscious is not a representation in fact inaccessible.[58]

This idea of the untouchable captures an essential mark of the act of touching. Merleau-Ponty extends this to the other senses also: the untouchable is also the invisible as it occurs in the context of seeing. The visible (touchable) and the invisible (untouchable) are in a reversible relation and in a fundamental sense, it is the invisible (untouchable) that grounds the visibility (touchability) of the world: 'it is the invisible *of* this world, that which inhabits this world, sustains it, and renders it visible'.[59] Underlying this is the idea that the invisible illuminates the visible: For example, as Dillon notes, 'the

[58] *Ibid.*, p. 254.
[59] *Ibid.*, p. 151.

invisible ideality of language illumine[s] the world and make[s] its
intelligibility apparent'.[60]

Derrida draws upon some of these ideas of Merleau-Ponty in
his idiosyncratic journey into the theme of touching. Following
Aristotle, Derrida identifies four aporias related to touch.[61] First is
the problem of whether touch 'is a single sense or a group of senses'.
Associated with this is the question about the organ of touch—is it
the flesh or is the flesh merely the medium of touch whose organ is
'farther inward'? Secondly, just like sound is the object of hearing,
what is the object of touch? Third is the problem of non-locality of
the sense of touch and, related to it, its relation to touching (tasting)
through the tongue—equivalently, the aporia is that the objects of
touch are both tangible and intangible. Fourthly, there is the sense
of immediacy related to touch and contact that distinguishes it from
other senses, such as sight, where we can perceive across a distance.
Furthermore, for Aristotle, touch or the tactile faculty is only potential and not actual. For Aristotle, touch cannot be dispensed with,
although all other senses can. The loss of this sense brings about
death—'touching, then, is a question of life and death'.[62] Also, excess
touch kills animals. Derrida extends this to point to the need for a
moderation of touch, a command such as 'thou shall not touch too
much' and so on, as the first law of prohibition. Ritual prohibitions,
he says, comes after this proscription.

The sense of touch is that which allows our conceptualization
of the body. While the relation between touch and body has been
discussed in terms of action, motility, and so on, Kant's argument
about conceptualization is somewhat different. For Kant (in the
Anthropology from a Pragmatic Point of View), touch is the most
important of the three objective senses—namely, touch, sight, and
hearing. It is the one that brings greatest certainty, and importantly
acts as the foundation for the other two objective ones. Sight and
hearing must 'originally be referred' to touch to 'produce empirical
knowledge'. Such a tradition, according privilege to touch, continues
even in Husserl. Derrida notes that for Kant, it is easy to find the

---

[60] Dillon (1997: 171).
[61] Derrida (2005).
[62] *Ibid.*, p. 47.

signification of touch since the hand (fingers and fingertips) is the essential 'organ' of touch—thus the enquiry is of the 'phenomenal experience of the hand'.[63] Also, for Kant, as for Heidegger and many others, animals do not possess anything like the hand: 'Nature seems to have endowed man alone with this organ so that he is enabled to form a concept of a body by touching it on all sides. The antennae of insects seem merely to show the presence of an object; they are not designed to explore its form'.[64] Thus, the hand through the sense of touch enables us to form the concept of a body. In a sense, this is a mechanism to embody the self who explores with the hand. This embodiment is of crucial importance as far as existing in the world is concerned. When untouchables are refused this capacity of exploration through touch, there is a fundamental gap in the way they conceive of themselves and of others.

There are two aspects of the untouchable in Derrida's book that are useful for exploring the nature of untouchability. First, Derrida suggests an intriguing relation between the untouchable and law. He makes this connection by beginning with 'tact'. In the notion of tact, he discovers the first notion of a law: 'the law is always a law of tact'.[65] The play on 'tact' is a typical play of ideas by Derrida. In our common usage, tact means, among other things, to be considerate, to hesitate. 'Tact' is also hidden in the 'tactile'. Tact is not to do something that one might be able to do or might want to do. To be tactful is to hold back—but hold what back? For Derrida, tact is something like 'touch without touching'. He goes on to add that in touching, 'touching is forbidden: do not touch or tamper with the thing itself, do not touch on what there is to touch. Do not touch what remains to be touched, and first of all law itself—which is the untouchable, *before* all the ritual prohibitions that this or that religion or culture may impose on touching'.[66] Derrida's concern with touch here arises from proscriptions such as those relating to touching another person, say a person of the opposite sex or somebody else's spouse. What is the notion of untouchable here? If I am tactless, I may just reach out and grab a

[63] *Ibid.*, p. 41.
[64] Quoted in *Ibid.*, p. 42.
[65] *Ibid.*, p. 66.
[66] *Ibid.*

person I do not know. Why is this tactile response tactless? Because I do not respect—I do not respect the law that separates us, the law of tact, and not just the person who is the object of my touch. The untouchable here is the law (of tact) and not the other person, for I could replace that person but I would still respect the law.

This Derridean reading of the untouchable is illuminating and also points to a difference with the practice of untouchability in the Indian context. For Derrida, the untouchable is understood with respect to a 'law', one that is not imposed by religion or culture but present in the very act of touching. The law is one that is governed by a sense of tact understood as 'knowing how to touch *without* touching, without touching *too much*'.[67] The tradition from which Derrida engages with untouchability is one that still privileges the individual, that still allows an autonomous agent to make choices about behaviours related to touching. Thus, the untouchable is part of the complex of ideas related to abstinence (a self-imposition), of respect, of codes, and so on. Derrida wants to suggest that there is a domain of the untouchable before any such act of an agent, something inherent in touch itself. The examples he gives are also illustrative of the agency involved: 'Not to touch the friend ... to not *touch him* enough is to be lacking in tact; however, *to touch him*, and to touch him too much, to touch him to the quick, is also tactless'.[68]

The problem about tact here is a problem about freedom, choice, and inability to decide how to act. So also acts of caressing are special acts of touching that are very different from the acts of 'touching/untouching' associated with untouchability. In the case of a caress, the situation is more complicated: Derrida seems to agree with Levinas that a caress is not reducible to the type of contact, to the specific modalities of touch. Levinas notes that 'what is caressed is not touched'.[69] Derrida also suggests that Merleau-Ponty's invocation of the untouchable is similar in that there is always the untouchability of the other. However, in these cases, untouchability seems to be synonymous with a gap. It only seems to say that a touch is not complete; that there are enduring gaps. So a caress, however tender

[67] *Ibid.*, p. 67.
[68] *Ibid.*, p. 75.
[69] *Ibid.*, p. 77.

it may be, still does not grasp or touch the other entirely. But this incompleteness is not the idea of the untouchable in the Indian context. Untouchability is not to be understood as 'incompleteness' of any kind here.

There are different ways of characterizing the difference between the way phenomenologists in the Western tradition have invoked the idea of untouchability and the practice of untouchability in the Indian context. One is that the meanings of the untouchable in the former case range from not being proper objects of touch (such as a concept or a law) to ever-present incompleteness and so on. Also, these examples assume the centrality of the autonomous subject. But in the case of untouchability as a practice, the impulse against touching is situated within the 'object', the untouchable person.

Perhaps one could extend these observations as follows. What is the difference in the untouchablility practised in not touching another man's wife as against not touching an untouchable person in Indian society? If seen in terms of proscriptions, then both can be seen to be part of a larger code of conduct imposed on the members of a society. However, there is a fundamental philosophical difference in these two acts. If both are consequences of a law, then they are in principle similar; but the untouchable that Derrida discovers is the untouchability of the law itself. Moreover, the wide range of activities that falls under touching—which has been extensively listed by Jean-Luc Nancy, including grazing, striking, stroking, pinching, biting, kneading, embracing, and so on—needs an analysis that is not offered in philosophical discussions on touch.

There is an immediate and obvious difference between touch and non-touch. There are different kinds of touch, as we saw above, but there is only one sense of not-touching. That is, whether we not-strike or not-stroke, there is no difference. The difference that is present in the many different types of touching gets erased when we consider the non-touch. Why? What is it about non-touch that all the distinctions that characterize the different types of touch vanish? It is in this particular act that one should situate untouchability. It is in this space that the Indian conception of untouchability should be seen. The way such a difference is negated—paradoxically—is by making non-touch itself a sense! Untouchability unifies all these diverse elements of touch and in this sense serves as a foundation of touch. Without the notion of the untouchable, there is no way to unify all these phenomenological actions as belonging to the sense of touch.

How do we understand a sense? If we refer back to our earlier discussion, we will see that 'objects of sense' were often the defining markers of sense. There are different objects of senses. In fact, this is one reason why philosophers (both in Indian and Western traditions) argue for the existence of many senses. (In particular, this is the argument against one view in Nyāya that touch is the only sense).[70] The point about non-touch or in general non-sense is that there are no clearly defined objects of these senses. The Western philosophers' reference to untouchability is not in terms of objects of non-touch. However, in the Indian context, the creation of untouchables as a category precisely does this job of creating a discursive set of objects—and these are objects of the sense of the non-touch or un-touch. Therefore, just as there are objects of vision and hearing, there are objects specific to the sense of un-touch—these are the untouchables.

PHENOMENOLOGY OF UNTOUCHABILITY

If non-touch is a 'sense', then we need to seriously consider the possibility of a phenomenology of the sense of non-touch or the untouched. The difficulty in framing a 'name' for this sense illustrates the problems with this 'sense'. One way to engage with the question as to whether there is a non-touch 'sense', which is not a non-sense, is to identify the objects of this sense. It will be my contention that the construction of the class of untouchables actually creates objects of this sense of non-touch. Thus, primarily the creation of the class of untouchables is a creation not of a set of people with some characteristics but a set of objects of the sense of non-touch. This constructed set of objects of sense allows us to enter into a phenomenology of untouchability. The starting point of such an inquiry must therefore begin with the nature of untouchable objects, since it is clear

[70] See also Chakrabarti (1992) and Jha (1984).

that the untouchables are but one special class of objects that are untouchable.

The most important characteristic of the untouchables is our recognition that they are potentially open to touch but yet are objects of non-touch. Untouchable is different from unseeable or untasteable, and this is another reason why there is a sense of non-touch. In the case of non-touch, there indeed are many objects of non-touch just as there are objects of non-sight. Space and time are two entities that are both untouchable and unseeable.[71] There are many other entities that are not objects of touch, but in the way I have formulated the objects of non-touch, it is easy to see that such entities are not objects of non-touch even though they are not objects of touch. Thus, merely not being objects of touch is not enough to make something objects of non-touch. Space, time, God, properties, and so on are not objects of touch but they do not become objects of non-touch. Thus they are not objects of the sense of non-touch and in this sense are not untouchables. There is another class of objects of sense that appear to be untouchable. For example, very far objects that we can see are untouchable, as are mirror images. And so is a stranger—especially if this person is of the opposite sex, then s/he is untouchable in most contexts but is not *an* untouchable.

The relation between the untouched and the divine also leads to a consideration of the untouchable. We can go back to Derrida's analysis of touch, where he makes an explicit connection between touch, salvation, and the divine. He notes that 'one can take the Gospels for a *general haptics*'.[72] The idea of salvation present in this religious tradition allows Derrida to recollect the relation between touching and salvation. Hence, salvation 'saves by touching, and the Savior, namely the Toucher, is also touched: he is saved, safe, unscathed, and free of damage. Touched by grace'.[73] Jesus is the toucher who saves through touch. He heals a leper by touching him, heals the blind by touching their eyes, gives the ability to speak to a deaf-mute man by

[71] As far as space and time are concerned, there have been different claims on the possibility of sensing space, ranging from Berkeley's view that it can be touched to the Nyāya view that it can be heard.

[72] Derrida (2005: 100).

[73] *Ibid.*

touching him on his tongue, and raises a dead person by touching the coffin. Derrida argues that it is not only his touching but the fact that he can be touched that is important—or at least that something of his (which has been in contact with him) can be touched. Derrida seems to draw away from this equation between salvation and physical touch when he claims that it 'is not the touch that is saving, then, but the faith that this touch signifies and attests'.[74]

He goes on to say that although these are the descriptions in the books of Mathew and Luke, the gospel according to John has no reference to these touchings. Derrida suggests that this is due to the fact that 'Jesus becomes momentarily *untouchable*'.[75] This example points to the importance of salvation through touch, one that has interesting resonance in the medical profession today! Haptotherapy is a growing field.[76] But the interesting question in this context is why do gods give salvation only through touch? Why didn't Jesus *say* I cure you of your blindness? Or why was his sight, his mere presence, or his mere wish or thought not enough? Why the touch? In the context of the untouchables, the relation between salvation and touch is most pronounced for the only way of salvation that is allowed to these objects of non-touch is when they are touched. That is, in the discourse of these objects, touch is the only mode of salvation. Here is an interesting reversal between what happens to Jesus and what happens in the creation of the untouchables.

The very idea of untouchability has many nested notions within it, such as the notions related to impossibility, what ought to be, negation, inability, and so on. At the most basic level, the notion of untouchability involves the possibility of touching and untouching. We say that a dish is untouched when the dish is in front of me and I do not touch it. I do not say that the dish is untouchable because if there is nothing that stops me potentially from touching the dish, then it is open to my touch if I so desire. So the untouchable is not the untouched, although those who are untouchables are also those who are forever untouched. But it is important that the word captures the potential inherent in that continued rejection. That is, it is not that

---

[74] *Ibid.*, p.101.

[75] *Ibid.*, p. 102; italics mine.

[76] See, for example, Leder and Krucoff (2008).

the untouchables cannot be touched but that they ought not to be touched. The difference in these two positions is indeed important—something that cannot be touched is outside the experience of touch, but something that ought not to be touched is a touchable entity that should not be touched.

Relating untouchability to objects of the sense of non-touch fundamentally distinguishes it from mere acts of untouchability such as not touching due to fire and disease. In none of these cases is there a negation of the sense of touch. In these cases, one does not touch because one decides not do so for various reasons. Often, a naïve understanding of the practice of untouchability reduces the act of untouchability to such reasons—for example, saying that one does not touch untouchables because they are involved in highly demeaning acts of cleaning human waste and so on. But this is to misunderstand the phenomenology of untouchability. There is also an inherent cyclicity of the argument: Do they clean human waste because they are untouchables or are they untouchables because they clean human waste? This ambiguity is very important, for it sustains these people as objects of non-touch. This is accomplished in various ways, including through invoking the claim that these characteristics are hereditary.

Thus, the phenomenon of untouchability cannot be reduced to functional reasons alone. Moreover, even for the untouchables, there is no negation of touch as a sense. They can touch themselves, they can touch each other, they touch their children, and so on. A clue to the larger philosophical problem can be found in the construction of the word itself.

Consider the use of the word 'untouchable'—how does this compound really work? Does it mean un-touch-able? 'Un-' is a negation operator. But as we know, with negation operators, the meaning of the compound drastically changes depending on where the negation acts. In this case, does the negation act on the sense of touch or on the 'ability' to touch? If the former, then it is the impossibility of touching (like touching space, say); but if the latter, then it is the impossibility of the act of touching. In other words, does the word untouchable translate into 'not-touchable' or 'touch-unable', that is, unable to touch? The primary difference between these two formulations is that they point to two different types of inability. In the former, it is the inability placed on the object of touch—the object of touch is such that it is inaccessible to the sense of touch (like space or God), whereas in the latter, it is such that the subject is unable to fulfil the act of touching. In the first case, it points to the nature of the object that is sought to be touched while in the second case it is the nature of the subject who is unable to touch. It is clear, therefore, that the case of an untouchable points to the inability of the 'toucher' rather than any inability of the touched person. *Thus, the real site of untouchability is the person who refuses to touch the untouchable.*

There are important consequences for the person who does not fulfil this potential of touching. The model of touching others is that of touching oneself. Thus, in the most primal sense of the term, denying oneself the fulfilment of touch leads to denying oneself the capacity to touch oneself. As much as touching fire causes burns, so also the denial of touching an untouchable causes an inability to touch oneself in a certain sense. That is, the person who refuses to touch an untouchable suffers from 'touch-un-ability'. This inability to touch is a characteristic of the toucher and not the touched. The moment one creates this inability to one's sense of touch, one loses an important aspect of touch. The impact of not touching is present on both the Brahmin and the Dalit—neither of them can fulfil the act of touching, but they have different phenomenological experiences of the same. In the case of the former, it could be associated with psychological feelings of revulsion, power, rejection, and so on, whereas in the latter, it is associated with feelings of humiliation, shame, and so on. What in the phenomenon of untouchability causes this asymmetry of response even though the act of untouchability is symmetrical (the person who doesn't touch is also not touched)?

To be able to answer this and related questions, we have to go back and inquire into some aspects of the sense of touch. As mentioned earlier, there is no localized organ in the body that does the job of touching. The organ of touch is the skin. If you do not like to touch something, then you have to 'close your skin'. But closing the skin is to close the first means of contact with the world. As many philosophers and biologists have pointed out, we cannot live without the skin, although we can live without the other senses. Simply put, the moment you close the skin, you die. It is the partial death or decay of the subject who practises untouchability that is the first consequence of practising untouchability. This happens not just because practising untouchability is morally wrong but because the person is denying himself a part of his ability, his capacity to engage with his own sense. In not touching others, he is not able to touch himself. Merleau-Ponty repeatedly voices this relation between touching and touching oneself: 'To touch is to touch oneself' and 'Tactile experiencing of the other is simultaneously self-experiencing, since otherwise I would not be the one experiencing'.[77] Extending this, we can see how the denial of touching what is touchable is a denial of touching what is touchable within oneself. This means that one can never practise untouchability only with respect to a defined other, but in so doing, one always and necessarily practises untouchability with respect to oneself. (Gopal Guru's invocation of the 'folded body' of the Brahmin is an illustration of this).

Unlike other senses, touch is an action. Our standard response towards objects is that we automatically reach towards them. But the untouchability experience conditions us to be more reserved towards touching any other and not just a set of people who are seen as the untouchables. So the very act of touching becomes problematical because every act of touching becomes reflective. There is an important consequence of this: Touching is no more an 'automatic' sense but becomes a judgement. In so doing, it gets modelled on vision. We know that in the case of vision, we see objects on the one hand, but we also see objects as something. 'Seeing as' is a reflective process associated with perception. In the phenomenology of untouchability, we see a similar move that makes touching a matter of judgement. So touching now becomes 'touching as'. Such a judgement is not about 'facts' alone; there is a moral code attached to it. This move explains my earlier comment about how touch becomes a 'moral sense'.

As a consequence, every person is first of all potentially an untouchable! Every act of touching is now imbued with this sense of doubt as to whether the objects of touch we reach towards could perhaps be an object of untouchability. This introduces the notion of *illusion in touch*. In fact, the creation of the idea of the untouchable person is indebted to metaphors of vision, thus reversing the classical understanding of vision as contact (particularly in the Indian

---

[77] Quoted in Chrétien (2004: 84).

philosophical traditions). In the case of vision, a mirage is seen by the eye but its status as a mirage, as an image and not as a real object, is grounded by the lack of the possibility of touching a mirage. When I reach out to a mirage and try to grasp the object I see in the mirage, I realize through the failure of the act of touching that the vision I see is actually a mirage. In the case of untouchability, an interesting reversal takes place: When I see an untouchable, I can see him but I do not reach out to him. I cannot use my sense of touch to validate the vision that I see. But I do not have the same kind of doubt that I have about a mirage. The untouchable is real but through the denial of touch, he is made into a mirage—this is the illusion of touch.

Thus, every touching is possible only if it first overcomes this potential untouchability. The primary sense that defines touch—particularly of humans—is not the capacity to touch but the potential of untouchability. This has profound consequences on the creation of the narrative of the self as well as on action.

As we saw earlier, the relation between the body and touch is very important. Touch has both an 'active movement and passive receptivity' and kinaesthetic touching is not only the basis of the body's intentionality but defines the action of the body, thereby making possible the Husserlian shift to 'I can' instead of 'I think'. As Paterson notes, there are important consequences of this phenomenology of touch: 'the dual aspect of touch (being transitive–intransitive, active–receptive) could usefully lead to explorations of subject–object dualisms, the biological facticity of the body and its relation to the felt coherence of somatic sensation, and the self-affirmation of the lived, sensible body through the example of reflexive touch, of one hand touching another'.[78]

Gibson focuses on the active sense of touching manifested in the exploratory as against the performatory aspect of touch—that is, an act of touch can arise in an exploratory moment when the body orients towards the object of touch in specific ways.[79] We can extend this to understand how we make sense of others through an exploration of the tactile sense. We often make judgements about how friendly a person is when we shake his or her hands. We get 'vibes'

[78] Paterson (2007: 31).
[79] Gibson (1962).

about others when we are engaged in physical contact with them, for example when we hug a person. Touching is an act of exploration, it is a reaching out to feel and to know. Untouchability is the obstacle to this movement, it is the inability of people on both sides of the fence who find that they cannot know or feel the persons who are untouchable to each other.

Finally, what distinguishes the phenomenological dimension of untouchability is the relation between *touching oneself* and *not touching another*. (Note that this is different from the relation between touching oneself and touching another, a view discussed earlier in the context of Merleau-Ponty). Not touching another is actually a manifestation of the problem of touching oneself—this shift is precisely what makes untouchability in the Indian context unique. This is what differentiates it from other objects that are beyond the sense of touch. *That is, in the most essential sense, untouchability is actually about the always-present, potential untouchability not of another but of oneself.* This is most clearly manifested in the way the structure of untouchability unfolds in the Hindu practice.

UNTOUCHABLE IN THE TOUCH: THE INHERENT UNTOUCHABILITY OF BRAHMINS

It has been argued that untouchability is a characteristic of the Brahmin community. Quigley, for example, emphasizes this characteristic in order to support a different reading of caste. He notes that Brahmins 'can *be* Untouchables, and Untouchables, as ritual specialists, are priests'.[80] His re-reading of caste critiques Dumont's observation that the hierarchy in the caste system occurs through the opposition of the pure and the impure. He finds Dumont's characterization of the opposition between spiritual authority (of the Brahmins) and the temporal authority (of the kings), which leads to the essential disjunction between status and power, as not being empirically supported. Based on this, Dumont constructs Brahmins and the untouchables as extreme contrasts.

[80] Quigley (2000: 16).

Quigley argues that the fact that the notion of impurity is very much a part of a Brahmin priest implies that one cannot use the pure–impure axis, following Dumont, to posit contrasts between different castes. First, Quigley points out that there are at least six types of 'Brahmin personae', such as the renouncer, spiritual preceptor, non-priest, personal priest, temple priest, and death priest.[81] He then goes on to discuss the various ways by which these Brahmin priests become impure, which leads to the members of other communities looking down upon the Brahmins who accept gifts and digest the 'sin, evil, and death of others'.[82]

Quigley's attempt is to make explicit the political dimensions involved in the creation of a hierarchy and in particular to emphasize the role of kingship in this act. His and other such similar attempts to rewrite the narrative of caste in India miss one essential point: an inquiry into the nature of the category of untouchability. To say that Brahmins are also untouchables (in the above sense) is to misunderstand the fundamental nature of untouchability as manifested in the untouchables.[83]

Ambedkar was aware of the presence of the impure among Brahmins and other castes, but he clearly points out to the many differences. First, he notes that there is only a notion of temporal untouchability in the case of Brahmins and others who are in a state of impurity.[84] There is no encoding of this state into one of a permanent stature. The acts of propitiation to get rid of the 'impure' state are not available to the untouchables. Pointing out that the Brahmins too had moments of untouchability cannot allow one to equate them with the untouchables. Rather than asserting this statement, we need to understand why this equation would not be possible. Ambedkar conceptualizes this difference in terms of the impure and the untouchable. So, what Quigley calls 'untouchable' in the case of Brahmin priests, Ambedkar would call as the state of impurity. Is

[81] *Ibid.*, p. 54.

[82] *Ibid.*, p. 80.

[83] Quigley's later book (2005) has a section on kingship and untouchability, but says little of value about the nature of untouchability and misses the fundamental import of untouchability in Brahmins.

[84] Ambedkar (1948).

there any merit to creating such a distinction? Ambedkar's distinction can be retained if we understand that *untouchability is not about
impurity* as well as recognizing that impurity is not untouchability.
How do we make this distinction?

First of all, note that the notion of 'untouchablility' among
Brahmins is not restricted only to priests or to the act of accepting
gifts or 'accepting' the death of others. The rituals concerned with
impurity begin with daily acts. There are many texts that describe
elaborate rituals of purification starting from the time one gets out
of bed.[85] It is also the case that there are states of *maḍi* where the
Brahmin is 'untouchable' to others and these states are present even
when not associated with impurity. Almost all the moments of auspi-
cious worship, festivals, marriages, and daily prayers have some rituals of maḍi associated with them.[86]

Maḍi is a characteristic of untouchableness. Certain rituals, which
includes most forms of prayers, have to be performed under this
condition. A common ritual associated with maḍi is the following:
The person who is doing a ritual must first of all wash his clothes and
hang them out to dry. Once they are dry, they cannot be touched
by any other person. The person who is 'in' maḍi cannot wear the
clothes unless he or she has had a bath. If the clothing has to be
moved, it is often done with the help of a stick. If anybody else or
the maḍi person touches the dried clothes before s/he has had his or
her bath, the clothes will have to be washed again.[87] When a person

[85] See Kashyap (2008) for references to untouchability in various
contacts.

[86] See Bean (1981) and Fuller (1979) for descriptions of maḍi in different
communities. These approaches, like most others, are primarily concerned
with understanding this practice in terms of purity and pollution. What I
am suggesting here is the need to focus on the concept of untouchability
as a primary term in this analysis, which then leads to a very different
reading of these practices as well as creating possibilities of new political
interventions.

[87] There are differences in this practice across communities. Also, there
are various subtleties present, such as the distinction between cotton and
silk cloth in relation to maḍi.

is in maḍi, nobody—including his own children—can touch him.[88]
What this means is that during family rituals, family members are
completely untouchable until the ritual is completed.

Following Ambedkar, we can actually note the important distinctions in such states of 'untouchability' of the Brahmins. While one
can designate the individual as being in a state of untouchability, the
characteristics of untouchability are fundamentally different. First
of all, in the Brahmin's case, the individual voluntarily takes on the
mantle of untouchability. This has an important consequence: such
an individual refuses to touch others because he believes that he is in
a 'purer' state. Untouchability in the case of such individuals is a mark
of *greater purity* and not of greater impurity. The fact that such an
individual takes it upon himself to be an 'untouchable' means that he
is the autonomous agent for such a decision. Secondly, in most cases,
such an individual can come out of this state. Thirdly, the punishment
for transgression is not one that is similar to what is imposed on the
involuntary untouchables. The Brahmin's state of untouchability is
that one does *not want* to be touched and not that one is refused the
touch. The touched–touching dichotomy that informs this position
is characteristic of touch. I agree with Ambedkar that these transient,
voluntary states should not be equated with the notion of being an
untouchable.

However, we should note here another class of Brahmins who
are 'permanent untouchables', and these are the Ācāryas. These
Ācāryas are permanently untouchable but since their untouchability
is already inscribed within the notion of autonomous untouchability,
they retain this 'superior' nature. Such Ācāryas will not eat food
that is cooked even by their wives (in cases where these people
are married). They too, like the untouchables, gain their status of
absolute untouchability through birth. The children, or at least one
son, of an Ācārya usually continue to be Ācāryas. Even Brahmins
in a state of maḍi cannot touch these Ācāryas, watch them eat, and
so on. Untouchability for these Ācāryas is not about attaining a
state of untouchability and then coming out of it. It is hereditary,
it is part of tradition, and they are in a permanent state of being an

---

[88] Similar states are applicable to the women also.

untouchable, even to their family and kins. Here, it is not about purity and impurity but about a *state of being*.[89]

What should catch our attention is the bipolarity in those who are untouchables. Agreeing with Ambedkar, we can characterize all those caste individuals who are in states of 'untouchability' as impure and not as untouchable. But the special case of the Āchāryas suggests something radically different. It is that the notion of being an untouchable is an essential and necessary component of being a Brahmin. To be a Brahmin is to be an untouchable. For the many varieties of Brahmins, these are only moments of untouchability. But for the most exalted spiritual leaders, the moments of untouchability are permanent. In fact, what distinguishes these Brahmin spiritual leaders is being a permanent untouchable, a characteristic that is passed on hereditarily.

Here is an intriguing paradox: What distinguishes the state of untouchability of these people in contrast to the untouchables of Ambedkar? Untouchability in the former case is obviously a positive virtue whereas in the latter case it is a negative 'fact'. What is it in the nature of untouchability that allows this accretion of value? And what is it that resists the inversion that would make the positive virtue a characteristic of all untouchables? While there are some social and political reasons that might explain this phenomenon, here I am interested in exploring the metaphysical consequences of the same.

[89] In the Brahminical Rāmānuja tradition, there are many stories of non-Brahmins (including Dalits) who occupy highly respected positions in this movement. The twelve Ālwars—the supreme spiritual figures for this community—include non-Brahmins. The *Divya-Prabandam* is the 'Tamil Veda' and is the central text for this community. Arguably, the most important part of this text is another text called the *Thiruvāimozhi*. Verse 3-7-9 of this text is roughly translated as follows: 'Those who do not belong to the known four castes but to the most backward called "Candālas"—not having anything to be admired of—if they are devotees of Lord Viṣṇu then not only they but their disciples too are my God' (translation by S.K. Sampath). There are other such sentiments in the text. Such references to the other castes, along with folk narratives of important non-Brahmin and Dalit personae in this Brahminical tradition, suggest once more the difficulty in understanding caste dynamics in terms of rigid distinctions based on some ideas of purity and impurity.

The importance of the idea of the 'untouchable' among the Brahmins is indicative of the essentiality of this notion to the very definition of what is it to be a Brahmin. A Brahmin is not one who belongs to a particular community—this is merely the sociological interpretation of being a Brahmin.[90] Being born into the community is not enough to be called a Brahmin unless the male member undergoes the investiture of the sacred thread. Different subgroups then have other initiations that are needed before one can become a full-fledged member of this community. (We need to reflect on this constant 'Brahminizing' of the Brahmins that is needed in order to continue to be a member of that community, in contrast to membership criteria in other castes). In the case of one sect of Brahmins, it is necessary for a person to have undergone the *panchasamskāram* (five purificatory/ initiatory rituals specific to the Rāmānuja tradition). Unless a person has done these five *samskāras*, he cannot perform most of the rituals associated with various states of impurity. For example, a person who hasn't done these samskāras cannot cook in various rituals. Orthodox Brahmins will not eat food that is cooked by anybody who hasn't undergone these samskāras.

Thus, one becomes a Brahmin in ways that are unique to that group. But the most important marker in becoming a Brahmin has to do essentially with the possibility of being an untouchable to members *of their own* community. Note this exclusiveness of untouchability in these cases. Untouchables are not untouchable to the members of their own community but only to certain others, but for the Brahmins in this state of untouchability, everybody is potentially untouchable and, moreover, the most exalted state is reached when one is in a permanent state of untouchability.

The above discussion clearly suggests that membership to a Brahmin community is not through heredity alone. It is a necessary condition that one is born into a Brahmin household but it is not sufficient. The sufficient condition that makes one into a Brahmin is related to the idea of becoming an untouchable. Thus, I would like to suggest here that the most dominant marker of being a Brahmin lies in the concept of untouchability, *lies in the potential of an individual*

---

[90] See Pandian's (2008) analysis of the creation of the Brahmin community in Tamil Nadu.

to become an untouchable. How so? A Brahmin is one who not only has access to temporal and potential untouchability but also to permanent, hereditary untouchability.

But then why is it that the Brahmin's untouchability is valorized whereas the untouchability of the untouchables transforms into most inhuman forms of treatment? The philosophical answer lies in the notion of supplementation, a concept that has been effectively used by Derrida in a completely different context.

UNTOUCHABILITY AND THE LOGIC OF THE SUPPLEMENT

Let me begin with the idea of a sign. A sign is that which stands for something else. Our access to the signified is mediated through representation through signs. But the dominant metaphysics underlying this process gives a primacy to that which is signified, because of which the sign is always placed hierarchically lower than the signified.

Derrida engages with this idea through the analysis of writing.[91] In Western thought, writing has dominantly been seen to be a derivative to speech, which itself is derivative to an originary thought, an essence, or presence. Whether it is Rousseau's comment that writing is a 'dangerous supplement' to speech or a more virulent opinion that writing is evil, there is a continued tradition of suspicion towards writing. Derrida's critique of the binary of speech and writing where speech is seen to be 'superior' to writing leads him to suggest that writing does not act as a mere 'supplement' to speech.

A supplement suggests that there is a lack in what is supplemented. But it cannot just be a mere representation of this lack or absence. What this process of supplementation points to is the fact that the supplemented is incomplete and necessarily depends on the supplement. It is the supplement that brings to presence the signified. The consequence of this move is that the signified is not accessible to us other than through the presence of the signifiers—every signified therefore is a trace of the signifier.

In the case of writing, thought—which is supposed to be represented by writing twice-removed—is not completely accessible

---

[91] For example, see Derrida (1976).

without writing. Not only is thought thus incomplete without the supplement, it is also the case that the supplement adds to the original thought. It is the supplement that makes the originary possible. Thus, Derrida says: 'The supplement is always the supplement of a supplement. One wishes to go back from the supplement to the source: one must recognize that there is a supplement at the source.'[92]

Speech is thus not 'independent' of writing; writing is not a mere supplementation of speech. As Culler notes, 'the thing supplemented (speech) turns out to need supplementation because it proves to have the same qualities originally thought to characterize only the supplement (writing)'.[93] The logic of supplementation gives us various possible alternatives of the relation between the supplement and the supplemented. Barbara Johnson suggests the following possibilities: If A is the supplement to B, then the relation between A and B can be one or more of the following—added to, substitutes for, superfluous addition to, makes up for the absence of, makes for deficiency of, usurps the place of, corrupts the purity of, necessary for restoration of, as that which the other is lost without, is a danger to, is a remedy to, protects against direct encounter with, and so on.[94]

Even this brief entry into the idea of the supplement points to its potential use in understanding untouchability in the Indian context. The popular understanding of caste, following Dumont, privileges the axial polarity between the Brahmins and the untouchables, also articulated along the pure–impure opposition. Like the speech–writing binary or man–woman, the Brahmin–untouchable binary is not only a constructed opposition but one in which the latter is inferiorized with respect to the former. This allows us to consider the possibility that the notion of untouchability acts as a supplement to the notion of a Brahmin. It is moreover a 'dangerous supplement' and one that is intrinsically 'dangerous' to the signified, the Brahmin. It further, to use one characterization of Johnson's logic of the supplement, 'corrupts the purity of' the Brahmin. To use another characterization, it 'protects against direct encounter with' the Brahmins. The discourse

---

[92] *Ibid.*, p. 304.
[93] Culler (1997: 11).
[94] Johnson (1990: 45).

of the untouchable illustrates its construction as a supplement in these various descriptions.

Derrida's argument that the supplement is all that there is, that the supplement is to be found at the source, allows us to engage with the dominant discourse of untouchability in a different manner. The discourse on Brahmins and untouchability clearly indicates that the notion of untouchability (like the notion of writing) is seen as a supplement to the notion of a Brahmin (speech). However, the critical analysis of the supplement suggests that it is impossible to sustain untouchability as a mere supplement. It, instead, is to be found in the source—the Brahmin—itself. The example of the permanent untouchable among Brahmins is an added illustration of the importance of the idea of untouchability among Brahmins. To be the highest Brahmin is to be an untouchable, but not of the kind that characterizes the untouchables as a caste group. In other words, the necessity to construct a group called the untouchables arises in large part due to the inherent presence of the notion of untouchability in the very idea of a Brahmin.

What then are the implications of this argument? It is first and foremost the recognition that untouchability as a notion is intrinsic to Brahmins, and this notion of untouchability is not about the rituals associated with impurity. It is actually about the characteristics of the non-temporal, permanent, and hereditary characteristics of untouchability. The creation of a supplementary community of untouchables is a necessary consequence of the inability of Brahmins to attain the 'pure' state of untouchable. But in creating this supplement, the pure state of untouchability that characterizes the Āchāryas, for example, is converted into a negative virtue. In other words, the untouchables are the supplemented Āchāryas and this supplementation is needed for the possibility of having a community of Brahmins whose members no longer carry the burden of 'pure untouchability'. Thus, if there were no creation of a supplemented class of untouchables, there would be no possibility of having a community of Brahmins. The untouchables are the supplemented Brahmins in the final analysis. In Derridean terms, the Brahmins are speech and the untouchables are writing. Ironically, the literal meaning of a Brahmin is essentially related to speech and the Dalits have been essentially reduced to possessors of a body—the material substratum on which writing is possible. Thus, we can see how the critique of speech suggests a way of critiquing the dichotomy between Brahmins and Dalits.

The distinction between the temporal and the permanent is also related to the logic of supplementation. Speech is temporary, transitory, and evanescent. Writing is permanent; it embodies the idea of 'hereditary'. The most horrendous aspect of untouchability lies not in moments of impurity or exclusion but in being in such a state permanently. The possibility of encoding this permanence in the untouchables clearly illustrates the logic of supplementation. The literal untouchability that characterizes speech (Brahmin) is actually transformed into the metaphorical untouchability of writing (untouchables). (That is, we literally cannot touch speech but can touch writing, but in an interesting twist, this literal untouchability gets supplanted as metaphorical untouchability on to the untouchables).

How exactly does this process of supplementation create a community of untouchables as something necessary for the sustenance of the idea of a Brahmin? This occurs through inverting the elements of the experience of touching. The supplementation occurs through the change from 'not wanting to be touched' to 'refusing to touch'. It is interesting that both these imperatives come from the Brahmin—that is, the untouchable Brahmin is one who refuses to let others touch him as well as refusing to touch others. In the case of the untouchables, neither is the case. I suggest that such a shift can happen only in the case of touch because of the touch–touched relation. It is in this sense that untouchability as we know it today arises entirely in consequence of the metaphysics of touch and the supplementation of the shift from being touched to touching. Since touching is always an integral part of being touched, they can only be in a reversible relation and not in a hierarchical relation, thereby suggesting that the Brahmins and the untouchables actually exemplify a reversible relationship between each other.

These are not just theoretical musings without empirical support! An interesting social phenomenon in Indian societies is the existence of communities who specialize in carrying the various burdens of other communities. The professional mourners of Rajasthan are a community of women of lower-caste who do the job of mourning when somebody from the upper-caste dies. In essence, these women are expressing the grief experienced by somebody else—they embody the emotion experienced by others. Public mourning is outsourced to these women. Quigley mentions the Mahabrahmins, whose job is to carry the spirits of the dead.[95] Indian society is filled with such examples of 'outsourcing'. In another book, where he relates kingship and untouchability, Quigley gives the example of Brahmins who hug a dying king in order to take the king's sin away.[96] Having absorbed the sins of the dying king, the embodied sinner leaves the kingdom, never to return. This practice continues to this day: Quigley cites the example of the royal murders in Nepal a few years back when similar rituals were performed. In the case of the untouchables, the untouchability of the Brahmins is *outsourced* to the Dalits who then carry that burden. Recognizing this move of supplementation is first of all a political recognition and enables specific political action.

Saying all this might not be saying much, given the inhuman practices associated with untouchability. However, we should also remember that the deconstructive moves initiated through the analysis of the logic of supplementation have generated new and liberative ideas that have been important in struggles against various types of hegemony. There is no reason that the same cannot happen in the case of the liberation of the untouchables also. Such a phenomenology of untouchability also does something else: It allows us to develop an ethics that is based on touch. While ethical responses to untouchability often draw upon political ideas such as individual freedom, there is a more foundational ethical response possible, one which is based on an ethics of touch.

[95] Quigley (2000).
[96] Quigley (2005: 130).

8

Archaeology of Untouchability*

Gopal Guru

> It may be in your interests to deposit your impurities in us, but how
> can it be in our interests to remain repository of your dirt (moral)?
>
> —*Babasheb Ambedkar*

Debating with Sarukkai acquires significance especially in an intellectual context where the discourse on untouchability in contemporary
times has received only lopsided attention from different quarters.
For instance, it has elicited some degree of academic interest among
historians[1] and substantially more attention from sociologists and
social anthropologists. Arguably, sociology and social anthropology
look impressive in as much as these disciplines offer quite a detailed
description of untouchability.[2] On the other hand, it is interesting to
note that untouchability as a social concern finds its most profound
expression in a different discipline—the non-Dalit[3] and Dalit literature.[4] On the flip side, in some of the more influential disciplines

---

* This chapter was first published in 2009, 'Archaeology of Untouchability', *Economic and Political Weekly*, XLIV (37): 49–56.
[1] Jha (1974).

[2] Desai (1976), Dumont (1988), and Shah *et al.* (2006).

[3] Mulkraj Anand's *Untouchable*, Shankar Pillai's *Scavenger's Boy*, Shivram
Karanth's *Chomana Duddi*, U.R. Ananthamurthy's *Samskara* are some
of the prominent literary texts that centrally touch upon the question of
untouchability.

[4] Bagul (1978), Walmiki (2002).

such as political science,[5] it factors only marginally, while in others such as economics and philosophy,[6] it faces a complete blackout. Even the sociological or anthropological description of untouchability, which may look fascinating to some, does not exhaust all the reference points. In other words, untouchability, which otherwise is a dynamic reality, tends to produce experience, but is always in excess of this textualized sociological and anthropological description. Hence, available descriptions are often inadequate to capture the totality of the meaning that emanates from this dynamism. This dynamism warrants a fresh perspective that could enable us to tap the excess meaning embedded in untouchability as a dynamic practice. At the moment, I can think of two such frameworks—the philosophical and the archaeological—that could reveal much richer and more nuanced meanings of the phenomenon of untouchability. Sarukkai's arguments in the previous chapter (Chapter 7), in my opinion, succeed in assigning both height and depth to the understanding of untouchability, thus elevating it from its mere descriptive/empirical, and therefore more routine and familiar, understanding to a much richer and wider philosophical context.

DEBATING SARUKKAI

Sarukkai offers a wider philosophical grasp of the notion of untouchability (Chapter 7). This he does by drawing on both Indian and Western philosophical traditions. In Sarukkai's understanding of untouchability, the idea of touch (and skin) becomes important. For touch and skin, as he says, form primal senses of the body. Sarukkai gives a fascinating insight into the phenomenological understanding of untouchability and argues that 'the notion of untouchability is an essential requirement of Brahminhood' (Chapter 7). For Sarukkai, Brahminhood, as a part of this requirement, seeks not just to outsource untouchability to others, but most importantly it also involves a philosophical move to supplement untouchability onto others. I

[5] Rudolph and Rudolph (1967: 132–54).

[6] It is only in Ambedkar's collective writings and speeches that one comes across a deep discussion on the impact of untouchability on economics.

would argue that Sarukkai's essay (Chapter 7), particularly this new understanding of untouchability as outsourcing and supplementation, questions the final vocabulary that has almost acquired a settled status, particularly in the authoritative sociological work of Louis Dumont. Sarukkai's take on untouchability thus provides a counter argument to Dumont's,[7] who says, 'It is clear that impurity of the untouchable is conceptually inseparable from the purity of Brahmin.' Sarukkai's perspective on untouchability thus provides a counter argument to this Dumontian understanding of untouchability. In addition to this, it also opens up the possibility of solving some 'sociological puzzles'.[8] Furthermore, his notion of outsourcing offers us an opportunity to theoretically understand the political dynamics of anti-untouchability movements led by Ambedkar and subsequently by the Dalit movement in India. Finally, it will not only help us in detecting the spaces that inhabit the upper castes' anxious self, but it also offers an opportunity to foreground the moral significance of this notion of supplementation and its contestation.

Sarukkai thus offers several insights embedded in his rather capacious reading of untouchability. However, the height and depth that he has assigned to the understanding of untouchability makes it all the more difficult to take on board all the important issues that he has raised in his analysis. Hence, in the first part of this chapter, I will engage with select issues such as the metaphysics of the body, the distinctive relationship between contact and touch, the concept of supplementation, and, finally, the structural logic that unites both the Brahmins as *deferential* or *ideal* (emphasis mine) untouchables and the Dalit as *despicable* or *real* (emphasis mine) untouchables. Let me offer another point in clarification that the choice to engage with some issues is informed more by my own convenience and less by the need to seek refutation of Sarukkai's argument. At best I could

---

[7] Dumont (1988: 54).

[8] The sociological puzzle could be understood in terms of the intense practices of untouchability that are found in regions with negligible Brahmin populations, or less-intense untouchability practices in places with larger Brahmin populations, particularly in Uttar Pradesh (UP). I have dealt with this issue in Guru (2007).

only claim that my own take on the issue under consideration is modestly aimed at seeking an extension of Sarukkai's position.

The second part of this chapter deals with the possibility of this expansion. I would like to argue that there are different types of archaeological methods deployed by different scholars for different purposes. However, I plan to choose one that would be more appropriate in making sense of the complex relationship between untouchability and caste. Taking a cue from Vitthal Ramji Shinde,[9] one of the leading non-Brahmin social thinkers from modern Maharashtra, who says, '*Asprushtechi malmal, manachy talashi dadun basil ahe*' (untouchability is a kind of repulsive feeling, a sort of nausea, that sits deep at the bottom of the Brahminical mind), I would like to argue that modernity forces untouchability to descend deep down to the bottom of the *Brahminical mind* (emphasis mine). As I would argue in the second part, the archaeological method seems to be the most appropriate one to detect the nausea-like attitude. It is also interesting to note that Sarukkai's understanding of untouchability goes close to the understanding of Shinde. As we have seen in the above section, Sarukkai also locates the source of untouchability in the Brahminical self.[10] I would further argue in the second part that due to the compulsion of the modern conditions, untouchability both as practice and as consciousness finds it difficult to remain on the surface of social interaction, as was the case in the feudal past. Modernity forces it to slide further down to the bottom of the hierarchical mind. Differently put, untouchability as a discursive practice plays itself out in much subtler forms than ever before. Untouchability in modern times is forced to hide itself behind certain modern meanings and identities. Hence, mere sociological or anthropological description does not seem to be effective enough to access the untouchability thus located. Archaeology as a method seems to be more effective in accessing this complex mind because it deals not so much with a need to invent but a need to discover an essence or truth of caste that gets covered with a subtle form of untouchability.

[9] Shinde (1976: 129).
[10] Sarukkai in previous chapter.

Let me initiate a dialogue with Sarukkai by engaging first with what
he describes as metaphysics of body and later explore what implications this idea has for untouchability when understood in the Indian
context. Sarukkai offers us different notions of body that, as he says,
appear in different Indian philosophical traditions. In the Nyāya
tradition, as he argues in Chapter 8, the body is the locus of the
senses and the body feels through the senses. He suggests the need
for further exploration in this regard but from the phenomenological
point of view. Sarukkai, quoting from Lang, further observes that
for the Buddha, the body was indeed the world in that it is within
the body that there is the arising and ceasing of the world. Sarukkai,
further quoting from Buddhism, particularly its Mādhyamika tradition from the Buddhist compendium, observes that the notion of
impurity of body is all pervading. From Buddhism, he elaborates five
impurities of body: womb, seed, body's nature, body's characteristics,
and corpse.

Taking a cue from Sarukkai, it is possible to make an extended
sense of the impurities of the body and argue that in addition to
these five impurities, the organic body also contains another set of
impurities, which seeks to undercut the moral significance of both
the sacred (in a ritual sense) as well as the perfect (in the physical
sense) bodies. All organic bodies contain within them negative properties, such as sweat, excreta, urine, mucus, and gases. In the material sense, they are the source of foul smells and unpleasant feelings.
Thus, at the metaphysical level, the organic body as the source of
impurities suggests a kind of ontological equality—that every body
is dirty, both in a moral sense as well as a material sense. Ontological
equality, suggesting equal distribution of these impurities or organic
refuse sitting underneath the skin of every body, is supposed to bring
out in every person a moral insight that in turn will compel him or
her to acknowledge this ontological equality. To put differently, this
insight is supposed to create a sense of self-realization among people,
who then can find no reason to produce a pernicious classification
of bodies into repulsive and attractive (of course this is bad news
for the cosmetic industry). This insight, which can generate a sense
of moral relativism, in effect creates the possibility to restrain and
perhaps totally eliminate the morally offensive capacity that a person
may use for producing the classification mentioned above. To put it

differently, moral relativism can make it difficult to produce a negative judgement, which often is deployed to seek condemnation of the
other's body as filthy.

The metaphysics of the body, leading to moral relativism, has significance in as much as it seeks to relativize the notion of the perfect
body or 'even out' the excess moral value that makes some bodies
superior to others. Assigning an egalitarian value to every body
becomes a possibility, what is called ontological mirroring of other
bodies. It is in this sense that my understanding of the metaphysics
of the body makes a complementary reading with Sarukkai's reading of the metaphysics of the body. I suppose both of us suggest a
re-description of untouchability that can have implications for the
discourse on disability.

PANCHAMAHĀBHŪTE AND UNTOUCHABILITY

Conversely, it is also possible to argue that every body is worthy of
respect simply because it is constitutive of five principles—air, fire,
earth, water, and orbit—that are present in every organic body in
equal quantity. These are earth, water, fire, air and ākāśa (space).[11]
In Indian philosophy (the Sāṃkhya school), these are called the
panchamahābhūte (five cosmic principles).[12] At the metaphysical
level, these panchamahābhūte assign affirmative meaning to the
'filthy' body, as mentioned above. These five principles, which are
naturally endowed with internal purity, form the necessary physical
conditions for the very organic existence of any body. It is in this sense
that the panchamahābhūte establish an ontological unity among
bodies across time and space. Ontological equality as an underlying
principle, therefore, should make all organic bodies worthy of respect
without discrimination. Thus, any cultural construction dividing
egalitarian bodies into pernicious gradations could be decisively
refuted by invoking the metaphysics of body. The metaphysics of body
in turn can create moral capacity among those who lack this capacity
that is so necessary for assigning moral worth to every body. Mutual

[11] See Sinha (1915).
[12] *Ibid.*

affirmation of bodies becomes a possibility through acknowledgement of the panchamahābhūte as an essential need of every organic body. Those who have the ability to use the panchamahābhūte to morally access the other's body ultimately acquire a moral capacity to shade off some surplus moral value that they attach to their own personality. Self-preservation as a morally integrated self finds its basis not in surplus moral value but equal worth—one person, one value. The lower-caste struggle was aimed at achieving this principle of 'one person, one value'. Thus, the panchamahābhūte can contribute to the creation of an egalitarian order in bodies. The panchamahābhūte, to paraphrase Aristotle, seek to provide an ontological mirror through which people can look at themselves not with the dominant sense of having excess moral value but as having the same value as the other (in the Aristotelian sense, a friend) would have.[13] This moral capacity that flows from these five principles in effect radically undercuts the very basis of Hobbsian self-preservation, which is ontologically related to the superior self.

The politics of self-preservation in the Hobbsian sense therefore suggests an unwillingness to step out from Brahminhood.[14] Interestingly, Brahminhood seeks to preserve itself through the process of Sanskritization. Sanskritization as a cultural process involves the efforts on the part of the individual at the lower layer to emulate Brahminhood. The lower social orders, instead of rejecting Brahminhood, seek to perfect it. Practitioners of Brahminhood seem to have adopted a very rigorous and all-pervading process that has helped them to preserve Brahminhood in an entrenched form. To put it differently, Brahminhood requires not just Sanskritization, which as a preservative option could be a little unreliable, but structurally a much more stable device to redeem this self-preservation.

This structural device involves the conversion of the ecological (five principles) into the sociological (hierarchical). In sociological reading Panchamahabhute acquire different and perhaps negative meanings through deploying the ideology of purity–pollution, which is so central to the former. This conversion is sustained by the asymmetries of power that robs the panchamahābhūte of their positive

---

[13] Shield (2007: 12–13).
[14] Honneth (1995: 7–10).

meaning. People do not follow the moral basis of the metaphysics of Panchamahabhute when they act. They are not sufficiently motivated by the exalted and therefore egalitarian meaning that is implied in the metaphysics of panchamahābhūte. In fact, their material interest and the cultural need to draw relative superiority over others seriously undermine the validity of metaphysics as the universal framework that provides moral orientation to social interaction among people. The failure of religio-theological discourse represented by different saint traditions proves this and has to be understood in terms of the corresponding failure of the common people to respond to the appeal of different saints, particularly Kabir. Put yet differently, the need to remain socially superior has led the upper caste to convert the ecological into the sociological or the natural into the cultural. Let me explain this in terms of the politics of converting the panchamahābhūte into instruments that are deployed to reduce some sections of society to 'walking carrion',[15] a degraded entity filled with a deep sense of repulsion. This transmutation, which is produced by the politics of the preservation of the hierarchically superior self, has serious implication for these five principles. They stand discredited; they are robbed of their egalitarian meaning. Let us see how.

According to the *Manusmriti*, the physical association of the upper castes—which are still under the social influence of ritual orders—with the earth is considered to be ritually polluting.[16] *Manusmriti*, further prescribes that members of the top layer in the social hierarchy are not supposed to soil their hands with either earth or mud.[17] Using ritual pollution to assign a negative quality to the earth goes completely against the Gandhian naturopathy,[18] which treats earth with much respect on account of its having a healing value. Gandhi considers it as healing in as much as it helps in pumping out the excess heat from the body; but the Manu strictures fail to convince the larger masses about the positive uses of earth. The earth in

---

[15] Naipaul (1988: 37).

[16] WSBA (1990: 258).

[17] *Ibid.*

[18] Gandhi had established a naturopathy centre at the village Loni near Pune. This centre teaches the importance of earth in natural cure.

Manu's scheme suggests a broad division based on purity–pollution, thus dividing the top rung of the twice-born on the pure side and the Shudras and *Atishudra*s on the impure side.

Generally speaking, the conversion of water as a natural and therefore pure substance into a polluted substance should be considered as objectionable. Conversely, the use of water for maintaining physical hygiene should not be considered as objectionable. But how can one understand the efforts made by some socially privileged sections to use water for constructing a morally painful asymmetry in social and cultural life? The upper caste, taking their cue from Manu's code, use water for constructing a perennial division, thus rendering some bodies ritually pure and other as eternally impure.[19] Such people treat seawater as ritually polluting[20] and also a source of ritual purification. According to this understanding, water—unlike earth—becomes a standard, by which it then becomes possible to measure how deeply the essence of caste has penetrated and perverted the social relations across castes. Water, unlike earth, is available to members of every caste, who use it to reproduce untouchability practices so as to retain relative social superiority on the scale of ritual hierarchy. Thus water determines the scale of untouchability. Water, in fact, forms the lifeline or provides the most important precondition for the survival of untouchability. Just imagine if there was no water: untouchability would not have originated in the first instance or it would have disappeared long ago if the water resources had dried up. Thanks to the water sources or long-living Himalayas, water is still available for practising untouchability!

According to the laws of Manu,[21] fire is considered as another source of purification. In Manu, fire is intrinsically pure, and this is proved by the social strictures that prevent a Hindu woman from mounting her deceased husband's funeral pyre if she is menstru-

---

[19] Dumont (1988: 51).

[20] In orthodox Hinduism, although there are umpteen references that suggest crossing the sea is a taboo, one can also argue that some of the orthodox Hindus do treat sea water as polluting, which is why they do not immerse the ashes of the dead into sea water, even if they are close to sea water (particularly in the coastal regions). For further details see Lederle (1976: 192).

[21] Dumont (1988: 50).

ating.[22] Fire, according to Manu's *Dharmashastra*, also acts as the purification agent.[23] The ritual practice among Hindus known as Agni Pariksha underscores the point. Within Hindu social or cultural practices, untouchables and women are forced to take this Agni Pariksha for different reasons. The upper castes use fire not only to punish untouchables but also to purify the vicinity through seeking displacement of the untouchables as 'walking carrion'.[24] The social history of caste riots in the past clearly shows how the upper caste have used fire for devastating the little shanty huts of Dalits all over the country. Thus, water purifies the upper-caste bodies while fire indirectly maintains the purity of space or ākāśa. Fire, as a weapon of the strong upper caste, is deployed by them to destroy not only the untouchables themselves but their dwellings as well.[25] In this regard, it is interesting to further note that fire as a purifying resource is also available to Ambedkar, but for emancipatory purposes.[26] As is well known, during the Chavdar water-tank struggle in March 1927 at Mahad in Ratnagiri district of Maharashtra, he set the *Manusmriti* on fire. However, it has to be noted that there is a difference between the two social usages of fire. The socially dominant deploy fire only to perpetuate the division between the ideal untouchable (the twice-born) and the despicable untouchable, while Ambedkar uses it to symbolically destroy this division.

Under what conditions should air become an objectionable substance? It can be objectionable only if it is converted from its being natural and hence as a pure substance into a source of contamination. However, air in itself does not constitute a source of contamination. On the contrary, it can become a source of contamination particularly when it is filled with foul smells, deadly gases, or dangerous bacteria, which are quite harmful to the general health

[22] *Ibid.*

[23] Dumont (1985: 50).

[24] Naipaul (1988: 37).

[25] There were 43 untouchable agricultural labourers burnt alive by the upper-caste landlord in Kilvenmani in the Thanjavur district of Tamil Nadu in 1962. Several houses of the Walmikis from Gohana in Haryana were set on fire by the upper castes in January 2007.

[26] WSBA (1990: 250).

of people. Thus, locating hazardous factories away from human habitation is quite understandable from a certain perspective. But how does one understand the location of Dalit *bastis* (locality) on the eastern side of the village? This location of the Dalits to the east of the main village has been empirically confirmed by several anthropological studies on India.[27] Is it natural or the part of a social design? I would like to argue that this morphology is part of the social design by the upper caste. Why? There is an ideology of purity–pollution working behind this morphology. The bastis of the untouchables on the eastern side of the village form the part of this deliberate design that is deployed by the upper caste to avoid pollution crossing over from the west to the east, should the Dalit bastis happen to be situated on the west side of the village. Since the upper caste cannot control the direction of air, which normally flows from the west to the east, they are forced to change the social morphology of the village in such a way as to situate themselves on the west while pushing the untouchables to the east. In certain anthropological reading, West can acquire positive connotation as well. (Veena Das, 1977)

According to the Nyāya philosophical tradition, sound accesses space. Even in modern times, one can actually measure the radial impact of sound. Excess production of sound leads to noise, which ultimately leads to noise pollution. Thus space comes to be filled with noise pollution. In this context, it might look completely bizarre to believe that at least a few decades ago, the sound created by untouchables was considered a source of ritual pollution. During the feudal social set-up, the untouchables in most parts of India were forced to announce their arrival before they could enter the main village.[28] The reason behind such a precautionary measure was that the upper caste sought to avoid listening to the untouchables' sounds, which the former considered as polluting. The notion of the sacred sought

[27] Karve makes this observation in her seminal work on Maharashtra (Khairmode 1990a). Even research on the Dignity Index in Maharashtra, Vikas Adhyayan Kendra, Mumbai, 2009, proves this point.

[28] This has been the common practice among the upper-caste Indians from different parts of India. Interestingly, Isaacs (1965) and Walzer (1983) also reconfirm this in their work.

to turn sound into the source of ritual pollution. Taking the evening meal was considered the most sacred occasion, particularly by the priestly class from the village.[29] The upper caste, particularly the Brahmin priest from the village, found the sound of an untouchable a source of interruption on this most sacred occasion. During the night, patrolling in the village, the untouchable was permitted to shout only using a low-pitched voice. This was done only to avoid the undesirable interruptions. The link between untouchability and the morphology of expression (different levels of expression) was firmly established and strictly followed by the upper caste in the village.[30] In one of the leading autobiographies of Babytai Kamble, the Veskar (the village servant) and the Mahars (from a former untouchable caste in Maharashtra) were not allowed to use high-pitched sounds during the evening as it was considered a major source of interruption in the sacred functions, as mentioned above.[31]

Sarukkai has argued that there is a contact between body and words. Thus, chanting words while bathing establishes this contact. But in case of the untouchables who are treated as 'walking carrion' with a concentrated expression of repulsion (even today some Indian people feel nauseated after seeing the untouchable and they cover their nose whenever they walk past the untouchables), there is a complete denial of this contact. This is because the words do not belong ontologically to the Brahmin body. They flow from the mouth of the walking carrion, a potent source of pollution. Thus, at one level, the untouchables were prohibited from producing high-pitched sounds as it was considered polluting as far as the 'pure untouchables' (Brahmins) were concerned. At another level, even the low-pitched sounds were considered polluting by the upper castes. Since sound accesses space, it can become the source of pollution as well. In order to avoid the 'menace of words' coming from the untouchables, the upper castes—particularly the Brahmins—forced the untouchables to eliminate the word and replace it with sound. This was done by forcing the untouchables to announce their arrival in the public

---

[29] Dumont (1988: 54).
[30] Kamble (2008).
[31] *Ibid.*, p. 58.

sphere, not by shouting their words but by beating the drum.[32] Just
to conclude the first part, the top rung of the twice-born seem to
have used these panchamahābhūte to produce 'walking carrion', a
concentrated expression of untouchability. Since the untouchable
was a walking danger, there was a need to quarantine this danger
into an isolated place called Chamrauti in UP, Halgeri in Karnataka,
Cherry in Tamil Nadu, and Mahar or Mangwad in Maharashtra.

MORAL SIGNIFICANCE OF BEING UNTOUCHABLE

In the above sections, we have seen that the panchamahābhūte do
have a capacity to assign universal meaning (ontological equality) to
a body that might look particular in terms of its outer constitution.
But at another level, it can also deny a particular body—for example,
an untouchable or 'walking carrion'—a moral significance. A walking
carrion can acquire moral significance in two major ways. First, it
(Panchamahabhute) can turn a passive, helpless, quarantined body
into a potent weapon—not so much to produce destruction, but
on the contrary for liberating the upper-caste bodies that otherwise
would remain folded into an estranged being: privileged untouchables. The touch of the despicable untouchable seeks to convert the
folded bodies into freely flowing bodies.[33] It can liberate the 'privileged untouchable', as Sarukkai would like to call them, from the
constraining sense of anxiety. The physical or corporeal or material
touch of the hygienic bodies could also be liberating for these bodies
folded into themselves. The touch, ranging from a simple handshake
to innocent hugging or intensive hugging (inter-caste marriage con-
summated as a result of sheer love or that which is led by conviction
and reason to produce a decent society) can democratize the very idea
of touch. Touch, therefore, can help overcome the mutual reification
of culturally folded bodies. Second, the untouchable as the real entity
ironically seeks to establish reverse control on the sacred bodies that

[32] *Ibid.*, pp. 58–63; this has also been confirmed by Mehbubhai from the
Behat block in Saharanpur district, UP, on 23 July 2009.
[33] Ananthamurthy (1978). This relates to the Kilvvenmani killings in
Tanjjavur district of Tamil Nadu and Gohana killings in Haryana.

are treated as 'ideal'. In other words, it is the ideal untouchable who feels vulnerable to the threat of the 'sociological danger' posed by the real.

Touch and contact can acquire mutually exclusive meanings depending on particular social contexts. Touch, which is active purely in a private and personal context, does not possess any special significance except that it has functional value. Thus, one hand touching another part of the body has only such a functional value. This touching the touched, as Sarukkai puts it, thus has a functional value. However, there is another context in which folding both the hands together acquires a definite social meaning. Thus the act of touching or folding both the hands can communicate different, perhaps contradictory, messages. For example, in the Indian context, greeting people with both the hands from a distance is considered safe as it serves the purpose of avoiding the touch of others, perhaps the repulsive other—namely, the untouchables. This point becomes relevant in the context of Sarukkai's observation that it is only contact with the other through touch that can define the touched and the untouched. Similarly, Sarukkai's attempt to elevate untouchability much beyond the binary of pure and impure by invoking the metaphysics of body, as mentioned earlier, plays an important role in collapsing the cultural hierarchy that divides these bodies. Also, his invocation of Merleau-Ponty becomes quite instructive to appreciate the role that an untouchable as invisible body plays in illuminating the touchable.

One can further build on to this insight and argue that the untouchable is forced to become the repository of the impurities of the touchable. While this elevation of untouchability beyond the contours of purity–pollution is desirable, at the same time it also tends to undermine the moral significance of untouchability based on the ideology of purity–pollution. I would like to argue that the untouchable as supplementation of the touchable has contradictory value. This is so because it is available for regressive as well as subversive purposes. In the regressive reading, it could be argued that untouchability has a moral significance. Just imagine what would happen to the touchable if the untouchable were to refuse to become the dumping ground for somebody's moral dirt or refuse to illuminate the touchable. It perhaps would lead to the moral decomposition or atrophy of the touchables' body or they would get crushed under the accumulated weight of these impurities. Thank God there has been an untouchable around to carry this burden! The untouchables as the repository of the impurities also have moral significance for another reason. The upper-caste politicians, including some of the Left politicians, should thank the untouchable for providing a vocabulary to express either their agony or anger against their political opponents or beat the opponents with untouchability as a poisoned weapon. Look at these expressions that political leaders use almost every day: 'We are not untouchable'; 'Do not treat us as untouchable'. They seek to undercut the social significance of the twice-born by making the latter realize that they are either parasites or the free riders resting their burden on the body of the untouchables. The moral depletion of these free riders becomes total when they refuse to take any responsibility for the untouchable after they deposit their moral dirt in the latter.

However, the idea of moral significance could be deeply problematic as far as the emancipatory project of the untouchable is concerned. A person who prefers to stay in untouchability just for the sake of moral significance summarily loses the capacity to question the asymmetrical social relationship between the touchable and the untouchable. In fact, moral significance becomes a possibility only in the context of this asymmetry. Hence, it lacks transformative potential. The sacrifice made for maintaining the superiority, for example, of the top layer of the twice-born may have only an instrumental value to the extent that it provides vocabulary to the self-serving politicians, but it hardly has any transformative value for the slave and the untouchable. Thus, staying in an asymmetrical relationship necessarily subverts the self-understanding that is fundamentally so important for the freedom and ultimate emancipation of the person in question. Those in question, however, do not stay tied to the master just because they get some spiritual advantage or moral significance. In fact, the force of new aspirations motivates them to walk out of this constraining relationship. They refuse to become the dumping ground for somebody's garbage. This new emancipatory rationality could be very well captured in the modern mood characterizing the subversive politics of Ambedkar and his followers. His mood could be paraphrased in the following sentence: 'It may be in your interest to deposit your impurities in us, but how can it be in our interest to remain repository of your dirt (moral).' In the post-Ambedkar Dalit movement, the critique of untouchability as supplementation (Sarukkai's expression) is best captured in the term *Ghamdya*[34] that subverts this Dalit rationality, which is the hallmark of Ambedkar's emancipatory politics.

Ambedkar's politics seek to annihilate caste. But before he attacks its roots, he very systematically seeks to prune its branches—the various untouchability practices. For carrying out this attack against casteism through untouchability, Ambedkar follows an archaeological method. That is to say, through the social struggle, he first seeks to question untouchability practices that are the manifestation of the essence of caste. Also, for Ambedkar, the solution lies not in morality; on the contrary, it is fundamentally political. It is because of this primacy of the political that he does not lose sight of caste while he attacks its existence—that is, untouchability. However, for Gandhi, the solution lies not in the political but in the moral.[35] Gandhi chooses the moral route that does not centrally take on the essence of untouchability—that is, caste. In the Gandhian moral framework of action against untouchability, the contestation, if any, does not encircle the essence of caste but its existence- untouchability. This shift in focus from essence to existence invokes naturally a moral response rather than a political one. *Seva* (service) as the moral category in Gandhian discourse on untouchability makes sense in the context of this shift. Seva, as a moral category, does not seek to attack the roots of the problem; instead it chooses to prune its rough edges. In Gandhi, it is pruning rather than uprooting, while in Ambedkar, the reverse is the case. Although Gandhi looks less interested in establishing the link between untouchability and its essence (caste), it has to be acknowledged that his moral category of seva looks certainly radical when compared to Vedantic thinking, which rules out resolution of untouchability through material and corporeal touch.[36]

[34] For more discussion, see Guru (1996). This term could also be understood through the literary imagination of Dalit writers such as Prahlad Chendwankar, who has written the poem 'Cup' (Guru 1987).

[35] Iyer (2001).

[36] Tendulkar (1968: 230).

Look at Gandhi's body language, which is so relaxed and flows freely across time and spaces. The reverse is the case for the Shankaracharya, whose body is folded into itself; it is completely frozen. It is in this sense that the significance of the corporeality of touch makes the Gandhian approach to untouchability analogous to Ambedkar, because both of them insist that untouchables must enter the temple with the physical body and not through the spiritual mind, which is what the Vedantic view suggests.[37] However, Gandhi and Ambedkar differ from each quite substantially on other counts. Unlike Gandhi, who finds the solution of untouchability in the moral surgery of the heart, Ambedkar suggests the annihilation of caste, of which untouchability is just the existence.[38] According to Ambedkar, the 'Brahminical mind' produces opaque forms of untouchability that can be detected either through sociology or anthropology.[39] But untouchability exists beyond mere description and hence requires archaeology that can access the untouchability which, as Shinde has very perceptively pointed out, sits at the bottom of this mind.[40] Ambedkar's thinking and politics follow the archaeological method of discovering the essence of untouchability.[41] Let us explore the question of what archaeology is and why it is relevant for understanding untouchability in 'elegant India'.

ARCHAEOLOGY OF UNTOUCHABILITY

Archaeology, in recent times, has become a generic term that appears in different fields of inquiry ranging from the social sciences to the humanities to physical sciences such as geomorphology. For example, medical practitioners have been using archaeology to understand the diminishing height (physical) of persons across generations. Parentage, with nutritional deficiency, leads to diminishing height

[37] Guru (2007: 221–38).
[38] Tendulkar (1968: 230); Ambedkar (1979: 47).
[39] Ambedkar (1990b: 32).
[40] Shinde (1976: 129).
[41] Ambedkar (1979: 7).

in successive generations. Similarly, in geomorphology, archaeology is an important method to access the natural substance that, due to changes in nature, gets hidden underneath waterbodies, earth, and snow.[42] In fact, changes occurring in the natural substance can best be captured with archaeology as a method of analysis. For example, in a region experiencing snowfall, one finds peaks getting covered with snow and becoming denuded during the hot weather. The importance of archaeology in history deals not so much with invention but with discovering historical evidence in different forms (artefacts and even quantitative data) so as to provide a background for making conjectures and refutations. The debate among the Indian historians over certain disputed historical structures proves this point quite adequately. Some sociologists also find archaeology a useful method to study social relations in India.[43]

Interestingly, archaeology also finds its relevance in debates between two leading Marxist thinkers: Hobsbawm and Althusser. Hobsbawm finds in Althusser an archaeological operation and identifies in the latter different layers of theoretical thinking, which had gradually accumulated on top of Marx's original thought.[44] Finally, and most importantly, in the Foucauldian sense, archaeology tries to define 'not the thoughts, representation, images, themes, preoccupations that are concealed or revealed in discourse, but those discourses themselves, those discourses as practices obeying certain rules. It does not treat discourses as document, as a sign of something else, as an element that ought to be transparent, but where unfortunate opacity must often be pierced if one is to reach at least the depth of the essential in the place in which it is held in reverse, it is connected with discourses in its own volume as a monument. It is not interpretative discipline, it does not seek another, better hidden discourse, it refuses to be allegorical'.[45]

[42] I benefited from a discussion I held with Prof. Harjit Singh, an expert in glaciology.

[43] *Ibid.*, p. 242.

[44] Hobsbawm (1994: 1).

[45] Foucault (1994: 136).

A Foucauldian take on archaeology would also help us to distinguish archaeology from architecture. In the Indian context, Dalits used the metaphor of the pyramid to describe the caste system and more particularly the varna system, while the Marxists put caste and untouchability as being located in the superstructure.[46] In the archaeological sense, caste and untouchability are not a kind of ordered or open design. In fact, as we shall see in the following pages, they play out quite secretly and subtly. For example, in public discussion, themes on Dalits come to be listed at the fag end of the seminar or conference or at the end of a research journal.[47] This preferential order looks natural because those who have the power to put Dalits in an irreversible order do not find it necessary to provide any reason for such a preferential arrangement. Thus, archaeology seeks to access this inalterability of the 'Indian Mind'.[48] It seeks to reveal or fathom the untouchability-ridden 'Indian Mind' that hides within itself a persisting element of caste. The Indian mind essentially operates through the subtle act of transferring value from one sphere to another. Thus, archaeology is a generic concept that appears relevant to different scholars in different contexts. However, covering and discovering or melting and freeing are essential and defining features of archaeology, common to all the perspectives on archaeology. Secondly, archaeology for its definition requires a hidden context with opacity or anonymity. That is to say, it does not become relevant in a transparent context. Let us explore what this context is for untouchability.

THE CONTEXT OF THE ARCHAEOLOGY OF UNTOUCHABILITY

Let me begin by arguing that archaeology as a method of discovering the essence or the truth of caste becomes intelligible only in certain contexts. For example, archaeology may become redundant in the rural context, where caste hierarchies play out openly through resorting to blatant untouchability practices, and hence caste does not

---

[46] Jha (1997: 27).
[47] *Biblio*, VII (9 and 10), September and October 2002.
[48] Foucault (1994).

require untouchability to adopt subtle forms for its own expression. Let me make this point further clear by citing some evidence
from some villages in Tamil Nadu and Maharashtra.[49] In these villages, where the upper castes have raised a physical wall of separation
between the touchable and the untouchables, archaeology does not
need to discover anything more. To put it differently, archaeology requires a spatially ambiguous context for its success. Similarly,
archaeology would be ineffective in the rural context where the
untouchables still have to appear in public with body markers (with
a broom, a basket of filth on the head, a certain dress code, or a black
ribbon on the wrist), constituting them as 'walking carrion'. To put
it differently, archaeology does not make sense particularly in the
face-to-face or intimate social context. Rather, archaeology becomes
intelligible in the social context where every other person appears a
stranger to every other person in an opaqueness of social relations.
The urban context makes it difficult for the pure untouchable to
remain in touch with the despicable untouchable. I am already suggesting, as does Sarukkai, that the despicable untouchable provides a
subjective condition for self-preservation of the 'pure untouchable'.
The growing dilution of the interactive sphere, leading to growing
anonymity, makes the domestic space within the urban context the
only sphere for the protection of the 'pure untouchable'. The domestic sphere provides an opportunity for the resolution of the anxiety
that continues to grip the urban upper castes. Let me further argue
how the domestic space offers a stable context for the pure untouchable to overcome his or her anxiety.

First, the domestic sphere offers the space for conducting purifi-
catory functions. The touchable or the twice-born persons use the
domestic sphere for both physical as well as ritual purification. It
is quite revealing to note that some parents hose down their kids
after they return home from school, not because their bodies are
mired in mud or dust, but because they might have messed with the
untouchable kids while in school.[50] Second, the domestic sphere also
provides an opportunity for the upper castes to feel sovereign over

---

[49] *Frontline*, December 2008.

[50] My own field work from the villages from Sawantwadi block, in the Tal
(deep) Konkan region of Maharashtra.

controlling the domestic space. Practising untouchability at home becomes the major source of the sovereignty. The need to realize that this sovereignty cannot be fulfilled in the public sphere, which can offer only an abstract sense of sovereignty to a citizen of the Indian republic, becomes clear from following the moves that the pure self makes in protecting the domestic sphere as a sphere of sovereignty. First, he invites those about whose background he is absolutely sure. He enjoys discretionary power. Second, the twice-born host uses money power to retain his ritual power in case the twice-born host commits a mistake by inviting a person of ambiguous social identity, gets stuff from the hotel, and, finally, if he knows the invitee is from a lower caste but cannot avoid inviting him, he then offers him tender coconut. The shell of the used tender coconut is a safe device for avoiding ritual pollution because the shell can be disposed of.

Interestingly, the axis between the domestic and the public spheres provides space for archaeological articulation. As mentioned above, the domestic sphere is the sphere of sovereignty for the member of the upper caste. He or she, due to the pressure of social vigilance, can enjoy partial sovereignty only in the fragmented time and space and not in continuous time. In fact, the pressure of social vigilance forces him or her to don universal masks while he is in the public domain. Thus, he or she becomes co-worker, teacher, citizen, consumer, and so on, depending on the spheres. In the journey back home, the sacred soul begins to drop each of these universal identities. He or she becomes completely denuded in the domestic sphere. This is analogous to the archaeology of the glacier as mentioned above. It is in this sense that the domestic becomes the sphere of deflation of pretension. For the untouchables, therefore, it is the domestic sphere that is the testing ground for the morally integrated or genuine personality. This has been further confirmed by some anthropologists.[51] How does one get an insight into this deflation of the 'pure self' who hides behind the universal identities? While there are several Dalit autobiographies that offer an insight into this archaeological insight[52], let me cite

[51] Khare (1984: 14).
[52] Walmiki (2002).

an interesting conversation between an upper-caste landlord and a prospective untouchable tenant.

Landlord: May I know your name?
Tenant: My name is Bhagvan. (This Hindu sounding name anticipates subsequent question from the landlord)
Landlord: You are from which region?
Tenant: I am a Maharashtrian. (This does not give any idea of his social background)
Landlord: Which language do you speak?
Tenant: Hindustani or English.
Landlord: Are you Veg. or Non-veg? (This is true in some regions only)
Tenant: Vegetarian. (This does not help the landlord to overcome landlord's reservations, and hence he uses the last question)
Landlord: Where do you work? (This is the last but sure source of knowing the caste of a tenant because as Harkishan Santoshi has observed in his testimonies, the caste of a person reaches to working place earlier than his/her transfer papers)[53]

The conversation between the landlord and the prospective tenant underlies an archaeological move that is deeply contradictory in nature. The landlord's archaeology involves a set of questions that are authoritative, irrational, and hence offensive. This archaeology, which is aimed at restoring inalienability between the sacred self and the modern enterprise, acquires an offensive character particularly on normative grounds. The prospective tenant, instead of rejecting the irrational question on rational grounds, chooses to cope with it by adopting a defensive archaeology, which involves universal answers for the particular questions. This withdrawal into guided universalism thus suggests a loss of self-esteem as far as the tenant is concerned. The tenant fails to put counter questions to the landlord, thus exposing the latter's failure to follow market rationality. It is due to this primacy of the irrational over the rational or ritual value over the monetary value that the offensive archaeology adopted by the upper-caste landlord cannot be reduced to mere psychology, because the landlord does not ask these questions to satisfy his psychological curiosity. In fact, in this case, offensive archaeology establishes an ontological link with the ritually superior self. Offensive archaeol-

[53] Guru (1986).

ogy, which operates through the coercive questioning, in the process tends to render the landlord completely denuded, of course on moral grounds. The prospective tenant also suffers from a painful skinning off of layers of different universal identities that he puts on himself as a defence mechanism. Thus, archaeology suggests a double bind.

This offensive archaeology has implications at three levels. First, at the phenomenological level, the social attitude of the ideal untouchable (the upper caste) does point to social relations rather than to knowledge conditions. Second, this archaeology suggests the irresolvable tension between a good citizen and a good person. To put it differently, an upper-caste person may be a citizen good enough to grant at least temporary recognition to an untouchable, but he or she may not be a good person. Third, an attempt on the part of the landlord to cordon off the private sphere eventually divests the sphere of being the space for healing and recuperating necessitated by the ravages of the public world.[54] Fourth, this Janus-faced ideal untouchable thus violates the Aristotelian principle that suggests interconnection between the private and the public, which are bound by the totality of the moral qualities of a good man.[55] Finally, the ideal untouchable and his or her attitudes towards the real untouchable confirm Sarukkai's main argument, according to which the self-definition of the upper caste or the ideal untouchable becomes possible only in relation to the ascriptive identity of the untouchable. This sacred self cannot exist without the presence of the other, the despicable untouchable. This tense coexistence becomes a possibility only through outsourcing untouchability to the other. However, those who supplement untouchability into others continue to suffer from endless anxiety. That is to say, they can neither completely detoxify themselves of an element of untouchability, nor can they brandish it openly. Ironically, the predicament makes the archaeological method inevitable for the detection of untouchability, which sits deep in the anxious self.

[54] Michel de Certeau, quoted in Gupta (2003: 56).
[55] Aristotle (1985: 13–17).

9

Conclusion

Gopal Guru and Sundar Sarukkai

In this debate about experience and theory we have tried to engage with themes which, in our opinion, are essential to the 'doing' of social science in India today. In the Introduction, we have suggested that two major asymmetries plague the theoretical discourse of the social sciences in India. One was the excessive dependence on philosophical concepts drawn from European (and the larger but more ambiguous 'Western') experiences to understand and theorize experiences that characterize Indian societies and cultures. The other asymmetry was the overall neglect, both within and outside, of Indian intellectual traditions in social theorizing. In other words, western philosophical and intellectual vocabulary drawn and developed from an engagement with their special experiences become part of a universal discourse applicable to all societies whereas similar vocabulary—even if developed from non-western societies—are at the most applicable only to those societies. These entrenched asymmetries have significantly impacted the competence as well as the confidence of countless students of social science. Adding to these problems, but not distinct from them, is the question of language in social science writing in India.

Now, at the end of this prolonged, and sometimes 'idiosyncratic' debate, we can ask whether our debate really attends to, even if only partly and prematurely, any of these concerns. We believe that this debate has been able to achieve the following: one, bring philosophy and the social sciences closer to each other in the context of social theorizing of Indian experiences; two, exhibit the contours of how we can draw on Indian intellectual practices to reflect on experiences; three, highlight a fundamental issue about theorizing that is far too often ignored, namely, the ethical stance that should explicitly characterize the act of theorizing; and, four, through these modes point explicitly to the politics of theorizing about human experiences. In a sense, then, this book is an exploration of the politics of experience and the ethics of theorizing.

We began the debate with the politics of experience which has become endemic to the practice of social science in India. Guru raised this question by invoking the theme of community and the prerequisites necessary for theorizing about that community. While we recognize that it is difficult to identity all Dalits as belonging to a homogenous community, it nevertheless pointed to a particular problem of doing theory itself. This problem was primarily the derivative status of theory-making in India. Theory was being dominated by an excessive dependence on concepts and vocabulary drawn from cultures and traditions 'foreign' to the Indian society. This in itself is not a problem although the excessive dependence leads to, among other things, undigested and uncritical use of these categories. Many times, this leads to unreadability, a trend which seems to have alienated many social scientists as well as activists in India. Equally importantly, our participation and dependence on these theoretical frameworks have not been 'accepted' by the West—in other words, Indian social scientists have become consumers of the knowledge games of the Western academic world and are not seen as equal partners in this enterprise. The startling absence of Indian thinkers in encyclopaedias, intellectual biographies, and in textbooks must definitely be a cause of concern to some at least!

The neglect of Indian theoreticians by the accomplished West continues the political agenda of all theorizing. We only need to remember here the enormous influence of Plato's idea of theory on contemporary understanding of the act of theorizing. For Plato, theory is an act of the Extraordinary. From the ordinary world, and mediated by Eros, theory occurs in the extraordinary realm. Coming back from the extraordinary realm, theory then illuminates the ordinary. Has the theoretical activity changed at all from this fundamental belief that there is a sense of the Extraordinary that is associated with it? Has theory moved away from this intrinsic relationship with desire and interest? If not, then there are serious consequences of an act that is driven by desire and the exclusion of the ordinary. Pre-modern accounts of knowledge in Indian and the European civilizations tempered the idea of theoretical knowledge by associating it with 'sins' of pride and vanity, among other things. For the traditional Indian thinkers, pure theoretical knowledge was undesirable not only on ethical but also on pragmatic grounds.

The theme which unifies the problems of theory and experience in India today is that of stakeholdership. In the context of theory, Western academics do not see Indian theory as having a stake in their discourse; hence, their 'unreasonable indifference' to work from non-western societies. And paradoxically, in the case of experience, they believe that their theoretical moves allow them to have a stake (and say) in describing Indian experiences. Theory and experience in the Indian context both become subservient to dominant ideologies and hence become political in a fundamental sense of the term. This is extendable to non-Western societies in general, and to Asia and Africa in particular.

These reflections on theory lead us to re-emphasize the point that the idea of theory itself is not universal and that it means something different in the Indian (and perhaps the Asian) context. Theory in these traditions, as was noted above, is not the platonic movement to the Extraordinary thereby devaluing the ordinary (the empirical, the experiential). Instead, the very idea of theory in Indian traditions is one that is always integrated with the empirical, the experiential and the ethical. More importantly, they point to the possibility that there is no one 'theory of theory'.

While scholars will accept that there are different theories, by and large, they tend to believe that there is only one kind of a structure that defines theory. For example, in this belief, fiction is not a legitimate mode of theorizing. Western intellectual history could as well be read as a concerted effort to legitimize one kind of theory as theory. Look at the European response to theory in Indian traditions. It is well exemplified by the dismissal of the availability of theory in the Indian traditions by thinkers ranging from Hegel to Gadamer, through Husserl. Moreover, this definition of theory also served political ends. As best illustrated by the colonial discourse, theory was used to legitimize the superiority of the European societies with respect to the colonized ones by claiming that the colonizers had 'theory' while the colonized did not possess the capacity for doing theory. (Guru's argument about theoretical Brahmins and empirical Shudras highlights this dichotomy by showing how it occurs within the practice of social science in India today).

What could any of these otherwise intelligent European thinkers have meant by saying that Indians (and the Asians, in general) had no idea of theory? Two of the essential models for theory in the West were logic and mathematics. The Greeks and the traditions that followed had a very specific idea of these two disciplines but interestingly these do not match the idea of mathematics and logic in Indian traditions. Indian logic has a special nature, one that essentially combines the empirical and the conceptual. For long, most European commentators on Indian logic argued that this was not logic since it did not differentiate the logical (formal) from the empirical. Similarly, there has been a long history of western scholarship that argued that Indian mathematics was not really 'mathematical' since it didn't possess important characteristics of mathematics as in the Western view. Indian mathematics remained embedded in the empirical and unlike the platonic tradition, which influences the understanding of mathematics even today, does not get associated with the transcendental and the theological. To claim that these platonic and theological underpinnings of mathematics are what characterize mathematics is to claim that one group's views on mathematics should be accepted as the universal definition of it. To claim that non-Western traditions have no idea of theory (and mathematics and logic) by defining these terms from one point of view is as absurd as saying that the West has no idea of mathematics and theory since they do not match the Indian formulations of these notions. However, we should note that the history of the idea of theory in the West has been a long and complex one. The culture of theory has been established through scholarly, analytical, and interpretative use of concepts and ideas from their past as well as creative reflections on their present. Theory in the West is established through the fertile use and abuse of earlier concepts, appropriation, and misappropriation of their intellectual history. Unless we, in India, learn to have this creative engagement with cultural and intellectual categories (both from the past and the present) we might end up depending on others to supply categories for our theorizing.

Our conclusion goes beyond merely saying that one has to use concepts from other non-western traditions, including those that speak of the experiences of people and communities who are theoretically 'marginalized'. We are also saying that the definition of a theory itself needs to be relooked at—definitions from other non-Western cultures on what constitutes the act of speaking for others, both human and nonhuman. In so doing, we hope that the readers will begin to reflect more deeply on the very nature of theorizing, the desire and motivation that accompanies this act, the emotions that are engendered by the belief that we, as theorists, understand much more than those who are not, the ethics of speaking for and on behalf of others, the troubling notions of vanity, confidence and 'arrogance' that lurks behind the theoretical stance.

The second major theme of this debate involves an attempt to find ways of articulating the problem of experience. This, in some sense, reverses our critique of theory by now enquiring closely into some accepted views of experience. In particular, the belief that some experiences are unique to communities, a belief that succeeds in grounding identity theories, has been debated quite extensively in this book. While we began with some preliminary ideas of lived experience as having some unique characteristics which resist appropriation by any and all, we have also over the course of the debate brought in various other aspects of experience. We do seem to suggest—by the end of the book—that completely 'pure' experiences without any sort of conceptual mediation may not be possible but at the same time, we also believe that it is necessary to theorize 'experience' as a category before we raise questions about the theory–experience relationship.

One way by which we have attempted to do this is by trying to use a different set of conceptual terms to talk about much-discussed experiences. We focus on Dalit experience and try and rearrange the contours of the extensive literature in this field. Guru's thematization of space in the context of Indian experience is a way of negotiating with concepts of contemporary interest in association with thinkers

such as Ambedkar and Gandhi. In doing this, Guru is also addressing the asymmetries discussed earlier—one, by bringing to the fore
a dialogue between contemporary thinkers and Indian intellectual
such as Ambedkar and Gandhi, and two, by suggesting how such
exercises can be of relevance to theoretical attempts to understand
Western societies. Sarukkai broadens this debate on experience by
illustrating different approaches to the notions of experience and
self. The four chapters, following the Introduction, are concerned
with these aspects related to experience. Although this debate began
with the idea of the uniqueness of lived experience and its opacity
to theory, the four chapters together create a much more complex
discourse of experience. The remaining chapters engage largely with
the idea of ethics in the act of theorizing. In attempting to discover
the ethical in the act of theorizing, we also discover the complexities
of the relationship between experience and theory, and the essential
intertwined nature of these two categories. We would like to make
a modest claim that the two chapters on untouchability reflect the
inherent richness in such approaches. Our debate on untouchability
was catalysed by our surprise that there has been almost no philosophical attempt to understand untouchability. But our debate goes
beyond merely attempting a philosophical description of it. Our
attempt is primarily to find ways to expand the conceptual categories
associated with untouchability and, in so doing, address the problems
of asymmetry as well as the ethics of theorizing and the politics of
experience inherent in the discourse on untouchability.

References

Achalkham, Rustam, 2006, *Tamasha Lok Rangabhumi*, Pune: Sugawa Publication.

Ada, Michael, 1989, *Machines as the Measure of Men*, Ithaca: Cornell University Press.

Ambedkar, B.R., 1957, *Buddha and his Dhamma*, Mumbai: Siddharth Publication.

————, 'The Untouchables. Who Were They and Why They became Untouchables?', in *Dr Babasaheb Ambedkar Writings and Speeches, Vol. 7*, Bombay: Government of Maharashtra.

————, 1987a, *Writings and Speeches, Vol. 1*, Education Department, Government of Maharashtra.

————, 1987b, *Writings and Speeches, Vol. 3*, Education Department, Government of Maharashtra.

————, 1989, *Writing and Speeches of Babasaheb Ambedkar, Vol. 5*, Mumbai: Education Department, Government of Maharashtra.

————, 1990a, *Writings and Speeches, Vol. 1*, Education Department, Government of Maharashtra.

————, 1990b, *Writings and Speeches, Vol. 7*, Education Department, Government of Maharashtra.

————, 1990c, *Writings and Speeches, Vol. 9*, Education Department, Government of Maharashtra.

————, 2001, *Writings and Speeches, Vol. 18*, Education Department, Government of Maharashtra.

————, 2002, *Writings and Speeches, Vol. 18, Part II*, Education Department, Government of Maharashtra.

————, 2003, *Writings and Speeches, Vol. 17, Part III*, Education Department, Government of Maharashtra.

————, 2005, *Writings and Speeches, Vol. 19, Part II*, Education Department, Government of Maharashtra.

Amin, Shahid, 1984, 'Gandhi as Mahatma: Gorakhpur District, Eastern UP, 1921', Ranajit Guha (ed.), in *Subaltern Studies 3: Writings on South Asian History and Society*, New Delhi: Oxford University Press.

Anand, Mulkraj, 2001, *Untouchable*, Delhi: Penguin.

Ananthamurthy, U.R., 1978, *Samskara*, (trans. by A.K. Ramanujan), Delhi: Oxford University Press.

Anderson, Benedict, 1991, *Imagined Communities: Reflections on the Origin and Spread of Nationalism* (revised and extended edition), London: Verso.

Aristotle, Nichomachean, 1985, *Ethics* (trans Terence Irwin), Indianapolis/ Cambridge: Hackett Publishing Company.

Bagul, Baburao, 1978, *Jevanha Mi Jat Chorali Hoti* (Marathi), Nagpur: Siddartha Publication.

Banerjee, Sumanta, 2000, *The Dangerous Outcast*, Kolkata: Seagull.

Baxi, Upendra, 1995, 'Emancipation as Justice: Babasaheb Ambedkar's Legacy and Vision', in Upendra Baxi and Bhikhu Parekh (eds), *Crisis and Change in Contemporary India*, New Delhi: Sage, pp. 122–50.

Bayly, Susan, 1999, *Caste, Society and Politics in India from the Eighteenth Century to the Modern Age*, Cambridge: Cambridge University Press.

Bean, Susan, 1981, 'Towards a Semiotics of "Purity" and "Pollution" in India', *American Ethnologist*, 8 (3): 575–95.

Berlin, Isiah, 1978, *Concept and Categories*, Henry Hardy (ed.), London: Hogarth Press, London.

Béteille, André, 1992, *The Backward Classes in Modern India*, New Delhi: Oxford University Press.

Bhattacharya, Amarnath, 2008, 'The Concept of Śarira: Sthūla, Sukṣma, Liṅga, Kāraṇa', in P.K. Sen (ed.), *Philosophical Concepts Relevant to Sciences in Indian Tradition*, New Delhi: Centre for Studies in Civilizations.

Bhattacharya, K.C., 2008, *Studies in Philosophy*, 3rd Edition, Delhi: Motilal Banarsidass.

Bhavare, N.G., 2007, *Waman Dada Kardak Yanchi Geet Rachana*, Parshuram Gimekar (ed.), Aurangabad: Kailash Publication.

Boivin, Nicole, 2005, *Orientalism, Ideology and Identity: Examining Caste in South Asian Archaeology, Journal of Social Archaeology*, 5(2): 225–52.

Broad, C.D., 1925, *The Mind and its Place in Nature*, New York: The Humanities Press, London: Routledge & Kegan Paul.

Bunge, Mario, 2007, 'The Ethics of Science and the Science of Ethics', in P. Kurtz (ed.), *Science and Ethics*, New York: Prometheus Books.

Burns, David, 1980, *Feeling Good: The New Mood Therapy*, New York: William Morrow and Co.

Butler, Judith, 1990, 'Performativity's Social Magic', Richard Shusterman (ed.), *Bourdieu: A Critical Reader*, Oxford: Blackwell Publishers.

Chadha, Monima, 2001, 'Perceptual Cognition: A Nyāya-Kantian Approach', *Philosophy East and West*, 51(2): 197–209.

Chakrabarti, Arindam, 1992, 'I Touch What I Saw', *Philosophy and Phenomenological Research*, Vol. LII, pp. 103–16.

———, 2000, 'Against Immaculate Perception: Seven Reasons for Eliminating Nirvikalpaka Perception from Nyaya', *Philosophy East and West*, Vol. 50, pp. 1–8.

Chattopadhyaya, B. and D.D. Kosambi, 2002, *Combined Method in Indology and Other Writings*, New Delhi: Oxford University Press.

Chakrabarti, K.K., 1999, *Classical Indian Philosophy of Mind*, New York: State University of New York.

Chatterjee, Partha, 1986, *Nationalist Thought and the Colonial World: A Derivative Discourse?*, New Delhi: Oxford University Press.

———, 2002, 'Institutional Context of Social Science Research in South Asia', *Economic and Political Weekly*, XXXVII (35): 36–12.

Chauhan, Surajpal, 2010, *Dalit Autobiographies in Hindi*, New Delhi: Vani Publications.

Chrétien, Jean-Louis, 2004, *The Call and the Response*, (trans. by Anne A. Davenport), New York: Fordham University Press.

Classen, Constance (ed.), 2005, *The Book of Touch*, Oxford and New York: Berg.

Colebrook, Claire, 2002, *Gille Deleuze: Routledge Critical Thinker*, London/New York: Routledge.

Collingwood, R.G., 1994, *The Idea of History*, London: Oxford University Press.

Connor, Steven, 2004, *The Book of Skin*, Ithaca: Cornell University Press.

Csikszentmihalyi, Mihaly, 1996, *Creativity: Flow and the Psychology of Discovery and Invention*, New York: Harper Perennial.

Culler, Jonathan, 1997, *Literary Theory: A Very Short Introduction*, New York: Oxford University Press.

Curtin, Deane W., 1992, 'Food, Body and Person', Deane W. Curtin and Lisa M. Heldke (eds), *Cooking, Eating, Thinking*, Bloomington: Indian University Press, pp. 4–7.

Cybil, K.V., 2009, ' Defining Untouchability in Relation to Body', *Economic and Political Weekly*, XLIV (51): 82–3.

Das, Veena, 1977, *Structure and Cognition*, New Delhi: Oxford University Press.

Datta, Srilekha, 2008, 'Gunas (Qualities) in Nyāya-Vaiśeṣika Ontology', in P.K. Sen (ed.), *Philosophical Concepts Relevant to Sciences in Indian Tradition*, New Delhi: Centre for Studies in Civilizations.

de Souza, P., 2002, 'Intellectuals and their Domain', *Economic and Political Weekly*, XXXVII (9): 890–2.

Deliege, R., 1999 (1995), *The Untouchables of India*, Oxford: Berg.

Derrida, Jacques, 1976, *Of Grammatology*, (trans. by Gayatri Chakravorty Spivak), Baltimore and London: Johns Hopkins University Press.

———, 2005, *On Touching, Jean-Luc Nancy*, (trans. by Christine Irizarry), Stanford: Stanford University Press.

Desai, I.P., 1976, *Untouchability in Rural Gujarat*, Bombay: Popular Publication.

Dillon, Martin C., 1997, *Merleau-Ponty's Ontology*, Evanston: Northwestern University Press.

Dumont, L., 1980, *Homo Hierarchicus*, Oxford: Oxford University Press.

———, 1988, *Homo Hierarchicus*, (trans. by Mark Sainsbury, Louis Dumont and Basia Gulati), Delhi: Oxford University Press.

Dyer, Helen S., 1900, *Pandita Ramabai: The Story of Her Life*, London: Morgan and Scott.

Eagleton, Terry, 2000, *Literary Theory: An Introduction*, Delhi: Maya Publishers.

Fay, Christian, 1996, *Contemporary Philosophy of Social Sciences*, Oxford: Blackwell.

Fischer-Tiné, Harald and Michael Mann (eds), 2004, *Colonialism and Civilizing Mission, Cultural Ideology in British India,* London: Wimbledon Publishing Company.

Fontes da Costa, Palmira, 2002, 'The Culture of Curiosity at the Royal Society during the First Half of the Eighteenth Century', *Notes and Records of the Royal Society of London*, No. 56, pp. 147–66.

Foucault, Michael (tr.), 1994, *Archaeology of Knowledge*, London: Routledge.

Fox, Nick J., 1998, 'Foucault, Foucauldians and Sociology', *The British Journal of Sociology*, 49 (3): 415–33.

Fuller, C.J., 1979, 'Gods, Priests and Purity: On the Relation between Hinduism and the Caste System', *Man*, 14 (3): 459–76.

Gadamar, H., 1960, *Truth and Method*, London: Sheed & Ward.

———, 2001, *The Beginning of Knowledge*, (trans. by R. Coltman), New York: Continuum.

Ganguli, B.N., 1973, *Gandhi's Social Philosophy: Perspective and Relevance*, New Delhi: Vikas.

Geetha, V., and S.V. Rajdurai, 1998, *Non-Brahmin Millennium*, Kolkata: Samya Publication.

Gellnar, E., 1982, 'Relativism and Universalism', in Martin Hollis and Steven Lukes (eds), *Rationality and Relativism*, London: Basil Blackwell.

Gellnar, E., 1984, *Relativism in Social Sciences*, Cambridge: Cambridge University Press.

Ghurye, G.S., 1965, *Caste and Tribes of Maharashtra*, Mumbai: Popular Prakashan.

Gibson, James J., 1962, 'Observations on Active Touch', *Psychological Review* 69 (6): 477–91.

Glucklich, Ariel, 1994, *The Sense of Adharma*, New York: Oxford University Press.

Gooptu, Nandini, 2001, *The Politics of the Urban Poor in Early Twentieth-Century India*, Cambridge: Cambridge University Press.

Goswami, Manu, 2004, *Producing India*, New Delhi: Permanent Black.

Gramsci, A., 1996, *The Prison Notebooks*, Hyderabad: Orient Longman.

Gross, A.G., 1990, *The Rhetoric of Science*, Cambridge, MA: Harvard University Press.

Guha, Ramachandra, 2001, 'The Absent Liberal: An Essay on Politics and Intellectual Life', *Economic and Political Weekly*, XXXVI (50): 4663–70.

Gupta, Bina, 1995, *Perceiving in Advaita Vendanta*, New Delhi: Motilal Banarsidass.

Gupta, Brahmananda, 2008, 'The Concept of "Indriyas" in Āyurvedic Texts with Special Reference to Karmendriyas', in P.K. Sen (ed.), *Philosophical Concepts Relevant to Sciences in Indian Tradition*, New Delhi: Centre for Studies in Civilizations.

Gupta, Dipankar, 2000, *Culture, Space and the Nation-State*, New Delhi: Sage.

————, 2003, 'Democratic Public: Tradition, Modernity and the Public Private Divide', in Gurpreet Mahajan (ed.), *The Public Private: Issue of Democratic Citizenship*, Delhi: Sage.

Guru, Gopal, 1986, 'Discrimination and Sanskritization: Some Theoretical Aspects', *Sociological Bulletin*.

————, 1987, 'Political Economy of Discrimination and Segregation in Urban Bombay—1930', *Social Science Probings*, New Delhi: People's Publishing House.

————, 1987, 'The Political Economy of Dalit Segregation and Discrimination in Pre-independent Bombay City', *Social Science Probings*, 4 (1), pp. 36–46.

————, 1996, *Dalit Cultural Movement in Maharashtra*, Mumbai: Vikas Adhyayan Kendra.

————, 2002, 'How Egalitarian are the Social Sciences in India?', *Economic and Political Weekly*, XXXVII (51): 5003–09.

————, 2007a, 'Power of Touch', *Frontline*, December.

Guru, Gopal, 2007b, 'Twentieth Century Discourse on Social Justice: A View from Quarantine India', in Sabyaysachi Bhattacharya (ed.), *Development of Modern Indian Thought and the Social Sciences*, New Delhi: Oxford University Press, pp. 221–38.

————, 2009, 'Archaeology of Untouchability', *Economic and Political Weekly*, XLIV (37): 49–56.

Harding, Sandra, 1992, *Subjectivity, Experience and Knowledge, Development and Change*, London: Sage.

Harris, Barbara, 2003, *India Working*, Cambridge: Cambridge University Press.

Harrison, P., 2001, 'Curiosity, Forbidden Knowledge, and the Reformation of Natural Philosophy in Early Modern England', *Isis*, Vol. 92, pp. 265–90.

Heller, Agnes, 1987, *Beyond Justice*, Oxford: Basil Blackwell.

————, 1989, *A Theory of Modernity*, Oxford: Blackwell.

Hobsbawm, E.J., 1994. 'Structure of Capitalism,' in G. Elliott (ed.), *Althusser: A Critical Reader*. Oxford: Basil Blackwell.

Honneth, Axel, 1995, *Struggle for Recognition, Moral Grammer of Self Respect* (trans. by Joel Anderson), Cambridge, MA: The MIT Press.

Isaacs, H.R., 1965, *India's Ex-Untouchables*, New York: John Day Company.

Iyer, Raghavan, N., 2001, *Moral and Political Philosophy of Gandhi*, New Delhi: Oxford University Press.

Jablonski, Nina, 2006. *Skin: A Natural History*, University of California Press.

Jackson, F., 1982, 'Epiphenomenal Qualia', *Philosophical Quarterly*, Vol. 32, pp. 127–36.

Jefferey, P., R. Jefferey, and A. Lyon, 1989, *Labour Pains and Labour Power: Women and Childbearing in India*, London and New Jersey: Zed Books.

Jha, Ganganatha, 1984, *The Nyaya-Sutras of Gautama, Vol. 3*, Delhi: Motilal Banarsidass.

Jha, Vivekananda, 1974, 'From Tribe to Untouchables: The Case of Nisada', in R.S. Sharma (ed.), *Indian Society Historical Probing*, New Delhi: People's Publishing House, pp. 67–84.

————, 1997, 'Caste, Untouchability, and Social Justice, Early North Indian Perspective', *Social Scientist*, 25 (111–112).

Johnson, Barbara, 1990, 'Writing', in F. Lentricchia and T. McLaughlin (eds), *Critical Terms for Literary Study*, Chicago: University of Chicago Press, pp. 39–49.

Kamble, Babytai, 2000, *Jinha Aamucha*, Pune: Sugawa Publication.

Kamble, Babytai, 2008, *Prison We Broke*, (trans. by Maya Pandit), Delhi: Orient Longman.

Karanth, Shivram, 1984, *Choma's Drum*, (trans. by U.R. Kalkur), New Delhi: Arnold Heinemann.

Kashyap, S. 2008, *Concept of Untouchability in Dharmashastra*, Delhi: New Bharatiya Book Corporation.

Kaviraj, Sudipta, 1995, 'Reversal of Orientalism: Bhudeio Mukhopadhyay and the Project of Indigenist Social Theory', in Vasudha Dalmia and Hvon Stiencron (eds), *Representing Hinduism*, New Delhi: Sage, pp. 251–79.

Khairmode, C.B., 1985, *Bhimrao Ramji Ambedkar, Vol. 6*, Pune: Sugawa Publication.

———, 1990a, *Bhimrao Ramji Ambedkar, Vol. 1*, Pune: Sugawa Publication.

———, 1990b, *Bhimrao Ramji Ambedkar, Vol. 3*, Pune: Sugawa Publication.

———, 1991a. *Babasaheb Ambedkarnache Charitra, Vol. 2*. Pune: Sugawa Publication.

———, 1991b. *Bhirao Ramji Ambedkar, Vol. 2*, Pune: Sugawa Publication.

Khare, R.S., 1984, *The Untouchable as Himself: Ideology, Identity, and Pragmatism among the Chamars of Lucknow*, Cambridge: Cambridge University Press.

Khatare, Anil, 2009, *Shivkal Ani Peshwaitil Maharancha Itihas*, Pune: Sugawa Publication.

Lang, Karen Christine, 2003, *Four Illusions: Candrakīrti's Advice for Travelers on the Bodhisattva Path by Candrakīrti*, (trans. by Karen Christine Lang), New York: Oxford University Press.

Leder, Drew and Mitchell W. Krucoff, 2008, 'The Touch That Heals: The Uses and Meanings of Touch in the Clinical Encounter', *The Journal of Alternative and Complementary Medicine*, 14 (3): 321–7.

Lederle, Mathew, 1976, *Philosophical Trends in Maharashtra*, Bombay: Popular Publication.

Lefebvre, Henri, 1984, *Production of Space*, (trans. by Donald Nicholson-Smith), Oxford: Blackwell.

Lieten, G.K., 1984, *Colonialism, Class and Nation*, Calcutta: K.P. Bagchi and Company.

Lysenko, Victoria, 2007, 'What is Immediate Perception? The Buddhist Answer', *IIAS Newsletter*, Vol. 44, pp. 20–1.

Mahajan, Gurpreet, 2009, Experience and its Implications for Theory, Paper presented in a seminar on Theory and Experience held at Centre for Political Studies, Jawaharlal Nehru University, 6 May.

Mansfield, Nick, 2000, *Subjectivity: Theories of the Self from Freud to Haraway*, New York: New York University Press.

Matilal, B.K., 1985, *Logic, Language and Reality: Indian Philosophy and Contemporary Issues*, New Delhi: Motilal Banarsidass.

————, 1986, *Perception: An Essay on Classical Indian Theories of Knowledge*, Oxford: Oxford University Press.

————, 1998, *The Character of Logic in India*, J. Ganeri and H. Tiwari (eds), Albany: State University of New York Press.

Mehta, Uday, 1999, *Liberalism and Empire*, New Delhi: Oxford University Press.

Merleau-Ponty, M., 1968, *The Visible and the Invisible*, (trans. by Alphonso Lingis), Evanston: Northwestern University Press (First edition).

Mohanty, J.N., 1992, *Reason and Tradition in Indian Thought: An Essay on the Nature of Indian Philosophical Thinking*, Oxford: Clarendon Press.

————, 2002, *Classical Indian Philosophy*, New Delhi: Oxford University Press.

Montagu, Ashley, 1971, *Touching: The Human Significance of the Skin*. New York: Columbia University Press.

Moon, Vasant, 1987, *Madhya Prant-Varahadtil Dr Aambedkarpurva Dalit Chalwal*, Pune: Sugawa Publication.

More, S., 1999, *Collection of Writings of Tukaram*, Pune: Sakal Publishers.

Morris, D., 1965, *The Emergence of an Industrial Labor Force in India: A Study of the Bombay Cotton Mills, 1854–1947*, Berkeley: University of California Press.

Mulhern, Francis, 1994, 'Message in a Bottle: Althusser in Literary Studies', in Gregory Elliot (ed.), *Althusser, a Critical Reader*, Oxford: Blackwell.

Nagel, T., 1974, 'What is it like to be a Bat?', *Philosophical Review*, Vol. 83, 435–56.

Nagaraj, D.R., 2010, *Flaming Feet, Dalit Movement in India*, New Delhi: Permanent Black.

Naipaul, V.S., 1988, *A Wounded Civilization*, New Delhi: Picador.

Natarajan, B., 2009, 'Place and Pathology in Caste', *Economic and Political Weekly*, XLIV (51): 79–82.

Omvedt, Gail, 1996, *Dalits and Democratic Revolution*, New Delhi: Sage.

Osler, Margaret J., 1970, 'John Locke and the Changing Ideal of Scientific Knowledge', *Journal of the History of Ideas*, Vol. 31, pp. 3–16.

Pande, G.C., 1994, 'Two Dimensions of Religion', in Deutsch Eliot (ed.), *Culture and Modernity*, Delhi: Motilal Banarsidass.

Pandian, M.S.S., 2008, *Brahmin and Non-Brahmin: Genealogies of The Tamil Political Present*, New Delhi: Permanent Black.

Parekh, Bhikhu, 1996, *Colonialism, Tradition and Reform*, New Delhi: Sage.

————, 2010, 'The Poverty of Indian Political Theory', in Aakash Singh and Silika Mohapatra (eds), *Indian Political Thought, Reader*, London: Routledge, pp. 19–30.

Paterson, Mark, 2007, *The Senses of Touch: Haptics, Affects and Technologies*, Oxford: Berg.

Patil, Sharad, 1982, *Satyashodhak Marxwadi, Vol. 5*, Dhule: Satyashodhak Marxist Publication.

Pawar, Daya, 1978, *Baluta*, Mumbai: Granthali Publication.

Pensky, Max, 1995, 'Universalism and the Situated Critic', in S.K. White (ed.), *The Cambridge Companion to Habermas*, Cambridge: Cambridge University Press, pp. 67–94.

Peters, E., 2001, 'The Desire to Know the Secrets of the World', *Journal of the History of Ideas*, Vol. 62, pp. 593–10.

Phadake, Y.D., 1988, *Mahtma Phule Samagra Wangmaya*, Mumbai: Maharashtra Rajya Sahitya ani Sanskruti Mandal.

Phillips, Stephen H., 2004, 'Perceiving Particulars Blindly: Remarks on a Nyāya-Buddhist Controversy', *Philosophy East and West*, 54 (3): 389–403.

Pillai, Sivshankar, (n.d.) *Scavenger's Son*, trans. by R.E. Asher, New Delhi: Orient Paperbacks.

Quigley, D., 2000, *The Interpretation of Caste*, Oxford: Clarendon Press.

————, 2005, *The Character of Kingship*, Oxford: Berg.

Raghuramraju, A., 2006, *Debates in Indian Philosophy: Classical, Colonial and Contemporary*, New Delhi: Oxford University Press.

————, 2010. 'Problematising Lived Dalit Experience', *Economic and Political Weekly*, 45 (29): 162–7.

Raina, D., 2000, 'The Present in the Past', in Romila Thapar (ed.), *India: New Millennium*, Delhi: Penguin.

Ram-Prasad, C., 2001, 'Saving the Self? Classical Hindu Theories of Consciousness and Contemporary Physicalism', *Philosophy East and West*, 51 (3): 378–92.

Rege, S.S., 1991, *Bhimparva*, Pune: Sugawa Publication.

Rudolph, L.I., and S.H. Rudolph, 1967, *The Modernity of Tradition: Political Development in India*, Chicago: University of Chicago Press.

Russell, R.S., 1916, *The Tribes and Castes of Central India, Vol. 4*, London.

Samrendra, Padmanbha, 2011, 'Census in Colonial India and the Birth of Caste', *Economic and Political Weekly*, XLVI (33): 52.

Saraswati, Pundita Ramabai, 1976, *The High Caste Hindu Women*, Westpost, Connecticut: Hyperion Press.

Sartre, Jean-Paul, 1993 [1943], *Being and Nothingness*, New York: Washington Square Press.

Sarukkai, Sundar, 1997, 'The "Other" in Anthropology and Philosophy', *Economic and Political Weekly*, XXXII (24): 1406–9.

——, 2002, 'Inside/Outside: Merleau-Ponty/Yoga', *Philosophy East and West*, 52 (4): 459–78.

——, 2005, 'Dalit Experience and Theory', *Economic and Political Weekly*, 42 (40): 4043–8.

——, 2005, *Indian Philosophy and Philosophy of Science*, Delhi: Motilal Banarsidass.

——, 2009a, 'Phenomenology of Untouchability', *Economic and Political Weekly*, XLIV (37): 39–48.

——, 2009b, 'Science and the Ethics of Curiosity', *Current Science*, 97 (6): 756–67.

——, 2011, 'Possible Ideas of Necessity in Indian Logic', *Journal of Philosophical Logic*, Vol. 40, pp. 563–82.

——, 2012, 'Translation as Method: Implications for History of Science', in B. Lightman, L. Stewart, and G. McOnat (eds), *Circulating Knowledge*, Brill Press.

Scott, James, 1990, *Domination and the Arts of Resistance: Hidden Transcript*, New Haven: Yale University Press.

——, 1991, 'The Evidence of Experience', *Critical Inquiry*, Vol. 1.

Scidler, Victor J. 1986, *Kant, Respect, and Injustice, The Limits of Liberal Moral Theory*, London: Routledge and Kegan Paul.

Shah, Ghanshyam, H. Mander, S. Thorat, S. Deshpande, and S. Baviskar, 2006, *Untouchability in Rural India*, Delhi: Sage.

Shankaran, Raman, 2006, *Framing 'India': The Colonial Imaginary in Early Modern Culture*, Stanford: Stanford University Press.

Sharma, Arvind, 1992, 'Is Anubhava a Pramāṇa according to Śaṅkar?,' *Philosophy East and West*, 42 (3): 517–26.

——, 1993, *The Experiential Dimension of Advaita Vedanta*, New Delhi: Motilal Banarsidass.

Shields, Christopher, 2007, *Aristotle*, London: Routledge.

Shinde, V.R., 1976, *Bharatatil Asprushtecha Prashna* (Marathi), Bombay: Social Welfare and Cultural Department, Government of Maharashtra.

Siderits, Mark, 2004, 'Perceiving Particulars: A Buddhist Defense', *Philosophy East and West*, 54 (3): 367–82.

Sinha, Nandalal, 1915, *The Samkhya Karika*. Delhi: Orient Books.

Smith, A.D., 2002, *The Problem of Perception*, Cambridge, MA: Harvard University Press.

Smith, John E., 1978, *Purpose and Thought: The Meaning of Pragmatism*, New Haven: Yale University Press.

Smith, Steven B., 1989, *Hegel's Critique of Liberalism*, Chicago: Chicago University Press.

Sokal, A., and J. Bricmont, 1998, *Fashionable Nonsense: Postmodern Intellectuals' Abuse of Science*, New York: Picador.

Sonkamble P.I., 1979, *Athwaniche Pakshi*, Aurangabad: Chetana Prakashan.

Sorabji, Richard, 1971, 'Aristotle on Demarcating the Five Senses', *The Philosophical Review*, Vol. 80, pp. 55–79.

Srinivas, M.N., 1996, 'Indian Anthropologists and the Study of Indian Culture', *Economic and Political Weekly*, XXXI (11): 656–7.

———, 2009, *Omnibus*, Oxford: Oxford University Press.

Steinvorth, Ulrich, 2009, *Rethinking the Western Understanding of the Self*, Cambridge: Cambridge University Press.

Strong, T.B., and F.A. Sposito, 1995, 'Habermas's Significant Other', in S.K. White (ed.), *The Cambridge Companion to Habermas*, Cambridge: Cambridge University Press, pp. 263–88.

Tendulkar, D.G., 1968, *Mahatma*, New Delhi: Publication Division, Government of India.

Trechek, Ronald, 1986, 'Gandhi and Democratic Theory', in Thomas Pantham and Kenneth Deutsch (eds), *Political Thought in Modern India*, New Delhi: Sage, pp. 305–24.

Van Maanen, John, 1988, *Tales of the Field: On Writing Ethnography*, Chicago: University of Chicago Press.

Varela, Francisco, 1999, *Ethical Know-How*, Stanford: Stanford University Press.

Walmiki, Omprakash, 2002, *Jhootan*, (trans. by Prabha Mukherjee), Kolkata: Samya Publication.

Walzer, Michael, 1983, *The Spheres of Justice, A Defence of Pluralism and Equality*, Oxford: Basil Blackwell.

Weinberg, Steven, 1993, *Dreams of a Final Theory*, London: Hutchinson Radius.

Wesleyan, F.A., 2002, *Levinas, the Frankfurt School and Psychoanalysis*, Connecticut: University Press of Connecticut.

Zelliot, Eleanor, 1992, *From Untouchables to Dalit*, New Delhi: Manohar.

Index